Generations, Inc.

From Boomers to Linksters— Managing the Friction Between Generations at Work

Meagan Johnson and Larry Johnson

AMACOM

American Management Association

New York • Atlanta • Brussels • Chicago • Mexico City • San Francisco
Shanghai • Tokyo • Toronto • Washington, D.C.

Bulk discounts available. For details visit:
www.amacombooks.org/go/specialsales
Or contact special sales:
Phone: 800-250-5308
E-mail: specialsls@amanet.org
View all the AMACOM titles at: www.amacombooks.org

This publication is designed to provide accurate and authoritative information in regard to the subject matter covered. It is sold with the understanding that the publisher is not engaged in rendering legal, accounting, or other professional service. If legal advice or other expert assistance is required, the services of a competent professional person should be sought.

Library of Congress Cataloging-in-Publication Data

Johnson, Meagan, 1970–
    Generations, Inc. : from boomers to linksters—managing the friction between generations at work / Meagan Johnson, Larry Johnson.
        p.   cm.
    Includes bibliographical references and index.
    ISBN-13: 978-0-8144-1573-3 (pbk.)
    ISBN-10: 0-8144-1573-3 (pbk.)
    1. Diversity in the workplace—Management.   2. Intergenerational relations.
3. Intergenerational communication.   4. Conflict of generations.   5. Personnel management.   I. Johnson, Larry, 1947–   II. Title.
HF5549.5.M5J65   2010
658.30084—dc22

                                                                            2009053579

About AMA
American Management Association (www.amanet.org) is a world leader in talent development, advancing the skills of individuals to drive business success. Our mission is to support the goals of individuals and organizations through a complete range of products and services, including classroom and virtual seminars, webcasts, webinars, podcasts, conferences, corporate and government solutions, business books, and research. AMA's approach to improving performance combines experiential learning—learning through doing—with opportunities for ongoing professional growth at every step of one's career journey.

Printing number

10   9   8   7   6   5   4   3

Meagan's Dedication

To Alex: My truly badass husband, who has made me the happiest bride ever.

Larry's Dedication

To CJ: My friend and spouse of forty years, who taught me how to love.

Contents

Acknowledgments

We would like to extend our heartfelt gratitude to the family and friends who listened to us talk about the book for the past year and still wanted to spend time with us. Many offered advice, encouragement, and insights but without the invaluable assistance of the following people, our book would never have become a reality. Our literary agent, Michael Snell, guided us in creating a marketable proposal. Our editor, Steve George, provided tireless enthusiasm and gave our book a cohesive, clear direction. The entire multi-generational Pillard family—Kathie, Gino, Jason, and Kylie—donated countless hours of their time discussing real-life examples and talking to people of all different ages to give us the best possible content. Heather Osborn, Lisa Phillips, Edd and Katie Welsh, Hannah Kuenn, Kelsey Wolf, Kirstin Robertson, Jasmine Truax, Mary George, Kasey Cave, and MargZ! Lawson all allowed us to intrude on their lives to proofread, look up facts, and answer hard questions. If you meet any of these people, please be sure to give them all a big smile . . . they deserve it!

Authors' Note

We wrote this book together to offer the perspectives of a father and a daughter on the issues facing members of different generations who work together. Because we wanted to offer our own individual opinions, as well as our combined observations, we interspersed the chapters with individual as well as joint reflections. In addition, since we can only offer personal perspectives from our respective generational roots (Generation X and Baby Boomer Generation), we interviewed members of the Traditional Generation, Generation Y, and Generation Linkster to gain their insights, which are included in the book.

Meagan Johnson and Larry Johnson
Contact Information:
Johnson Training Group
24626 North 84th Street
Scottsdale, AZ 85255
1-800-836-6599
email: info@JohnsonTrainingGroup.com

Generations, Inc.

Signposts: Harbingers of Things to Come

"Life is rather like a tin of sardines—we're all of us looking for the key."
—Alan Bennett, British author, actor, humorist, and playwright

. . . .

Meagan Remembers

When I was six years old, I went to the grocery store with my father. He bought an item priced at $1.69, but the cashier misread it and only charged him 69 cents. (This was 1976. Scanners had yet to be invented, and cashiers manually entered prices.) My father alerted her to her mistake. She thanked him and charged him the extra dollar.

I was dumbfounded! At the time, my weekly allowance was a dollar. My father had just thrown away what it took me a week to earn. So I said, "Dad, that was dumb. All you had to do was keep your mouth shut and you could have saved a whole dollar." "Yes," he replied, "but how I feel about myself is worth more than a dollar."

My memory of that event has followed me all my life. It helps me decide how to handle situations in which I must determine the right thing to do. It taught me that there is more to life than material gain. I've even used it as a standard for picking the company I keep. Would I want a friend who would have kept the dollar? I think not. Thanks, Dad, for the great life lesson.

Larry Responds

You're welcome, Meagan, but gosh, I don't even remember this big event in your life. In retrospect, it seems I was able to convey a simple life lesson for a pretty small price. If it had been a million dollars at stake instead of one, I hope I would have acted as nobly.

It does remind me that early experiences can have lasting influences on our lives. I attended YMCA summer camp when I was ten years old. My family didn't have a lot of money and couldn't afford the tuition, but I was an enterprising sort. I secured a position as a dishwasher that allowed me to go for free.

For some reason, an adult counselor at the camp considered tuition workers second-class citizens. On an overnight excursion, after a long day of hiking, this counselor told the kitchen crew to wait until all the paid campers got their food from the chow line before eating. I waited and waited. When I saw some of the paid campers queuing up for seconds, I got in line. This counselor grabbed my arm and jerked me out of line. In front of all the other campers, he dressed me down, reminding me that I was just a "dishwasher," and I had to wait for the "real" campers to eat.

My humiliation was unbearable. I burst into tears, threw my plate in the counselor's face, and ran into the woods, hoping I would get lost and starve to death just to show them how unjustly I'd been treated.

Luckily, a more sympathetic counselor tracked me down and escorted me back to camp, where he gave me something to eat. He told me not to take the counselor who had been mean to me seriously because he had some personal problems that caused him to act that way. In retrospect, he should not have been allowed to work with kids, problems or not, but I did gain something positive from the experience. In the years since, I've traced any empathy I have for people less fortunate than I to that unpleasant incident. It gave me a small taste of what it feels like to be discriminated against. It was a painful, but beneficial, event in my life.

Personal and Group Signposts

We call these kinds of events *personal signposts*: experiences in our lives that significantly contribute to who we are. They are personal because they are unique to each individual. They are signposts because they influence our future decisions, reactions, attitudes, and behaviors.

Other signposts have just as much impact on us, but these spring from the experiences of the groups to which we belong and the society in which we live. These *group signposts* can have a strong effect on us because they are magnified by the power of numbers. For example, if you are a member of a racial minority, you may or may not have endured racism yourself. However, the fact that your friends, family, and colleagues probably did will affect how you view the issue of discrimination. And, if you combine this *group signpost* with one or more *personal signposts* associated with race, the effect can be very powerful.

Larry remembers an experience he had when working for a large organization. He and his boss, Irene, were conducting interviews to fill a position that would report directly to Larry. It came down to two finalists: one Larry liked, and one Irene liked. Since Irene was the boss, Larry yielded, and they hired her choice.

It turned out to be a mistake and they eventually had to let the woman go. In discussing it later, Irene graciously claimed responsibility for the fiasco. She said that she had let a prejudice hidden deep within her affect her judgment. It turns out that Larry's preferred choice was white, and Irene's was black. Irene herself is also black.

Larry was surprised. Irene had never struck him as being racially motivated. After all, she had hired him, a white guy, when there had been several minority candidates from whom to choose. She also had a sterling reputation as the consummate HR professional. Larry asked her to explain.

Irene replied that she hadn't preferred her candidate because she was black, but because the white candidate's Southern accent grated down at her "very core." As a young black woman growing up in the South, she associated many negative experiences with a Southern drawl. The combination of a *group signpost* (being black) and the *personal signposts* (these negative experiences) affected Irene's ability, years later, to be fair and impartial. To her credit, she promised to make a conscious effort not to let this prejudice affect her judgment again.

Irene's story illustrates the good news about signposts. They can have very positive effects on our lives, as did Meagan's experience with Larry at the grocery store, or they can have very negative effects, like Irene's reaction to a Southern accent. *But they can be changed.* Signposts are not life sentences. Irene proved the point. She learned from her insight and made a conscious decision to move in a different direction.

Generational Signposts

A *generational signpost* is an event or cultural phenomenon that is specific to one generation. Generational signposts shape, influence, and drive our expectations, actions, and mind-sets about the products we buy, the companies for which we work, and the expectations we have about life in general. Generational signposts mold our ideas about company loyalty, work ethics, and the definitions of a job well done.

Meagan's grandfather, Joe, was from the Traditional Generation (the parents of Baby Boomers born before 1946). He came of age in the 1920s and struggled to raise a family during the Great Depression, a major signpost for his generation. Joe, like most of his cohort, believed that if you were lucky enough to have a job, you owed absolute loyalty to the company that hired you—always. Joe worked for Procter & Gamble for forty years. Throughout his employment and his retirement, he insisted that everyone in the family buy only P&G products. If P&G made it, they bought it.

Compare that attitude with that of people from Generation Y (born after 1980). Their average job turnover rate is approximately 30 percent.[1] Some employers tell us they feel lucky if newly hired Generation Yers stick around past lunch. This lack of job loyalty can be traced to many factors including that the job often pays very little so the only way the Gen Yer can make more is to move elsewhere or the job itself is not his or her calling in life, it's just something to do until he or she finds a career path. For many, however, they simply don't need to work because they still live at home and are being supported by Mom and Dad. That phenomenon can be associated with a major signpost for them: They are the offspring of what we call "helicopter parents." We'll explain many of the implications of that parentage in Chapter 6, but suffice it to say that these kids are often overly indulged.

Life Laws

When Meagan was a young child, Larry traveled every week. She and her mother loved to surprise him by meeting his plane at the gate. It became a Friday night family tradition. However, for every generation born after September 11, 2001, that family tradition now takes place outside the security area. Today's young people have no recollection of being allowed to enter an airport concourse without submitting to a TSA screening. For them, this necessity is a *life law*.

Life laws are events that have social, political, or economic influence on our lives but occurred before we were old enough to remember any difference. We've talked to many members of Generation X and Generation Y who take for granted the fact that schools are not segregated by race. They can't imagine a time when it was otherwise. Consequently, they often have little appreciation for the sacrifices made by their Traditional elders that led to the 1954 Supreme Court decision of *Oliver L. Brown et al. v. the Board of Education of Topeka (KS) et al.*—a decision that outlawed segregation in schools. Nor do they remember the subsequent struggle by the civil rights movement to turn the ruling into a reality. For them, school integration is a life law. It's always been that way.

Life laws are important because they often affect how one generation views another. If you were part of the civil rights movement of the 1960s, you may have little patience with 18-year-olds who take their civil rights for granted. Likewise, if you are from a younger generation, you may have little patience for an older worker who is still bringing those struggles to work and sees the world through that lens. For example, we know a Gen Xer who found it irritating when she was pregnant that her Baby Boomer boss said she should be grateful the company was letting her come back to work.

Generation Defined

During a speech, Meagan mentioned that she is part of Generation X. An audience member yelled out, "Aren't you getting too old to be a Generation Xer?" That's a risky question to ask anyone and, to her credit, Meagan resisted the temptation to snap back, "Aren't you a little old to call yourself a Baby Boomer?" Instead, she clarified that generational groups are not determined by the present age of the members, but by the social events and demographics that were happening at their inceptions. Traditionals are defined as people born before the end of World War II. Thus, although people grow older, the period in which they were born always remains the defining time period that determines to which generation they belong. So if you are a Traditional, you'll always be a Traditional. If you are a Baby Boomer, you'll always be a Baby Boomer, and so on.

As it applies to groups in society, Merriam-Webster's online dictionary offers four variations on the word "generation." We start with this one—*a group of individuals born and living contemporaneously*—and then expand it a bit. Here's our definition:

> **Generation**: *A group of individuals born and living contemporaneously who have common knowledge and experiences that affect their thoughts, attitudes, values, beliefs, and behaviors.*

Absolutely no consensus exists on how to determine when one generation ends and another begins. The most common definition is based on major fluctuations in the birthrate. For example, World War II forced millions of Traditionals to postpone starting families. At the war's end, after long separations, these folks were ready to marry and produce children. And, aided by the nation's unprecedented postwar prosperity, produce they did!

In 1946, live births in the United States surged from 222,721 in January to 339,499 in October. By the end of the 1940s, 32 million babies had been born, compared to 24 million in the 1930s.

U.S. Birthrate Chart

When the surge ended in 1965, the Baby Boomer Generation included 78.2 million members—the largest American generation on record.

In the 1960s and 1970s, the Pill gave women more control over reproduction, while the women's movement increased their educational and career opportunities. As a result, many postponed having children and the birthrate declined. Only 49 million babies were born in the United States between 1965 and 1980, making Generation X the smallest American generation on record.

About the same time, the biological clocks of childless Baby Boomers started ringing. Additionally, many of those who already had children were divorcing and starting second families. So the birthrate climbed until 1996, when Generation Y recorded a head count of 70.4 million, almost as big as the Baby Boomer Generation. Starting in 1997, Generation Xers and some Yers began to have children and the birthrate started to climb again, creating what we call the Linked-In, or Linkster, Generation.

See the U.S. Birthrate Chart in Figure 1.1.

Figure 1.1. U.S. Birthrate Chart[2]

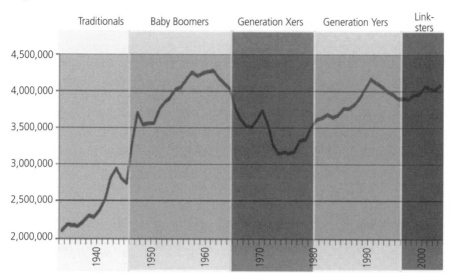

Five Generations at Work

History is in the making. Never before have five generations occupied the workplace as they do now. The three main groups are:

➢ Baby Boomers, aka the Woodstock Generation, born between 1946 and 1964
➢ Generation X, aka Latchkey Kids, born between 1965 and 1980
➢ Generation Y, aka the Entitled Ones, born between 1981 and 1995

A few members of the Traditional Generation are also still working (aka Depression Babies, born before 1945), and we're beginning to see the first of the Linkster Generation appearing on the job site (aka the Facebook Crowd, born after 1995). In reality then, five generations are now present in the workforce. This is rapidly changing as more and more Traditionals exit and more Linksters enter, creating a four-part milieu that will be with us until all the Baby Boomers retire. And, according to a host of studies, many Baby Boomers plan to continue working long past the age of 65, so this four-part milieu is likely to be the state of business for many years.

In this book, we will refer to members of each of the five generations as those born in the years just described. We will also discuss various generational subgroups that have been identified by historians and social commentators as they come up.

Each generation has widely differing sets of expectations and perceptions of what the working environment will provide, how they should behave as employees, how managers will manage them, and how they will manage others.

The same differences apply in one's personal life as well. To a great extent, how you get along with your young children, your adult children, and your parents is affected by the generation in which you reside.

Cuspers

People born close to the dividing line between generations are known as cuspers. They have the advantage of having one foot in two generational worlds. According to Lynne C. Lancaster and David Stillman in their book, *When Generations Collide: Who They Are. Why They Clash. How to Solve the Generational Puzzle at Work,* cuspers have a natural ability to identify with multiple generations' beliefs and interests.[3]

Gino, a project manager in the digital control system industry, was born in 1964. He is an example of a cusper who successfully straddles the line between Baby Boomers and Generation X. He serves as a bridge between the senior technical advisers, who are almost all older, salaried, professional-level staff, and the journeymen, who are hourly employees new to the company and the industry.

The senior technical advisers know Gino is reliable. He has had enough years in the industry to build a solid reputation as a project manager and has proven himself a reliable team member. The younger journeymen respect Gino's experience, but his relative youth makes him less intimidating than some of the senior members. Journeymen now take questions to Gino for quick resolution, therefore freeing up the time of the senior technical advisers.

Much of the glue that bonds Gino to both generations is language. Senior technical advisers trust Gino because he can "talk their language." He knows industry terminology and maintains composure under tight deadlines. The journeymen also trust him. One described Gino this way: "The dude calls it like it is. I figured someone with Gino's experience would act, more, you know . . . like corporate. He's not at all like those suits [senior technical advisers]."

Not all cuspers identify with both sides of the generational dividing line. Many adopt the values of one side and conduct themselves accordingly. Meagan's aunt Maureen was born in 1944. Her sister CJ, who is Larry's wife and Meagan's mother, was born in 1947. They both came into the world on either side of 1946, which divides the Traditional and Baby Boomer generations. Maureen went to junior college, married young, had three children right away, remained a devout Catholic, voted for Nixon, and was crazy about Perry Como and Andy Williams. CJ went away to college, dropped out of the church, lived a hippy lifestyle, voted for McGovern, and loved Van Morrison and the Rolling Stones. Both were born close to the border separating two generations. Maureen went Traditional and CJ went Boomer.

White Bucks, Duck Tails, and Generation Jones

Authors have identified subgroups with characteristics unique to a certain time period in their generation. For example, we often associate rock 'n' roll music with Baby Boomers. They grew up listening to Elvis Presley, the Beatles, the Who, Jimi Hendrix, and Janis Joplin. The term "rock 'n' roll," however, was first used for commercial purposes in the early 1950s by Cleveland disc jockey Alan Freed (aka Moondog). He discovered that increasing numbers of young white kids were listening to and requesting the rhythm-and-blues records he played on his nighttime radio program, records called "rock 'n' roll." Freed promoted "rock 'n' roll revues," concert tours featuring black artists who played to a young, racially mixed audience.

In most cases, however, the white kids requesting this music were far too old to be Baby Boomers, whose eldest members at the time were six years old. Technically, these teenagers were members of the Traditional generation, but their *generational signposts* did not include the two signposts that most defined the Traditional Generation: the Great Depression and World War II. We call this interim group the "White Bucks and Duck Tails Generation" after the shoes made popular by Pat Boone and the hairdos of many doo-wop groups. They became teenagers in the 1950s, dancing to Bill Haley and the Comets and living the life portrayed in *Father Knows Best*. If young daughter Kathy on that show represented the coming Baby Boomer Generation, her older brother, Bud, was a White

Bucks and Duck Tail guy. They identified with some of the events that would define Boomer culture, but their main connection was with their Traditional parents.

Another *interim generation* that has attracted recent attention is Generation Jones. Coined by Los Angeles–based cultural historian Jonathan Pontell, the members of Generation Jones were born between 1954 and 1964.[4] They entered their adult buying years during the 1980s, the decade known for its over-the-top, decadent living style, when keeping up with the Joneses was de rigueur. They barely remember the strife of the 1960s and 1970s that so influenced early Baby Boomers. Today, they are moving into the halls of power in corporations and government. They represent the younger end of the Baby Boomer Generation—think Barack Obama (born 1961) versus Hillary Clinton (born 1947). In fact, they are also known as Generation Obama.

Other Generational Definitions

Some people believe generations should be defined by their generational signposts. For example, Salon.com columnist Dave Cullen recently described Generation Y as the "Columbine Generation," referring to the Columbine High School massacre that took place in Littleton, Colorado, on April 20, 1999.[5] He feels that the shooting marked the end of Generation X and the beginning of Generation Y.

Others define generations by the president who was in power when they were born or when they became aware of who he was. People born between 1970 and 1980 often call themselves the Carter Generation. Many born in the late 1970s and the 1980s refer to themselves as Gen-Reagan: They were too young to vote for Reagan, but they can remember their grade school principals announcing that the president had been shot and wounded.

Generational Signposts Bond Us

Generational signposts create shared values and serve as built-in bonding mechanisms among the individuals of a group.

Meagan's mother, CJ, worked for AT&T during college, first as an information operator and then, after graduation, as a service representative for business accounts. She was very bright, graduating from college with a 4.0 GPA. She was well liked by customers and coworkers, and she understood the AT&T system inside and out. CJ's supervisor, Alva, recognized her potential and often assigned her to train other representatives, as well as all the candidates going through AT&T's executive development program.

CJ was honored to do this, but she was also frustrated. She knew that she would eventually be promoted to a position similar to Alva's, but she also knew she would never be admitted to the executive development group she was training because of her gender. At the time, AT&T was the nation's largest employer of women and also one of its most rigidly gender segregated. The working ranks were filled with women, but the management positions were reserved for men. In 1973, a discrimination suit filed with the FCC forced AT&T to change, but not before CJ had resigned in disgust and pursued another career.

Recently, CJ bumped into Alva, who had chosen to stay on at AT&T. With the end of its discriminatory practices, Alva had gone on to enjoy a 30-year career as an AT&T executive.

The bond between CJ and Alva was instant. Both had suffered under discriminatory practices that were common for their generation. They spent the afternoon talking about the pros and cons of staying at the company, and what had happened to all the people they knew. To this day, CJ has a special relationship with Alva that is particular to their shared signpost.

Whether it's the memories of Boomers overcoming the discriminatory practices of the 1970s or the commonality of two Generation Xers who have bittersweet memories of Kurt Cobain's death, generational signposts serve as mechanisms that bring people together. The downside of this generational bonding is that those whose pasts do not contain these signposts can be seen as "outsiders."

Most Baby Boomers remember where they were on the day Neil Armstrong walked on the moon. They remember the names of the people in the room and how important it was that the United States got to the moon ahead of the Soviets. Ask a Generation Y person where she was on that day, and she's likely to roll her eyes and remind you that she wasn't even alive then. For her, a man walking on the moon is about as impressive as a man walking to Wal-Mart: It's something to which she just doesn't give much thought.

This is not to say that Generation Yers are insensitive. It's just that the importance of one generational signpost is often lost on others who didn't experience it. They simply weren't there. For them, any lingering effect from this historic event is a life law.

When Signposts Become Life Laws

Generational signposts can create ripple effects that often lead to the creation of life laws. For example, the 9/11 attacks became a generational signpost for Traditionals, Baby Boomers, Gen Xers, and those Gen Yers old enough to remember them. For these folks, the events of that day probably cross their minds regularly and have had a significant impact on their lives: from airport security to perceptions of Muslims by non-Muslims to the wistfulness one feels when looking at a picture of the New York skyline sans the World Trade Center towers. For those too young to remember 9/11 and for those born after, however, the subsequent changes in the world will always be life laws. Something to which one doesn't give much thought.

Not all these ripples are negative. When Meagan was eight years old, she asked her babysitter why she had a small indentation on her left arm. The sitter explained that it was from her smallpox vaccination. Meagan asked, "What is smallpox?" With a tear in her eye, the babysitter replied that it was absolutely wonderful that Meagan had to ask that question. She went on to explain that she had a brother who had suffered from polio during the Great Depression and that polio, along with smallpox, had both been eliminated through massive inoculations of schoolchildren. For the babysitter, the *generational signposts* of polio and smallpox inoculations, combined with the *personal signpost* her brother represented, had a great deal of emotional significance for her. For Meagan, it was an interesting story, but not particularly memorable. For Meagan, the absence of those diseases was a *life law*.

Signposts Affect Everyone—Just Not in the Same Way

Of course, generational signposts are not applicable to every member of a generation in the same way. For example, when we think of young Baby Boomers, images of long-haired students rioting in Grant Park during the 1968 Democratic convention or young people cavorting naked at Woodstock may come to mind. In fact, most young people of the era considered themselves to be much more conservative than those images convey. Most were members of what Richard Nixon's campaign manager, Pat Buchanan, called the "silent majority."[6] And, it was this group of conservative Republicans who elected Nixon on a campaign promise to "restore law and order"—mostly in response to those unruly student protesters. So in fact, the generational signpost represented by the "silent majority" is as applicable to the Baby Boomer Generation as are the radical '60s.

Meagan is a member of Generation X. A major generational signpost for Gen X is that many came home after school to an empty house. They would let themselves in with their own key, thus acquiring the title of "latchkey kids." Meagan was a latchkey kid.

Why did this happen? When Gen Xers were young children, their Baby Boomer parents were coming into their 30s, entering what Daniel J. Levinson and his research team called "the settling down period,"[7] when you grow up and start taking responsibility for yourself. They became focused on supporting their families, accumulating wealth, and maximizing what they could accomplish in life. It was as if hippies, previously dedicated to social change and justice for all, had morphed into yuppies, dedicated to long working hours and a new BMW.

Television, ever the barometer of social trends, reflected the change. *All in the Family,* which was about the clash in values between Baby Boomers and their Traditional parents, gave way to *thirtysomething,* which focused on Baby Boomers' fascination with themselves. The no-nonsense *Dragnet,* whose detectives drove police-issued Chevys and wore sensible shoes, was replaced by *Miami Vice,* whose detectives drove Ferraris and wore Armani jackets.

The new focus on materialism required more and more families to have both parents working. For this to happen, parents had to give their children a fair amount of independence. When Meagan saw the movie *Home Alone,* her response was, "What's the big deal? I was home alone every afternoon from the time I was 8 until I was 18."

The impact today from the latchkey generational signpost is that Generation Xers tend to be highly independent workers. After all, they've been looking after themselves since they were very young. This has powerful implications for those managing them and for those working and living with them. We'll talk more about that in Chapter 4. On the other hand, not every member of Generation X was a "latchkey kid." If you're a Generation Xer, maybe you had your mom or dad waiting for you after school. Or maybe you went to after-school programs or you had a babysitter or you spent time at a friend's house. Still, it's likely that you were affected by the latchkey phenomenon. You may have been allowed to ride your bike to the store, take the city bus across town, or walk to the mall alone when you were eight or nine years old—freedoms that, for safety reasons, you might not extend to your own children today.

Likewise, not every Traditional who lived through the Great Depression suffered economic hardship, but anyone immersed in a culture where people all around you were struggling to make ends meet was affected by it.

During the 1930s, Larry's great aunt Josephine was married to a successful businessman. They lived in one of the biggest and fanciest houses in town. They belonged to the country club, played golf with the mayor, and drove a Buick. Until her death 60 years later, however, Josephine kept the thermostat set at 65 degrees in the winter and 90 in the summer. She reused paper towels until they were in shreds, and she continually reminded Larry and all the other nieces and nephews to save their money. Even though she didn't experience it much directly, the Great Depression was a generational signpost for her.

Generational Myopia

In our work as organizational consultants, we often hear managers complain that young people today have little or no work ethic. To tar an entire generation with one descriptor misses the tremendous value young people can contribute. Like them or not, young workers are the future of our companies, our communities, and our world. We call this tarring of one generation by another *generational myopia*.

Merriam-Webster's online dictionary tells us that myopia means "a lack of foresight or discernment: a narrow view of something." When one generation judges the merits and faults of another through its generational lens, it often takes a narrow view of how that generation thinks.

Let's suppose you are a Baby Boomer raised to believe that doing a good job means taking responsibility for seeing that your work is complete before you go home. It's likely you will take offense if you see a young person walk out the door at 5:00 P.M. when some task critical to a project is still undone. First, he's violating your generational signpost that says, "Grown-ups take responsibility." Second, he's violating a generational signpost common to Baby Boomers that we call *kumbyaism*, which means being a good team player is an absolute must.

Meanwhile, the young person in question has a different perspective. Up until now in his life, if something needed to be done, someone in charge would usually tell him to do it. Consequently, the task is not even on his radar. So, while you are projecting your ire at him, and by proxy, at all young people, he interprets your bristling as the typical weird behavior of old guys. It's generational myopia raging on both sides.

New Generations of Leaders

Recently, we heard a radio interview with an environmental expert. The host asked him why we should care about environmental issues when the economy is struggling so badly. He replied, "The environment doesn't care about the economy. The environment will continue to decline or improve regardless of our financial situation." Likewise, our generational challenges will continue regardless of the economy or the environment. Companies and organizations that ignore this reality do so at their peril. According to a survey of 578 companies by the Boston College Center on Aging and Work, only 33 percent say they have analyzed workplace demographics and made projections about the retirement rates of their workers.[8]

Because of aging and health issues, fewer and fewer Traditionals remain in the workplace. Meanwhile, Baby Boomers are retiring at an accelerating rate, leaving a gaping hole in America's management and employment ranks. There are currently approximately 69.2 million Baby Boomers. Simple math tells us that each day, the 10,540 Baby Boomers who turn 60 are thinking about doing something with their lives other than leading or managing in their organizations. Shortages of airline pilots, engineers, doctors, social workers, professors, managers, and senior executives, to name a few, loom on the horizon.

Although this prospect has been delayed by the drastic reduction of retirement nest eggs during the recession that started in 2008, it is coming. Smart companies are preparing Generation Xers and fast-tracking Generation Yers to take the place of disappearing Traditionals and retiring Baby Boomers.

How these folks are led and managed will impact the success of all organizations. According to a survey by Aon Consulting, 60 percent of companies say their business performance is suffering from a failure to prepare workers for leadership.[9] As Generation Xers and Generation Yers become the core of the world's workforce, their values, likes, and dislikes will determine how they respond to any efforts to direct, motivate, and inspire them to perform.

They are looking for something very different from their Baby

Boomer predecessors. According to Jobfox.com CEO Rob McGovern,[10] the top four motivators for Generation Y are:

1. **Balance**. "They don't embrace the value of the Boomer-created, nine-to-five work week. They work best when they can set their own hours."

2. **Leading edge**. This generation understands that technology is changing rapidly. If not updated continuously, their skills promptly become obsolete, so they are very interested in continual skill development.

3. **Instant contribution**. "They do not want to be treated 'as junior anything.' They want to begin contributing right away. Companies must do a better job of helping younger workers see how their work is vital and how that work relates to the bottom line of the company."

4. **Stability**. Generation Y workers can be loyal team players as long as they can balance work and life goals, gain new learning opportunities, and feel like they are supporting company goals.

McGovern goes on to say that the employers who will be most successful over the next two decades will be the ones who can best inspire and engage this challenging generation. The question is: How ready are you to motivate your Generation Yers and future Linksters?

Larry Comments on Intergenerational Miscommunication

Meagan and I strongly believe that the principles and approaches we describe in this book can be applied to your day-to-day interactions with people of different generations, regardless of where you encounter them. For example, I recently had an encounter with a member of the Traditional Generation, about which I wrote the following story for the e-zine we publish, "Tips For Today's Managers." (You can subscribe at no charge by going to http://www.larry-johnson.com.)

Bicycle Seats and Generational Disharmony

I'm an avid cyclist—not very good or very fast, but I like the exercise, and the fresh air you get from riding every day is invigorating. Yesterday, after my standard 12-mile jaunt, I stopped for coffee at Starbucks. Sitting at one of the umbrella-covered tables out front was a group of men who appeared to be from the Traditional Generation. They were all dressed in the same funny-looking bike clothes that I was wearing, so I stopped to talk bikes.

After the usual pleasantries about where we had ridden that day, one of them noticed the seat on my bike, which is one of those skinny, Lance Armstrong types. He said, "At your age, you ought to change out your seat and get one like this," pointing to his bike. His seat was one of those fat, cushy, gel-covered types with a split in the middle to relieve pressure on the rider's groin. Real bikers sneer at those miniature La-Z-Boys® as the mark of a beginning biker.

For me, it's not being a biker snob (although I know I'm guilty of being one). I've researched the subject and there are solid reasons why "real" cyclists ride a skinny saddle (the proper term for a bicycle seat):

1. It's lighter so there's less weight for the rider to propel.
2. It's designed for the rider to put his weight on the sit bones that lie under the gluteus maximi, so it forces you to ride in proper position. (If you're feeling pressure on your groin, you aren't seated properly.)
3. On rides longer than 10 miles, it doesn't chafe the way those cushy seats do.

So I replied to the fellow, "Those seats are okay for leisurely riding, but they are killers if you're going more than 10 miles." At that point, he shrugged his shoulders, as if to say, "Suit yourself." One of the other members of his group then said, "Charlie here ought to know what's the best seat: He rides 50 miles per day. At 75, he looks like a man in his 50s, don't you think?"

It was true. Charlie did look young and fit. But he wasn't looking at me. He was staring off in another direction in a way that told me he had disengaged from the conversation. I made a few more comments, wished them a good day, and went on my way.

In retrospect, I realize that my quick response to Charlie's comment had cost me the opportunity to get to know him—to maybe gain a new riding partner—all because I'd jumped in and offered my opinion without ever having given due respect and a fair hearing to his. At that point, instead of engaging in further discussion or debate with me, Charlie had simply written me off as a jerk.

It reminds me that all people want to be heard and to have their opinions respected, but more so the older members of our society. The greatest gift they offer us is the wisdom of their accumulated years—a gift that Charlie offered me and I casually tossed aside in my quest to show him how smart I was.

If I could repeat the conversation with Charlie and his friends, I would do it differently. When he told me that I should get a different saddle, I would have asked him to tell me why he likes the wider saddle. I would have inquired about its features and if there was anything about the seat that he didn't like. I would have asked him about his riding habits, what his favorite routes are, and if he had tried any other kind of seat. And throughout this inquiry, I would have listened to his opinions and not have argued, denied, or negated anything he said.

Then, once I was sure that Charlie felt like I had truly listened to and respected what he had to say, I would have offered my opinions about the type of saddle I use and why it works for me. My guess is that even then, I probably wouldn't change Charlie's mind, but the odds would have risen that he would hear me out with a semiopen mind. And had I done so, maybe I'd have a new biking partner. I guess I'll never know.

The lesson we can take from this story is simple: You will build better relationships with anyone from any generation when you are willing to listen to that person and respect his or her opinions, even if you disagree. Our journey to respect begins with a better understanding of why the members of different generations think and act the way they do.

CHAPTER 2

Baby Boomers: The Elephant in the Python

"We started off trying to set up a small anarchist community, but people wouldn't obey the rules."
—*Alan Bennett,* Getting On *(1972)*

Critical Events in the Lives of Baby Boomers

1960 John Kennedy elected
1961 Bay of Pigs
1961 Cuban Missile Crisis
1963 John Kennedy assassinated
1964 Passage of the Civil Rights Act
1968 Martin Luther King, Jr., and Robert Kennedy assassinated
1968 Chicago Democratic Convention riots
1969 Janis Joplin and Jimmy Hendrix die
1969 Man walks on the moon
1969 Woodstock
1973 Watergate
1974 Nixon resigns and is pardoned
1974 Arab oil embargo
1976 Jimmy Carter elected
1979 Hostages taken in Iran
1980 Reagan elected; Iran hostages released
1980 John Lennon assassinated
1984 Macintosh introduced

Larry Confesses

I don't remember a time growing up when I wasn't expected to finish high school and go to college. This was not unusual for my generation. With the postwar prosperity of the 1950s, the emerging middle class had the luxury of educating its children beyond the basics. There was no need to quit school and work to help support the family, as there had been for our Traditional parents. Fathers, and sometimes mothers, had jobs, and both had a desire to create better lives for their children. That included encouraging us to go to college. At the same time, the space race, initiated by the Soviet Union's successful launch of *Sputnik I* in 1957, created widespread demand for engineers, rocket scientists, and anyone else who could contribute to the cause.

In our family, the emphasis on education was stronger than in most because both my Traditional Generation parents were college graduates. Attending a university after high school was a given. That didn't mean I was motivated to excel or college was important to me. Instead, I saw it as a way to get a student deferment so I could avoid going to Vietnam, as well as to get away from home and have some fun.

Although I managed to make respectable grades, my real major in college was drugs, sex, and rock 'n' roll, combined with a lot of narcissistic navel gazing. Fortunately, by the time I received my bachelor's degree and began graduate school, I had outgrown that phase of my life and buckled down to work—but it sure was fun while it lasted.

Meagan Replies

When I was a kid, you expected me to finish high school and go to college, too. But you also made a big deal about my *not* doing any of that stuff you did—like drugs and sex. I guess you thought the rock 'n' roll was okay.

In fact, when I was 12, you offered me a deal: If I made it to age 21 without smoking, drinking, or using drugs, you would pay me $1,000 for abstaining from each. Don't you think it was hypocritical of you to be so against all these "fun" behaviors when you were Mr. Hippy Party Animal?

Larry Responds

True. It might have been hypocritical of me, but when I made the offer I was a parent, not a college student. Your mother (who did her share of partying, too) and I were responsible for raising you the best way we could and that meant helping you avoid our mistakes. And it worked. You collected $3,000 from us on your 21st birthday, and we patted ourselves on the back for parenting you through your teen years without a major disaster.

But you make a good point, Meagan. Many Baby Boomers have faced the conundrum of telling their Generation X and Generation Y children not to behave as they did during the rebellious 60s and 70s. We have Baby Boomer friends who just don't mention that period to their kids. Others confess, but explain that they were foolish and should not be imitated. Some just fabricate a more innocent picture of themselves. Bill Clinton, for example, told us that he had smoked marijuana but didn't inhale. Right! Has anyone ever smoked marijuana and not inhaled?

It was a special time for Baby Boomers. Not only were we the first generation whose parents could afford to send us to college, we were the first generation who had the time and inclination to question Traditional authority while we were there. And we were given lots of good reasons to do so.

Each night on the news we saw our high school friends being maimed and killed in a war that supported a corrupt regime in Vietnam. We watched policemen attacking peaceful black demonstrators with fire hoses and dogs. We witnessed the Ohio National Guard gunning down student protestors at Kent State University. So our rebellion was about more than just drugs.

To paraphrase Bob Dylan, "The times, they were a changin'."

The Postwar Baby Boom

As mentioned in Chapter 1, World War II forced the Traditional Generation to postpone having children. When the soldiers came home in 1945, the birthrate began to soar. Medical advances in the management of pregnancy and childbirth helped this phenomenon. Doctors learned to induce labor, reducing the number of stillborns. The Tuohy needle was developed, which allowed childbirth epidurals to be more easily administered. The number of scans used to detect problems early in pregnancy increased. More vaccines were created to control childhood diseases and overall infant and maternal nutrition improved. Consequently, between 1940 and 1960, infant mortality in the United States dropped 51 percent for whites and 59 percent for blacks.

The unprecedented surge in the economy following the war also helped the baby boom. Many feared that the immense drop in military production that would come at war's end, combined with the return of millions of service members, would create unprecedented levels of unemployment and force the economy back into the Great Depression. These fears turned out to be groundless.

The auto industry, which had been enlisted to make tanks, jeeps, and trucks during the war, easily converted back to making vehicles for domestic use. In 1950, the United States produced more than 80 percent of all noncommercial vehicles worldwide.[1] Clothing manufacturers that had made uniforms for the military transitioned back to making civilian apparel. Food processors, which had produced K rations for the infantry, started making frozen TV dinners. And so it went with every other industry that had been enlisted into the war effort.

Technology developed during the war was applied to consumer goods and services. For example, after the war, Boeing marketed the first pressurized airliner, the Stratoliner, which was a derivative of the B-17 bomber. The 33-seat Stratoliner, which could fly as high as 20,000 feet and reach speeds of 200 miles per hour, revolutionized the postwar airline industry.

Driving this conversion from wartime to peacetime economy was an unprecedented, pent-up demand for goods. Returning soldiers and their soon-to-be spouses needed washers, dryers, kitchen appliances, furniture, clothing, high chairs, cribs, lawn mowers, and cars. It was a great time for American manufacturing. If you could make it, you could sell it. And it didn't hurt that there were no overseas competitors to worry about. While the industrial complexes of Europe and Asia had been decimated by the war, American industries were left untouched.

Most of all, these new families needed houses. Facilitated by the FHA (Federal Housing Administration) and the GI Bill, it became easier than ever for couples to get mortgages and buy homes. This spurred an unprecedented spike in home building. In 1940, 43.6 percent of American families owned their own home. By 1960, that number had jumped to 61.9 percent.

Seemingly overnight, housing developments sprouted around every major city, giving rise to a new phenomenon on the American landscape: suburbia. Shopping centers multiplied, rising from just eight at the end of World War II to 3,840 by 1960. At the same time, the nation's gross national product rose from around $200 billion in 1940 to $300 billion in 1950 and to more than $500 billion in 1960.

But mostly, the postwar baby boom was driven by all those lonely, affection-starved soldiers coming home to lonely, affection-starved wives and girlfriends. From 1946 to 1965, the U.S. birthrate climbed at a record pace, creating the largest generation on record.

Signposts for Baby Boomers
Signpost: The GI Bill

At the end of World War II, more than 7 million soldiers took advantage of the GI Bill to further their educations and skill levels at universities, trade schools, and business programs. By 1947, veterans made up 49 percent of all college students. Consequently, as they graduated and began raising children (Baby Boomers), they expected their children to also go to college.

Baby Boomers React: The Expectation of Higher Education

The impact of the GI Bill is measurable, and it is significant for both Traditionals and Baby Boomers:

> ▷ From 1940 to 1964, the percentage of people between the ages of 18 and 22 who attended college tripled.
> ▷ In 1970, more than 6 million people were enrolled in postsecondary education, four times the number enrolled in 1940.[2]
> ▷ From 1965 to 1985 the number of students in American colleges and universities doubled to 12 million.[3]

More Baby Boomers went to college than in any previous generation because more of their parents had gone. They became the best-educated generation the country had ever seen, and much of the credit goes to the GI Bill. When working with Boomers, this fact can be a springboard for a relationship-building conversation. If you know that the Baby Boomer you're working with is probably the first of his family to go to college, he might appreciate your asking about how he came to go to school and if his parents encouraged him to do so.

Signpost: *Dr. Spock's Baby and Child Care*

In 1946, the book *Dr. Spock's Baby and Child Care*[4] by Benjamin Spock, MD, changed the way the Traditional Generation viewed raising and developing their Baby Boomer children. Previously, the general belief was that emotions and affection should be withheld from children for fear of spoiling them. They were to be seen and not heard. Dr. Spock's book redefined this paradigm. He encouraged parents to express affection toward their kids, to talk to them, and to encourage them to talk back. He popularized the idea that having a happy childhood is essential for growing into a healthy adult.

According to Dr.Spock.com, Dr. Spock's book was so successful because in postwar America "parents were in awe of doctors and other childcare professionals. . . . Spock assured them that parents were the true experts on their own children. He told them that parenting could be fun, that mothers and fathers could actually enjoy their children and steer a course in which their own needs and wishes could also be met. All this and much more, including a wealth of helpful medical advice, was delivered in a friendly, reassuring, and common-sense manner, completely at odds with the cold authoritarianism favored by most other parenting books of the time."[5]

As a result, *Dr. Spock's Baby and Child Care* became a worldwide best seller. It has been translated into more than 40 languages and has sold more than 50 million copies. *Life* magazine named Dr. Spock one of the 100 most influential people of the 20th century, and millions of U.S. parents called him "the nation's baby doctor."[6]

Ironically, Dr. Spock's philosophy that children were to be celebrated, cherished, and developed to the greatest extent possible led to severe criticism of him when these children later went to college and started protesting the Vietnam War. Many accused him of spoiling an entire generation of Americans, a charge that followed him all his life.

Baby Boomers React: Kinder, Gentler Spirits

Rolfing, est, *I'm OK, You're OK*, yoga, the Esalen Institute, aromatherapy, self-actualization, finding oneself. These and many other practices became synonymous with Baby Boomers in the 1960s and 1970s. In fact, 1960s activist Todd Gitlan called the Boomer quest the "voyage into the interior."[7]

Having been raised in families where they were celebrated rather than tolerated, Boomers constantly received messages from their Spock-educated parents that they were special. Consequently, they often entered young adulthood believing they actually were without understanding why. They became obsessed with looking inward to discover who they were and the spiritual meaning to life. In a survey of 300,000 college freshmen in 1967, 86 percent said "developing a meaningful philosophy of life" was an essential life goal. In 2004, only 42 percent of college freshmen agreed with that same statement.[8]

Of course, it helped that their parents, for the most part, were providing financial aid while they attended college. When you're not struggling to pay your rent or buy food, you can cast your attention to more intellectual interests like civil rights; protesting the Vietnam War; and finding your true, spiritual self.

As Baby Boomers approach retirement, many are returning to their search for answers to life's mysteries. Whether they "found themselves" or not when they were young, most went on to marry, create families, pursue careers, sue for divorces, and have more families. Now that they're older, many are thinking once again about the universe beyond themselves. Some are returning to Traditional religion while others are looking at non-Traditional answers to life's spiritual questions. And all this searching, to some degree, can be traced back to their parents embracing the kinder, gentler spirit of *Dr. Spock's Baby and Child Care.*

Consequently, Boomers are often interested in creating a better world. So when you pitch a product to a Boomer customer or try to sell your Boomer boss on a new idea, in addition to addressing the bottom line, you might want to explain how your product, project, or idea will make the world a better place to live in.

Signpost: The Soviet Union Goes Atomic

. . . .

Larry Remembers

Like the publication of *Dr. Spock's Baby and Child Care,* this example is another signpost that we Baby Boomers don't remember but that had a far-reaching impact on us. As a child in the 1950s, I remember the air raid siren that went off at noon every Saturday to make sure it would work if the Russians invaded. I also remember the air raid drills at school that were designed to prepare us for nuclear attack. We were told to duck under our desks and not look at the windows because we might be blinded by the blast's bright light or the flying glass. That seemed reasonable until the teacher showed us a film about the atomic bomb that included shots of actual tests in the Nevada desert.

Faux buildings with mannequins and vehicles placed around them were set up at various distances from ground zero. High-speed cameras filmed the buildings in slow motion as they were hit by shock waves from the blast. The buildings flattened while the mannequins and the vehicles evaporated. I was not all that bright, but I was smart enough to realize that during a nuclear attack, whether or not you looked at the windows of the classroom was a moot point. Everyone was going to die!

That realization caused me to question, for the first time, what the authority figures in my life were telling me. Either they were lying about what would happen if an attack occurred or they had no clue. Either way, I was not reassured. I was nine years old.

From that point on, through high school and college, I suspected that I would never live past 30 because the world wouldn't last that long. The fear was compounded when the federal government recommended that we install a fallout shelter in our backyard. According to civil defense authorities, a concrete block basement shelter could be built as a do-it-yourself project for $150 to $200.[9] That may not seem like a lot of money now, but back then we struggled to make our house payment, which was only $60 per month. I was sure my parents wouldn't spend $200 on a bomb shelter, and I was right.

The 1960 TV images of Soviet Premier Nikita Khrushchev banging his shoe on the table at the United Nations proclaiming that the Soviet Union would "bury us" didn't help either. When we came to the brink of nuclear war with the Soviet Union during the Cuban Missile Crisis in 1963, I remember thinking, "Well, the end has finally come."

Meagan Responds

Wow, Dad, I didn't realize you were so fatalistic about the future. You always struck me as pretty upbeat about life and what could be

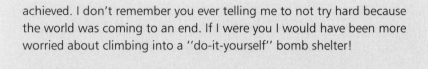

achieved. I don't remember you ever telling me to not try hard because the world was coming to an end. If I were you I would have been more worried about climbing into a "do-it-yourself" bomb shelter!

Baby Boomers React: Questioning Authority

For many Baby Boomers, the 1960s was a time of disillusionment with and disappointment in the people and institutions that had been the bed-rocks of their upbringing. As they grew into adulthood, they began to see the foibles and imperfections of their parents, teachers, religious leaders, and government officials. To a certain degree, this is a normal part of maturation. It's been said that we have reached adulthood when we can forgive our parents for not being perfect.

For Baby Boomers, the fatalism and cynicism generated by the nu-clear arms race exacerbated these sentiments, an attitude that was reaf-firmed with the assassinations of John F. Kennedy, Martin Luther King, Jr., and Robert Kennedy, and the killing of four students during the Kent State protests.

Signpost: Overcrowded Schools

Demographically, the post-WWII baby boom has been described as an elephant swallowed by a python. American school systems were the first to feel the elephant in 1953 when the 3.8 million Baby Boomers born in 1947 turned six years old and set off for school. Seventy-five million more followed in the next 17 years. From 1946 to 1956 the number of students in the first through eighth grades increased 50 percent.[10] Crowded class-rooms were common, and it was not unusual for students to share school supplies, books, and even desks. During the 1950s, California opened an average of one new school per week, and still didn't have enough classrooms.[11] Forty-five percent of today's U.S. public schools were built between 1950 and 1969.

Baby Boomers React: Working Well with Others

Attending school in these crowded conditions, Baby Boomers quickly learned the value of teamwork. Report cards, for the first time, included "works well and plays well with others" as a graded category. Involvement in team sports like basketball, baseball, and football was encouraged for boys and girls were urged to become cheerleaders or join clubs.

This familiarity with the team concept served many Boomers well after leaving high school. Those who worked for social change on college campuses found that doing so as a team helped their causes. Those who pursued a traditional path found that teamwork helped them succeed with school projects, especially if they belonged to a sorority, fraternity, or some other group. Those who went to Vietnam learned quickly that teamwork was essential for survival.

Consequently, as Baby Boomers moved into management positions in the 1980s, teamwork began to occupy a greater and greater role in company operations. It was during this period that we first heard about quality circles, high-performance teams, self-directed teams, and executive teams. Remember "There is no 'I' in TEAM"?

Before the 1980s, most companies were top-down, command-and-control systems. Management made decisions, and employees were expected to unquestioningly follow. As Baby Boomers entered management positions, they challenged and changed this system. A 1987 study of Fortune 1000 companies revealed that 70 percent had moved to a team model to solve problems and 27 percent relied on self-managed work teams (SMWTs) to complete work. The study was repeated six years later and found the use of problem-solving teams had increased to 91 percent and the use of SMWTs had jumped to 68 percent.[12]

Baby Boomers got an "A+" for working well with others. Which means that they have an inordinate appreciation for the power of teams and for working in harmony with others. Taking a team approach with a Boomer goes a long way toward cementing your relationship with him or her.

Signpost: *Brown v. Board of Education*

The oldest Baby Boomers were only seven when this landmark decision was made, so few of them remember the actual event. Its subsequent impact on American education and on their lives, however, was substantial.

Sponsored by the Topeka, Kansas, chapter of the NAACP, and named for Oliver Brown, one of the plaintiffs, the class action suit challenged an 1879 Kansas state law that permitted segregated elementary schools in certain cities of the state, based on the grounds that separate, but equal, facilities were provided to black children. The plaintiffs were 13 parents of 20 black children who had attempted to enroll their children in all-white schools and been denied. The court found that the 1879 law "violates the 14th amendment to the U.S. Constitution, which guarantees all citizens equal protection of the laws." The court determined that "separate but equal is not equal." The statement "Separate but equal is not equal" became a catchphrase for the ruling and the civil rights movement that followed. The decision forever changed the landscape of American education.

Of course, the decision was not immediately followed by implementation. Only after a host of subsequent lawsuits and attempts at forced desegregation did the issue finally appear somewhat resolved 30 years later, in the mid-1980s.

Brown v. Board of Education was the first major legal step toward racial equality to which Baby Boomers could relate. The decision gave moral justification for the civil rights movement for many white Boomers who, as they entered college in the 1960s, otherwise might not have cared. After all, if it was unconstitutional to segregate schools, it should be unconstitutional to segregate lunch counters, busses, and all other aspects of public life. For most Boomer blacks, of course, the issue was more personal and most likely didn't require legal justification. Even so, *Brown v. Board of Education* lent a great deal of legal weight to the movement.

For many Baby Boomers who became parents in the 1970s, school desegregation was personal. Many schools bussed students across district lines to comply with *Brown v. Board of Education.* This was met with great resistance from many parents, especially white parents. Most notable was ROAR (Restore Our Alienated Rights), organized by Louise Day Hicks in 1974. ROAR organized marches, motorcades, demonstrations, and protests to stop the bussing while facing opposition from the NAACP and other African American organizations.[13] In the end, the schools achieved some semblance of integration, and life went on.

Baby Boomers React: Decreasing Racial Discrimination

It's safe to say that racial discrimination, while not completely eliminated from the American landscape, has been substantially reduced. Before 1967, no major U.S. city had elected a black mayor since a number of southern cities did so during Reconstruction.[14] As of October 24, 2008, there were 641 African American mayors in the United States, with at least one in every state.

In 1967, the Supreme Court struck down Virginia's "Racial Integrity Act of 1924," which made it illegal for blacks and whites to intermarry. Since then, black-white marriages have increased from 65,000 in 1970 to 422,000 in 2005.

We also elected our first African American president in 2008.

As the first major Supreme Court decision in modern times to strike down a discriminatory law, *Brown v. Board of Education* can claim to be the starting point for these remarkable changes. Although most of the changes were initiated and driven by visionary members of the Traditional Generation, such as Thurgood Marshall, who argued *Brown v. Board of Education* for the plaintiffs, President Lyndon Johnson, who championed the Civil Rights Act of 1964, and Martin Luther King, Jr., who had the dream to make it all happen, many of the marchers, protesters, and advocates were Baby Boomers who deserve some of the credit for this dramatic paradigm shift.

The result is a generation that prides itself on embracing change, whether it be in changing the office procedures to be more efficient, changing the corporate culture to be more productive, or changing the mission of the company to better serve the community. If you work with Baby Boomers, you can often gain their support for projects or initiatives by pointing out how the project will change things for the better.

Signpost: Television Reflects Our Angst

In 1954, 54 percent of all American homes had a television set. By 1960, 90 percent had one.

As noted earlier, entertainment reflects the values of society. The 1950s are often remembered fondly as a time when America was at peace and there was little controversy to rile up ordinary citizens—assuming we ignore the Korean War, the McCarthy witch hunts, the Soviet Union's brutal crushing of the Hungarian Revolution, and the overthrow of the Batista regime by Fidel Castro.

Television in the 1950s usually reserved controversy for Edward R. Murrow and his colleagues on the evening news. Prime-time programming portrayed American life in fairly bland terms. TV taught young Baby Boomers many of the values they still hold dear. Davy Crockett showed the importance of never telling a lie. Mexican heroes the Cisco Kid and Pancho taught the value of ethnic diversity. Ozzie and Harriet showcased how a family should look, all wholesome and nuclear. Lucille Ball and Desi Arnaz showed that mixed marriage could be fun, and Sergeant Joe Friday taught that crime doesn't pay.

This bland but wholesome fare continued into the 1960s with programs like *The Andy Griffith Show, Bewitched, Gilligan's Island, I Dream of Jeannie,* and *My Three Sons.* The few bright spots in terms of innovative thinking and creative programming came from shows like the *Twilight Zone* and *Star Trek.*

As the 1960s unfurled, however, television started to reflect a society in turmoil. *Laugh-In* poked fun at everything from government decisions to social trends, as did *The Smothers Brothers Comedy Hour*, which, after a two-year run of biting antigovernment satire, was abruptly cancelled for refusing to submit scripts to network censors before being aired. *All in the Family* debuted in 1971, followed by *The Jeffersons, The Mary Tyler Moore Show*, and *Maude*, all of which dealt with issues of bigotry, race, women's liberation, and abortion. Meanwhile, the evening news was showing unparalleled levels of graphic violence live from the rice paddies of Vietnam. Like the Baby Boomers it served, television had evolved from the sweet days of *Leave It to Beaver* and *Father Knows Best* to *M*A*S*H**, *Kojak*, and *Saturday Night Live.*

Baby Boomers React: A Worldview Shaped by TV

According to George Gerbner, dean of the Annenberg School for Communication at the University of Pennsylvania, and his colleagues, "Television is a centralized system of storytelling. Its drama, commercials, news, and other programs bring a relatively coherent system of images and messages into every home. That system cultivates from infancy the predispositions and preferences that used to be acquired from other 'primary' sources."[15]

In other words, television can replace or at least compete with family, organized religion, school, and peers in its contribution to our views of the world. Baby Boomers were the first beneficiaries (or victims) of this process, evidenced by their nostalgia for "the good old days" and content with their distrust of the very establishment under which those good old days flourished.

Signpost: *The Feminine Mystique*

The Feminine Mystique by Betty Friedan was published in 1963, the same year that President Kennedy signed the Equal Pay Act, guaranteeing equal pay for the same work regardless of the worker's gender. The following year, President Johnson signed the Civil Rights Act of 1964, which prohibited discrimination by employers on the basis of race, color, religion, sex, or national origin.

These three events mark a major signpost for Baby Boomers' attitudes about the equality of men and women.

Betty Friedan graduated summa cum laude from Smith College in 1942. She married Carl Friedan in 1947. After working as a journalist for two years, she became a housewife. While attending a 15-year reunion at Smith College in 1957, Friedan surveyed 200 alumni and discovered that most were unhappy housewives. The experience inspired her to write *The Feminine Mystique*.

Her book described the dissatisfaction many women felt with their lives as homemakers. She compared articles from women's magazines published before WWII with those same magazines published after the war. Freidan noted that the stories in the prewar publications featured confident and independent heroines, many of whom were involved in careers. The postwar stories, however, focused on "happy housewives," describing them as women whose only ambitions were marriage and motherhood.

Freidan called this homemaker ideal of femininity "the feminine mystique." She went on to describe her own voluntary submission to this model of the "ideal woman" and examined the various factors, from Sigmund Freud to Madison Avenue, that influenced her and others to make the same choice. She ended the book by outlining a New Life Plan for women where scrubbing floors and washing dishes was not considered a career.

The Feminine Mystique became an instant best seller. Betty Friedan went on to help start the National Organization for Women (NOW). Her book was followed by a host of other feminist books and publications including *The Female Eunuch* by Germaine Greer, *The First Sex* by Elizabeth Gould Davis, and *Our Bodies, Ourselves* by the Boston Women's Health Book Collective.

And then there was *Ms.* magazine. Originally an insert in the *New York Times* magazine section, *Ms.* morphed into a monthly women's magazine that focused on issues like unequal pay for women, career opportunities for women, and job-related sexual harassment. After the first regular issue hit the newsstands in July 1972, network news anchor Harry Reasoner commented, "I'll give it six months before they run out of things to say." Within weeks, *Ms.* had received 26,000 subscription orders and over 20,000 reader letters.[16] In the mid-1980s, its circulation reached as high as 550,000. Today, almost 40 years later, it is not the popular powerhouse it once was, but *Ms.* is still in business as a quarterly publication with a circulation of about 110,000.[17]

During the 1950s and 1960s, women earned approximately 30 percent less than their male counterparts for performing the same jobs. Certain jobs were considered appropriate for men but not for women, and vice versa. This dichotomy was reflected in the want ads of most newspapers, which were divided into jobs for men and jobs for women. Positions that could be filled by either sex would be listed in both columns, but with a lower pay scale for women. The Equal Pay Act of 1963 made gender-based pay differentiation illegal, which was progress, but it did not address the issue of sex discrimination in hiring as reflected in the separate advertising for male and female jobs.

When the Civil Rights Act of 1964 came to Congress, feminists lobbied hard for the addition of an amendment prohibiting sex discrimination in employment. After much debate, Title VII was added, making it illegal for employers to discriminate on the basis of sex, as well as race, color, religion, or national origin. The EEOC (Equal Employment Opportunity Commission) was formed in 1965 to enforce Title VII. Pushing for its formation was Betty Freidan and her cohort of feminist activists.

· ·

Meagan Comments

When I was six years old, my Baby Boomer mom had a T-shirt that read, "Sometimes the Best Man for the Job Is a Woman." There was a picture of the Mona Lisa wearing overalls underneath the slogan. I loved the image because I had a pair of overalls and if the Mona Lisa liked them, she was okay in my book. I did not understand the slogan, however, so I asked my mom to explain. "A woman job candidate is just as good as a man candidate," she replied. That annoyed me. I thought to myself, "Well, duh, of course a woman is just as good as a man." The idea that women were treated any differently than men was inconceivable to me.

Larry Responds

Your mom will have to take credit for instilling that attitude in you. She's always believed in the equality of men and women. Resigning from AT&T because there was a glass ceiling was typical of her. (We talked about that in Chapter 1.)

• •

Baby Boomers React: Women as Equals

President Eisenhower was once asked by a journalist from the *New York Times* if a woman would make a good president. The crowd laughed when the president responded, "A woman would have the good sense not to want to be President."[18] (Nice sidestep, Ike.)

The year was 1954. There were no women running for president. In 2008, one almost *became* president. Progress has been slow, but it *has* been made:

> ▷ Back then, there were no women on the Supreme Court. As of this writing, there are 2.
>
> ▷ There were only 12 female members in the House of Representatives and 3 female members in the Senate. Today, 76 Representatives and 17 Senators are women.
>
> ▷ In 1954, there were no female state governors. Today, there are 6.
>
> ▷ In 1969, women accounted for 19 percent of all medical school students in the United States. Today they represent 48 percent.

A lot of this progress can be traced to *The Feminine Mystique*, NOW, and the efforts of a host of feminists and visionary leaders who worked tirelessly to pass the Equal Pay Act of 1963 and the Civil Rights Act of 1964. Not that the women's movement and NOW are, or ever were, perfect. Many religious leaders and conservatives vilify them because of their stances on contraception, abortion, and the "proper" role of women in society. Talk radio host Rush Limbaugh often refers to feminists as "femin-nazis."[19] But whether you support their causes or not, Betty Freidan and her feminist allies deserve credit for making it possible for the 68 million women working today to have a chance at positions equal to that of their male counterparts.

If you are a young woman working today, and you want to connect with a successful Boomer woman, you might ask her to describe her climb up the corporate ladder. Her trials and tribulations can offer you insights into managing your own course, plus give you an appreciation of what she went through. If nothing else, she may appreciate the effort and be more likely to help you succeed.

Signpost: Watergate and Vietnam

In the early hours of June 17, 1972, five men were arrested for breaking into the Democratic National Committee headquarters in the Watergate Hotel and Office Complex in Washington, D.C. It was later discovered that they were part of a secret task force that was carrying out a political spying mission on behalf of the White House. In subsequent hearings, tape recordings of White House meetings proved that President Richard Nixon had authorized the break-in and then lied about it to the American public. After two wrenching years of accusations, denials, and hearings, and with the threat of impeachment and sure conviction hanging over his head, Richard Nixon resigned in disgrace from the presidency on August 9, 1974.

Meanwhile, the Vietnam War, which had dragged on for eight years, drew to a close. One of Richard Nixon's last major acts as president was to end the long, bloody, and highly unpopular war that had killed more than 50,000 Americans and untold numbers of Vietnamese. It had also wreaked havoc on a small country half a world away, and torn this country apart as supporters and opponents rioted in the streets of America.

Baby Boomers React: Losing Confidence in Their Government

For many Baby Boomers, Watergate and the Vietnam War shattered their unquestioning faith in American institutions. For those against the war, the fact that we were spending lives and resources to prop up a corrupt regime in South Vietnam was absurd. For those in favor of the war, the fact that our military leaders weren't allowed to win it outright but could only maintain the status quo seemed equally absurd. Watergate only confirmed the opinions that our leaders were corrupt and inept.

A 2002 study by the AARP (formerly known as the American Association of Retired Persons) compared the results of a 1970s phone survey with the results of a 2002 Internet survey. The same questions were used in both surveys. The results confirm that Baby Boomers still carry remnants of their disillusionment with government. In the 1970s survey, only 3 percent of Boomers said they were very confident in what government leaders told them. Thirty years later, that number had doubled to 6 percent.[20] You could argue for significant improvement since the number doubled, but 6 percent seems pretty lame to us.

Of course, if you or a loved one was a participant, Vietnam had an even more significant impact on you. Despite doing their duty to serve their country, returning Vietnam vets were often treated not as heroes but as villains. Called "baby killers" and "warmongers," they became targets of the pent-up anger the war had sparked in the civilian population. And their government did little to change that reality. For the veterans and their families, the Vietnam War was, and still is, a powerful signpost that influences their lives.

Watergate, the Vietnam War, and other events of the 1960s and 70s pushed many Baby Boomers to view promises made by the government and other authority figures with suspicion. On the other hand, Baby Boomer levels of trust in their fellow Boomers and others have remained high. In his book *The Moral Foundations of Trust,* Eric M. Uslaner points out, "Boomers had very sharp declines in trust in the early 70s, but by the late 80s had become the most trusting cohort."[21] Trust in each other, that is.

Signpost: Civil Rights Movement

Larry Remembers

When Meagan was nine years old, she told us about Julie, a new friend she had made at school. For the next month, Julie was all we heard about. "Julie said this." "Julie said that." "Julie's mom doesn't make her eat green beans." "Julie has two dogs. Can we get another one?"

Finally, CJ and I suggested that she invite Julie over on Saturday for what Gen X mothers today call a "play date." When Julie arrived, we were surprised to see that she was African American. After she left, we asked Meagan why she hadn't told us Julie was black, and Meagan replied, "What's black?" It made me realize how far race relations have come, at least within our family.

As a child, I remember my grandmother using the "N" word in casual conversation. I don't think she did so maliciously. In her world (she came from a West Texas ranching family), it was what you called black people. In fact, I remember her bringing soup to Hattie, the black woman who did her ironing, when Hattie took sick. Of course, my grandmother would never have invited Hattie to come to a dinner party at her house or accompany her to church. It just wasn't done. And the idea of her daughter dating Hattie's son would have given her a heart attack. My grandmother bore no ill will toward black people, but she firmly believed the two races should stay separate.

My mother, on the other hand, was a Depression-baby liberal who maintained her membership in the ACLU until she died at the age of 83. She would never have used the "N" word and she slapped my face the one time I did. She would have invited Hattie to lunch, if she'd had the chance, but I don't remember any black people ever coming to our house unless it was to fix something. As far as going out with Hattie's son, my mother once told me that despite her liberal leanings, she drew the line at interracial dating and marriage, so she wouldn't have done it.

I was a middle-class white kid who went to college in the 1960s and played at being a hippie. I never used the "N" word because I found it repulsive. I made a conscious effort to maintain a nonprejudicial attitude toward everyone, especially black people. As for dating Hattie's daughter, I would have done so without hesitation. In fact, before I was married, I dated a black woman. Had it worked out, I might have married her. I think I'm as open-minded and nonracist as you can get, but when I am with someone from another race, especially African American, I am aware that he is black. I find myself taking care to not say something that would offend him, and I wonder what he's thinking, as a black person, about what I am saying. So, for me, to some extent, race is still an issue.

I don't think race has ever been an issue for Meagan. She includes people in her life of all colors and backgrounds. Her being oblivious to her childhood friend Julie's color gave me great hope for the country and the future of race relations.

• •

It's hard to pin down exactly when the modern civil rights movement began. Some people point to President Harry Truman's executive order in 1948 stating, "There shall be equality of treatment and opportunity for all persons in the armed services, without regard to race, color, religion, or national origin."[22] Others point to the *Brown v. Board of Education* decision in 1954 that made racial segregation illegal. For others, it was the arrest of Rosa Parks in 1955 for refusing to move to the back of a Montgomery, Alabama, bus. In our experience, however, when most people think of the civil rights movement, they think of Dr. Martin Luther King and the "I Have a Dream" speech he delivered to 200,000 people on the Capitol Mall on August 28, 1963.

Marked by protests, both peaceful and violent, there's no doubt that the civil rights movement advanced the rights of minorities in America and changed the way we do business. And the struggle continues. As recently as 2008, Senator Edward Kennedy (D-MA) introduced the Civil Rights Act of 2008. Some of the proposed provisions included ensuring that federal funds are not used to subsidize discrimination, holding employers accountable for age discrimination, and improving accountability for other violations of civil rights and workers' rights.[23]

Baby Boomers React: Stamping Out Racism

Today, it's not surprising to find that your doctor, lawyer, priest, accountant, local politician, or undertaker are neither white nor male. African Americans, Latinos, Asians, and other minorities populate professional, managerial, executive, and governmental positions far beyond the levels of the 1960s. A new, black middle class has emerged, and Latinos are the largest minority in the country and growing rapidly.

Racial discrimination is certainly still with us but it is refreshing to note that not only is it illegal, but responsible companies and organizations consider it an abomination. Cultural norms that say it's okay to tell a racist joke or make a racially derogatory statement have gone the way of smoking on airplanes and drinking while you drive. It's just not cool to do it.

In 2006, during a comedy routine at a Los Angeles nightclub, the highly talented comedian Michael Richards, of *Seinfeld* fame, was caught on tape angrily spewing racial epithets at a heckler. The tape instantly appeared on YouTube.com and Richards's career came to a crashing halt, with good reason. Such blatant racial bigotry simply isn't tolerated anymore. We have to ask ourselves if his tirade would have crushed his career before the civil rights movement. We think not. When it comes to racism, discrimination, and bigotry, things are not perfect, but they have gotten much, much better. We have a host of visionary Traditionals and their activist Boomer children to thank for the improvements.

Signpost: The Decadent 1980s

The stagflation of the 1970s continued until 1982, when interest rates finally declined and the economy rebounded. By 1984, the United States was enjoying significant economic growth.

Boomers React

Baby Boomers who had railed against the establishment in the 1960s and 70s began to change their attitudes. It became socially acceptable to vote Republican and pursue financial prosperity. Symbolic of this change was the transformation of 60s radical Jerry Rubin, one of the Chicago Seven who stood trial for inciting the riots that disrupted the 1968 Democratic Convention. He became an investment banker in the 1980s. He organized networking seminars for Wall Street professionals and conducted a series of debate tours with fellow '60s radical Abbie Hoffman titled "Yippie vs. Yuppie," during which he argued for exchanging the values of radicalism for the benefits of capitalism.[24]

The 1980s saw the morphing of Baby Boomers into what humorist Alice Kahn called "yuppies," a modified acronym of "young urban professional."[25] They have been defined as people between the ages of 25 and 39 with incomes of at least $40,000 (a healthy income in 1984) and with a professional or management job. Yuppies were estimated in 1984 to be 20 million strong. On December 31, *Newsweek* declared 1984 "The Year of the Yuppie."

Not surprisingly, the 1980s became known as the "decade of consumption." QVC was pumped into our homes. Automobiles sported bumper stickers that read "I Owe, I Owe, So Off to Work I Go," "Shop Till You Drop," and "He Who Dies with the Most Toys Wins." (We recently saw a variation of the "toys" bumper sticker that read, "He Who Dies with the Most Toys . . . Still Dies.")

The Bottom Line

According to a survey conducted by leading-edge gerontologist Ken Dychtwald for Merrill Lynch, 76 percent of Baby Boomers intend to keep working and earning in retirement.[26] That's good news for employers who dread the brain drain and experience void their eventual leaving will create. It's not such good news if you are a Gen Xer or fast-tracking Gen Yer looking to move up in your organization.

Either way, Baby Boomers can be an enormous resource for you and your company. Living through the tranquil '50s, turbulent '60s, disillusioning '70s, decadent '80s, booming '90s, and financially seesawing 2000s has given them wisdom and insight that will be sorely missed when they finally leave. If you work with Boomers, take this opportunity to learn from them. Ask them to teach you their strengths: dealing with change, navigating politics, and working in teams.

If you live with Boomers, know that they plan to be around a long time. In 1900, the average life expectancy for both sexes of all races was 47.3 years. As of 2005, it was 77.8 and climbing. That may be the statistical reality, but the RIC (Rehabilitation Institute of Chicago) released a study in 2004 showing Baby Boomers expect to live much longer. RIC polled 1,000 respondents nationwide between the ages of 43 and 57. Fifty percent expect to live beyond age 80 without serious limitations on their activities and more than 75 percent have turned to medical science to enhance the quality of their lives with physical rehabilitation, prescription medication, surgery, chiropractic, and acupuncture as treatment options.[27]

It will take a long time to work this elephant through the python.

CHAPTER 3

Managing Boomers

"Two reasons to hire Boomers: They don't expect to be complimented for breathing and they're unlikely to take the week off because someone broke their heart."
—Cindy Cooke, Director of Boomerz[1]

Pushing Back Retirement

As they prepare to retire, many Baby Boomers are looking forward to either starting new careers or engaging in active retirements. Unfortunately, because their stock investments and retirement accounts took such a drastic hit during the economic meltdown of 2008, many Baby Boomers will have to wait to do either. In an AARP survey published in May 2008, 27 percent of workers ages 45 and up said the economic slowdown had prompted them to postpone plans to retire.[2] The good news for employers is that they will continue to be in the workforce for some time to come. The bad news for Gen X and Gen Y is that Baby Boomers will continue to be in the workforce for some time to come, potentially blocking their path to advancement.

Most Baby Boomers have much to offer. They have the experience to successfully get their jobs done while avoiding the pitfalls that come with gaining that experience. Unfortunately, some may be on "cruise control," just waiting to exit. Worse, some may have already retired without actually leaving the building. Whatever the case, the challenge for any manager is to maximize the contributions they make before they leave while minimizing the damage some may cause by staying.

Take Bill, for example. He's a Baby Boomer account executive for a heavy equipment supply company. He knows the likes and dislikes of all the buyers to whom he sells. He sees many of them at church and the Rotary Club. He sends their kids birthday cards and congratulatory texts when they hit a Little League home run or have a piano recital. He knows never to call on one certain customer in the mornings because the fellow is usually hungover. He never calls on another in the afternoon because her mood tends to worsen as the day progresses.

Bill always exceeds his quota and makes his bonuses. Bill manages his internal relationships as carefully as his external relationships with his customers. He has friends in packing, production, and shipping. These carefully built connections allow Bill to expedite orders for his customers and excel as a salesperson.

No one is irreplaceable, nor should they be, but replacing Bill when he finally retires will be costly. The longer you can keep the Bills of the world around, the greater the benefit to the organization and your team.

Not that Bill is perfect. Despite the great value he adds to the organization, he sometimes stands in the way of progress because he's slow to adapt to new technology. Long after his company was using electronic ordering, he was still doing his orders on paper and having someone else enter them on the computer. He often voices his opinions loudly when he thinks things are going in the wrong direction, which can be positive when he's right but distracting and time wasting when he's wrong.

Anyone managing Bill would need to have some strategic goals in mind:

> Keep him motivated and excited about the job he's doing so he continues to contribute and make sales.

> Ensure that he trains and mentors a replacement so his hard-earned "tricks of the trade" aren't lost when he leaves.

> Help him overcome his resistance to change so he doesn't stand in the way of progress.

Tips for Managing Boomers

1. Don't Ignore Them

Since these folks have been around for a while, they probably have the ability to get along on their own without much interference. It's tempting to leave them alone and direct your attention to the more demanding Generation Xers and Generation Yers. That can be a mistake.

This is the generation that craved teamwork. They practically invented it. They often have more to contribute than anyone else. Leaving them alone risks losing their insights into the team process, organizational politics, and operational intricacies.

That doesn't mean looking over their shoulders. Given their experience on the job, Baby Boomers are particularly sensitive to feeling micromanaged. Engage them when you need their help but avoid holding their hands.

2. Make Them Mentors

Assigning a *sempai* (mentor) to a *kohai* (mentee) is a common practice among Japanese companies. A promising young manager, the *kohai,* is assigned to an older, more experienced manager, the *sempai.* The *sempai* is usually outside the *kohai*'s chain of command and functions much like a "godfather" to him or her. In addition to his normal managerial duties, the *sempai* helps the *kohai* succeed in all areas of work from technical know-how to operational issues to organizational politics.

There's a wonderful scene in the movie *Tampopo* in which a group of Japanese businessmen go to lunch at a fancy French restaurant. As is the custom in Japanese culture, everyone waits for the CEO to order and then they all order the same thing. When the waiter gets to the youngest member of the group, however, he grills the waiter about all the options on the menu, asking which wines go with which entrées, and finally orders a meal three times more expensive than that of the CEO. As he does this, his *sempai* is kicking him under the table, trying to keep him from killing his career.

You may wonder why you wouldn't just have the young person's manager be the *sempai.* Isn't it the manager's job to mentor her people? To a degree, that's true, but the manager must often make decisions that adversely affect the *kohai.* She may have to pass him over for a promotion or place him on an assignment that is necessary but won't contribute to his growth. Her first responsibility is not to the *kohai* but to the work unit.

On the other hand, because the *sempai* has no responsibility for the success of the *kohai*'s work unit, but is only accountable for the success of the *kohai,* he or she can focus on helping the *kohai* do well. It's a matter of incentive. The manager is rewarded when the group is successful. The *sempai* is rewarded when the *kohai* is successful. If the manager has to fire the *kohai,* it becomes a black mark on the *sempai*'s career.

Consequently, the subordinate is rewarded because he can be more open with someone who is not part of the chain of command. The *sempai* can get at the real reasons an employee is flailing, not just the politically correct, pat answers one might give to the boss. Together, they can address the real issues. Wouldn't you have loved to have had a mentor with that level of interest in your success early in your career?

Our suggestion is to create a system that assigns Baby Boomers to serve as *sempais* for promising Gen Xers and Gen Yers. Include it as an assigned duty on the contract that is the basis for the Baby Boomers' performance reviews. Be sure to involve each Baby Boomer *sempai* in the process of selecting the *kohai*, identifying the *kohai*'s goals, establishing the criteria for her success, and clarifying personal preferences so the Boomer doesn't feel like he didn't have a say in whom he was assigned or what he was supposed to accomplish.

When a Gen X *kohai* achieves success by mastering a skill, completing a project, or getting promoted, be sure to invite her Baby Boomer *sempai* to the recognition party and applaud him for his part in the success.

3. Ask for Continuing Contributions

Art, a heavy equipment mechanic for a city government, was a Baby Boomer four years away from retirement. According to his Gen Xer boss, Jan, Art had been on cruise control for some time. His production numbers were down, although they weren't below acceptable levels. He came to work, did his job, and went home. If he talked about anything, it was about how anxious he was to retire or how crappy the equipment was at work.

Take the system for removing engines. The organization only had cherry-picker-type removal devices. They were fine for pulling engines on cars and pickup trucks, but to pull an engine on something big, like a fire engine, the mechanics had to jerry rig a cherry picker to make it work. It was awkward, time-consuming, and not safe.

Tired of listening to him gripe, Jan asked Art to head a committee of mechanics to develop a better solution. Reluctantly, Art agreed. He and the group decided the shop needed an overhead crane system, but the budget deficit—it was early 2009, California was going broke, and all governmental agencies were screaming poverty—made it unlikely that such a high-cost item would ever be approved. Jan told Art that if his committee could figure how to justify the investment, he would be leaving a legacy that would benefit his fellow mechanics and the city for years to come.

With that, Art was hooked. He dove into the project, working on it during his lunch hours, after work, and on weekends. He and his team ran time-in-motion studies and gathered statistics comparing cherry pickers to overhead cranes. They contacted other equipment management centers to get their input on the best, most cost-efficient equipment, and they created blueprints for the installation.

When the team was ready, it presented its proposal to the City Council, which was, at the time, the only body that could approve such a large expenditure. After a brilliant presentation, in which Art and his team showed the short- and long-term return on investment for the project, the council approved it. Art and his team worked with the city contracting office, the architect, and the contractor to ensure the finished product met their specifications.

Since that project, Art has led two other special projects that have been successful—in addition to fixing cars, trucks, and fire engines on his regular job. Best of all, he doesn't just show up for work every day. According to Jan, he now seems to dive into every day with gusto. He still gripes about the equipment, but now he offers solutions—and he rarely talks about retirement.

Asking Baby Boomers to recommit themselves to their jobs in new and creative ways will often recapture their hearts and stimulate them to contribute until the day they leave.

4. Don't Give Up on Them

According to a survey of more than 2,200 employees ages 17 to 81 and representing 9 organizations in different industries, "older Baby Boomers (ages 53 to 61) reported significantly less support from their supervisors to acquire additional training to further their careers than did workers ages 27 to 52" (Generation Xers and younger Boomers). They also reported less access to flexible work options than did Gen Xers and Gen Yers. In addition, "those with the least amount of job tenure (0–3 years) felt more supported by their supervisors, and that they had greater access to learning and development opportunities than those with more than three years on the job."[3]

Neglecting the growth needs of Baby Boomers is understandable. They seem to be successful doing what they are doing, so why would they need the attention? After all, they'll be leaving soon, so why waste money training them when it can be better spent on someone younger?

That can be a mistake. With many Boomers planning to extend their careers because they can't afford to retire or simply like working, they may be around longer than you think. Since most Gen Xers and Gen Yers view their jobs as temporary assignments, paying to train older employees may be the safer bet. Even if the Boomer retires before you get a return on your investment, you may be able to recover that investment with some creative planning.

We know a Baby Boomer telecommunications engineer who oversaw the installation of large phone systems for big corporate customers. Six months before her retirement, her company significantly upgraded these systems, which required extensive new training for installers and the completion of a certification process. Her boss made a deal with her: He would send her to the training so she could be certified if she would agree to be on call for one year after retiring at her regular salary, prorated to a daily fee. It was a win/win. The company got the benefit of her certification for the last year she was there, plus a full year of being an on-call contractor. She got the benefit of being able to charge other consulting clients more after she retired because she had this certification.

Whether or not you can work such a sweet deal with your Baby Boomers, it would serve you well to think twice before automatically writing them off for training, no matter how close they are to leaving.

5. Deal with Resistance

The good news about Baby Boomers is that they have a wealth of experience and a long organizational memory. They know what has worked and what has failed. They know how to use the system to get things done.

The bad news is they may be convinced that what worked in the past needs to continue, regardless of whether it's still the best way to do business. They can drag their feet when it comes to change. Overcoming that resistance is important. For example, they may not take advantage of the training necessary to advance to the next level or to master new systems. They may figure, "Why bother? I'll be out of here in six months anyway."

If you simply let them resist, figuring they will retire soon, you risk eroding your credibility with the Gen Xers and Gen Yers who are watching. Down the road, you may want them to make a change they don't want, and they'll remember how you handled change with your Boomers. Your failure to insist that the Boomers "get with the program" may come back to bite you. More important, by allowing a Baby Boomer to opt out of a change effort, the organization and the team are cheated out of any increases in productivity the reluctant Boomer would have delivered with the new system or approach.

A Boomer's Perspective on Overcoming Resistance to Change

Larry Comments

If you have ever moved from one house to another, you know that change can be painful. Packing up stuff, notifying everyone that your address will change, setting up services at the new house, arranging for the movers to come: What a hassle! Not to mention the day of the move, which is exhausting.

Some years ago, our family went through this painful experience after a lot of urging on the part of Meagan's mother, CJ. We had lived in our old house near downtown Phoenix for 10 years. I was perfectly comfortable there. It was affordable, and the house had the charm that comes with homes built in the 1920s. The landscaping was lush and verdant, it had real hardwood floors, and it was close to the airport.

However, it wasn't perfect. The bedrooms were small, and since my office was in one of them, it was a bit crowded. It didn't have a pool, which would have been nice, but otherwise, I liked the house a lot.

CJ found the old house and its leaky pipes, drafty windows, and small bedrooms less charming than I did. She wanted to move to Scottsdale, an upscale suburb of Phoenix. I resisted her every effort. I argued that Scottsdale was too far from the airport, the homes didn't have the charm of our old house, and it was too expensive. She argued that the houses and the closets were bigger in Scottsdale and a new freeway would be opening soon that would make the drive to the airport almost as short as the one from our old house. I would counter with another argument, and the discussion would continue until I'd say, "Hey, how about those Phoenix Suns? Aren't they awesome this year?'' And she would stomp out of the room.

One Sunday, CJ suggested we go to brunch at a resort in Scottsdale that serves all the champagne you want for free. I noticed CJ wasn't having any, but she assured me that I could have all I wanted because she was driving. As we walked to the parking lot, she asked if I would mind stopping at an open house. Feeling a bit loose, I said, ''Sure.''

We went to several before walking into a house that had hardwood floors, a charming floor plan, lush landscaping, huge bedrooms, and a large wing that had been tastefully added to serve as an office. The wing had French doors overlooking the pool. I was dazzled.

When we got home that afternoon, I looked around the old house and thought, ''This place ain't so hot.'' We moved shortly thereafter.

Looking back, I realize that CJ had applied a key principle in overcoming my resistance to change that I now teach in my seminars. The principle is based on a song that was popular following World War I:

How ya gonna keep 'em down on the farm after they've seen Paree?[4]

You were probably thinking the principle had something to do with champagne, right? No, CJ made sure I saw for myself the benefit the change would bring to me. When I did, my resistance melted and it had nothing to do with the alcohol . . . I think.

· ·

Show Them Paree

We have a client who applied the "Show Them Paree" principle to a car dealership he owns. In an effort to make the culture more customer oriented, he contracted to send his employees through the Ritz-Carlton new employee orientation, so they could learn how to live the Ritz-Carlton mission: "Ladies and gentlemen serving ladies and gentlemen." The owner reported that the biggest changes came from some of the most hard-bitten, Baby Boomer salesmen. They returned to work with a new attitude about serving customers and a willingness to try new approaches that the owner had never seen before.

If your Baby Boomers are resisting changes, forcing them should be your last option, especially if they're close to retirement. They can simply wait you out. If you can help them see, and actually experience, the benefits they will get from embracing the change, the odds increase that they'll jump on board, even if retirement is just around the corner.

6. Confront Negative Behavior

Occasionally, a Baby Boomer may adopt a less-than-positive attitude as she approaches retirement. It may be based on unhappiness with the company or her circumstances or on mixed feelings about leaving. Or, it may simply be a product of "Short-Timer Syndrome," in which her mind and spirit have moved on to the next step in the road. Whatever the cause, if it's creating a problem that is affecting the quality or quantity of output, profitability, customer satisfaction, or team morale, the manager must deal with it.

Talking with her is the first step. In a private conversation, we recommend using the Six-Step Conversation:

1. **Describe the problem.** "Jan, I've noticed that in the last few months your reports have been late and, on two occasions, they had to be completely revised because they were inaccurate. I've also received complaints from three different clients that you're not returning their phone calls or emails. You don't seem to be attentive during staff meetings. Yesterday, Tim asked you about delivery status on an order, and it was like you didn't hear him."

2. **Explain your concern.** "I'm concerned. It's affecting our productivity and, with other people noticing, it's having a negative impact on team morale. Most of all, I'm concerned about you. You've always done a terrific job, and this change in behavior is really puzzling. I understand that retirement is not far off for you. Does that have anything to do with this or is there something else going on?"

3. **Listen to and acknowledge the person's issues.** The key here is to listen without passing judgment or saying anything except to repeat back what she says and how you think she feels. This can be an interactive discussion, but you should do most of the listening. It may require flexibility on your part to accommodate her specific situation. For example, she may have a spouse who is sick and her concerns about him have dominated her thoughts. If so, you may want to adjust her schedule or alter her workload to help her if it's appropriate. It is important, however, that you keep the conversation focused on the issues at hand and not allow this unacceptable behavior to be excused or to continue.

4. **Ask for an agreement to change.** "Jan, I really need your head in the game while you're still here. What can I do to help you?"

5. **Clarify what's been agreed on.** "Okay, so you're going to make sure your reports are timely and accurate and you'll return calls and texts to customers within an hour. I will see that you're put on a flextime schedule so you can be with your husband more. Do we have an agreement?"

6. **Express confidence and confidently expect change.** "Jan, I appreciate your help here. Like I said, you've always been a great contributor, and I truly appreciate your turning this around."

From this point, observe Jan to see if the changes occur. If they do, express your appreciation in a quiet and unobtrusive manner, preferably in private. You don't want to embarrass your wayward Boomer by congratulating her for getting her act together in front of others. If, on the other hand, the behavior continues or worsens, don't hesitate to discuss the issue again, this time outlining the consequences of her noncompliance. It may be a good time to consider arranging early retirement for her or pursuing disciplinary procedures that are endorsed by your Human Resources department.

7. Offer Opportunities to Volunteer

Many Baby Boomers have reached a point where they want to give back to society, perhaps to fulfill unrealized desires to change the world that have been dormant since the 1960s or because they feel it's time to balance the scales of karma. In 2005, nearly one-third of all Baby Boomers volunteered with formal organizations, which the Corporation for National and Community Service called the highest volunteer rate of any American group.[5]

According to the U.S. Committee on Education and Labor Web site, the recently passed Edward M. Kennedy Serve America Act will triple the number of volunteers nationwide to 250,000.[6]

You can tap into this desire to serve and enhance your company's image at the same time. Start by involving your Baby Boomers and other employees in identifying the organizations they want to support. Put Boomers in charge of communicating with these organizations to find out what they need and sharing that information within your company.

Work with your leaders to develop guidelines for how your company will support these volunteer efforts.

Baby Boomers want to serve. Helping them fulfill this desire will re-energize them, not only for the volunteering they are doing but for the company that supports them.

Tips for Younger Managers Working with Boomers

Nearly all managers must oversee people older than they are. If you are a Gen Xer or Gen Yer with Baby Boomers to manage, your success, to a large degree, is tied to how well they perform. You can help them do their best by understanding the key signposts that shaped their generation, as described in Chapter 2, and what they need from a manager at this stage of their careers.

1. Respect Their Experience

Acknowledge their experience by asking for advice. All of us like to think we have value. To a Boomer, much of that value comes from having decades of experience. Be careful, however, not to come across as pandering. Most people can tell when a manager is saying something he doesn't really mean. Focus on the work, and ask legitimate questions that acknowledge the older person's experience.

We know a Gen X sales manager who makes it a point to ask his Baby Boomer sales reps how they have handled specific customers. For example, he will say, "Hey, Jane, the buyer over at Dickenson's is giving our new sales rep a hard time. He won't give her the time of day and when he does, he tries to flirt with her. I understand you've had success dealing with him. What would you suggest?"

2. Give Them Room Without Abandoning Them

Most Baby Boomers should be at a point in their careers where they don't need much direct supervision. Too much, and they may accuse you of micromanaging. It's a matter of personal perception. You may think you are keeping your distance and not following your Boomer's progress on a project closely enough. He, on the other hand, may think you're always in his hair.

We suggest you have a frank conversation about boundaries and communication requirements early in your relationship. Make sure he knows you won't stand in the way of getting his job done. Rather, that you are there to support him and get him what he needs to achieve his goals. On the other hand, be clear about how often you want to hear from him, how quickly you want to be notified of any problems, and what kind of support you expect.

For example, how often do you expect him to inform you about day-to-day events? How do you want him to do so? Phone? Email? Twitter? At what point do you expect him to involve you in a problem? Immediately, so you can be involved in the solution, or only after he's tried to fix it and notifies you that he needs your help? How serious should the problem be before he calls?

These kinds of issues should be discussed early in every manager/subordinate relationship to avoid misunderstandings and conflicts down the road. For the young manager/older employee relationship, however, it's even more important, because the potential for misunderstanding and hurt feelings is so much greater than when the age difference is reversed.

3. Prove Yourself Through Performance

You are younger than the Boomers and that won't change. For a while, you will be perceived as "just a kid." Accept it and have a sense of humor about it. You will gain respect by your performance.

For example, a brilliant young software engineer we know was promoted to lead a team of senior scientists because they were working with advanced systems in which he had expertise. When a disagreement would arise about how to handle a problem with the system, he made it a practice to ask for their opinions first. If their solutions seemed right to him, he'd say something like, "Great, that makes sense to me." If he disagreed, he would often make a comment like, "I'm the one with the least experience, but I have an idea. What do you think about. . . ? In your experience do you think that would work?" and then present his case. As the Boomers got to know him and trust that he really understood what he was talking about, he was able to drop the humorous disqualifiers and engage with them as equals. He said it took about a year to get to that point.

4. Practice "Radar O'Reilly Management"

If you ever saw the television series *M*A*S*H*, you probably remember Radar O'Reilly, played by Gary Burghoff, a cute, naive young man who slept with a teddy bear and drank Nehi® sodas. His title was Company Clerk and Bugler. His real job, however, was to get the surgeons and nurses what they needed to do their jobs well. If they needed scalpels, he tracked them down and delivered them. If they needed a generator but none was available, he'd wheel and deal with clerks from other companies to score one. If they needed strings pulled with some top general so they could get some R&R in Tokyo, he'd persuade Colonel Potter to do it even if it was against the colonel's best judgment. One way or another, Radar got the job done and earned the respect of the others in camp, despite the fact he was only a corporal and looked 12 years old.

As a manager of people older than yourself, you want their perception to be that you are doing a great job for them. This is especially true when they observe how you deal with those above you. All your direct reports are looking to you to see how you deal with the "suits" upstairs. If you do this well and get them what they need to do their jobs well, their respect for you will climb.

5. Capture the Wisdom Boomers Offer—Before It's Too Late

When a Texas Instruments technician making control boards on a radar equipment assembly line accepted early retirement, she took with her the only knowledge about correct assembly procedures in her area—the errors in the printed documentation were all in her head. The problem was easily fixed once the faulty documentation was recognized, but the temporary loss of this knowledge cost the company $200,000 and lots of customer goodwill.[7]

This story comes from *Lost Knowledge: Confronting the Threat of an Aging Workforce* by David DeLong. In an interview, DeLong stated that most companies across the United States and around the world have Baby Boomers with deep knowledge of complex business processes, technical systems, advanced scientific processes, and complicated global management practices that are critical to the futures of their respective businesses. Their departure will likely have a major impact on the ability of these organizations to sustain high levels of performance.

Between 1969 and 1972, NASA completed six missions to the moon, DeLong points out. We could not repeat the same feat today because the people who made it happen have either died or retired and, unfortunately, the knowledge they acquired was never passed on. He suggests five key steps companies should take to minimize the costs of the looming brain drain caused by Baby Boomer retirements:

1. Recognize that not all retiring Baby Boomers are equal in terms of critical knowledge. Identify those whose departure will have the greatest impact on the organization.

2. Clarify how much time you have before specific individuals leave. This will determine your options and tactics for transferring essential knowledge.

3. Recognize the double-edged sword created by the recession of 2008. On the one hand, it makes it easier to retain Baby Boomers. Their 401ks have been decimated, so they need the money. On the other hand, it makes them reluctant to share their know-how because, as long as the knowledge is locked up in their heads, it's more likely they will keep their jobs. Your challenge is to reassure them that transferring what they know to younger employees will not raise the odds they'll become redundant.

4. Identify specific types of knowledge at risk. DeLong says there are three types of knowledge to consider when planning a knowledge transfer program for your company:

   ➤ *Explicit knowledge*—includes facts, figures, procedures, and sequences. It's all the things that can be easily transferred by reading, watching videos, and attending lectures.

   ➤ *Implicit knowledge*—easily articulated if you ask the right questions. For example, since we deliver close to 200 speeches and seminars every year, we are often asked how to give a good talk. Much of it we don't really think about, but if you asked us specifically how we handle a tough question from an audience member, we could probably tell you a story about how we handled one, and then clarify how we did it.

   ➤ *Tacit knowledge*—information you know in your gut, which is best transferred through mentoring and learning by doing. What a project manager does every day to keep her projects on time, on target, and on budget is a good example.

5. Continually connect knowledge transfer efforts to important business outcomes. Whose departure will impact you most, based on your desired strategic outcomes? For example, if your company is driven by innovation, the product developers in R&D may be where you want to concentrate your efforts. On the other

hand, if your company is more focused on growth, maybe you should focus on the retiring salespeople who are most successful.

The important thing is that you take the looming exodus of Baby Boomers seriously. We recommend DeLong's book for all organizational executives, whether in business, health care, government, or not for profit. The future is coming, and the Baby Boomers won't be around to help you deal with it, so now is the time to prepare.

6. Motivate Them on Their Terms

The owners of a Harley-Davidson motorcycle dealership wanted to reward their lead mechanic, a Baby Boomer who had been with them for 20 years, for his loyalty and dedication. They decided to give the mechanic and his wife an all-expenses-paid vacation to Hawaii. At a special luncheon, they described the mechanic's stellar performance over the years and then awarded him the trip.

From the look on his face, they could tell he was not thrilled about the award. Later, they asked him what he thought of the trip. He replied that he didn't mean to be ungrateful, but his wife had recently left him for another man, and he didn't particularly want to go to Hawaii with her or anyone else. The flabbergasted owners asked him what he would prefer instead, and he said he really liked the fancy toolbox the Snap-on sales representative had tried to sell him recently. The owners offered the toolbox instead of the Hawaii trip, and the mechanic felt better—not great—but better. It would have been better to have checked with him before the public ceremony.

What motivates people is highly individualistic, especially for Baby Boomers who have lived long enough to have a wealth of experiences. In choosing special awards or incentives for them, increased contributions to a 401k, flexible schedules so they can start developing postretirement interests, and opportunities to be recognized and applauded for their achievements make sense for most, but that doesn't mean all Boomers will want those things.

The obvious step is to ask the Boomer what reward would best recognize his contribution and then listen. For example, a Generation X manager wants to reward a Baby Boomer employee for good work, so she offers him some time off to spend with his family. He declines, noting that he has a big project he's trying to complete and taking time off would just add to his stress. The smart manager would ask, "How can I reward you for your terrific work?"

7. Leverage Strength in New Ways

Baby Boomers have had long careers to hone skills that can very often be put to use in new and innovative ways. Give them the opportunity to do so; it will help them restart their motors and renew their commitment to the organization.

The Medical Records department at Health Central in Ocoee, Florida, had poor turnaround time that impacted Accounts Receivable days and unbilled discharges. Patient and physician satisfaction was poor because the department was not timely in releasing medical records for continuity of care. Employee morale and satisfaction were extremely low and turnover was high. Internal customer satisfaction was also very low. To make things worse, the department had recently implemented an electronic medical record system, and users had not been trained to use it. The department director had resigned and the hospital was looking for a replacement.

The director of the hospital's Quality Management Department, Kathy Deel, suggested that she could run Medical Records, as well as Quality Management. Kathy had successfully combined these two departments at another hospital.

The executive committee gave her the go-ahead. Kathy, who was 55 years of age at the time, told us that the challenge was like a shot of adrenaline for her. Under her leadership, the newly combined department was prospering within a year. Medical record turnaround time was reduced from 4 days to 24 hours, well below the industry benchmark. She focused the staff on eliminating waste and revamping processes, which improved efficiency so much that she did not fill the vacancies that occurred with attrition. She also let some nonperformers go and didn't fill their positions. Today, the department operates with one-third fewer employees, patient and physician satisfaction is up, and the department is recognized as one of the best medical records units by its electronic medical record vendor. Most of all, says Kathy, the staff members who remained have an attitude of pride and team spirit that was missing before she took over.[8]

Managing Up the Age Ladder: The Dilemma of Xers and Yers Managing Boomers

1. Arrange for Recognition and Credit

Late, great Alabama football coach Bear Bryant was once asked to identify the secret to his success. He replied, "If anything goes bad, I did it. If anything goes semigood, then we did it. If anything goes real good, then you did it. That's all it takes to get people to win football games."

Like any generation, Baby Boomers like to be recognized for their achievements. To the degree you can make that happen, you will reap the rewards of their loyalty. You must be careful, however, not to sound fawning. The chances of this happening are directly proportional to the difference in your ages. If you are more than 10 years younger than the Baby Boomer you are praising, see if you can enlist the help of another Boomer from whom the praise will carry more meaning.

For example, during a team meeting, Judy, the Gen Y team leader, commented that Jack, the Baby Boomer, had really gone the extra mile to resolve a customer problem. She said, "And it's not the first time. Bill was telling me about what you did on the Anderson account, right Bill?" At that point, Bill made a comment supporting Jack's abilities. It gave Jack a double dose of praise, and it built Judy's credibility because she (1) did her homework and (2) proved she's willing to give credit where credit was due.

2. Find Your Veteran Sergeants

We have a friend who survived three tours in Vietnam as a Marine officer. He went over as a second lieutenant and left as a major. He said the most important lesson he learned was to hook up with each platoon sergeant assigned to him and ask what he needed from him to be successful. He did this when he arrived in Vietnam, and the first veteran said, "Watch our backs and don't get us killed." Not knowing quite how to do that yet, our friend said, "Okay, if you'll give me a straight answer when I ask you for help." They shook hands on the deal.

The next night they went on their first patrol. Our friend took the veteran aside and said, "You know this country better than anyone, especially me. How do you think we ought to approach this patrol?" The veteran gave him the advice he sought, and the patrol went without incident. The next morning, he said to the veteran, "In the future, if you think I'm wrong or I'm making a mistake, I want you to take me aside and tell me. I can't promise I'll always do what you suggest, but I want to hear what you have to say." It was the beginning of a three-tour partnership and a lifelong friendship.

All great leaders surround themselves with advisers who may have wisdom in areas they lack. Making an ally of a Baby Boomer who holds the respect of the team will do the same for you. It will enhance your credibility with the entire team and give you support when things get rough. Best of all, the Baby Boomer with whom you build this adviser/advisee relationship will tend to feel more vested in your success and in the success of the group.

The Bottom Line

Every generation adds value to an organization. Baby Boomers may be nearing retirement, but that doesn't mean they should be shunted to the side and ignored. They have the experience that can provide historical perspective for the decisions you face. They have overcome many obstacles and that tenacity can help your organization meet new challenges. They are team players who can enhance any group in which they participate.

But they need to be engaged. They need to feel they are still valuable to the organization. They need the freedom to act on their accumulated knowledge and skills without being micromanaged—but they don't want to be left totally adrift.

Successfully managing Baby Boomers means keeping them motivated and excited about their jobs, communicating—and listening—to ensure that they are aligned with the goals of your group and organization, and giving them the support they need to continue to perform at the highest levels.

And don't forget to capture their knowledge so all is not lost when retirement calls.

Big Bird, *Wayne's World*, and *Home Alone*: Signposts for Generation X

"Parents often talk about the younger generation as if they didn't have anything to do with it."

—*Haim Ginott*[1]

Critical Events in the Lives of Generation X

1973	First cellular phone call
1978	Jonestown mass suicides
1981	President Ronald Reagan assassination attempt
1986	*Challenger* disaster
1987	Stock market crash (Black Monday)
1988	Pan Am Flight 103 crash
1989	*Exxon Valdez* spill
1989	Fall of the Berlin Wall
1990	Gulf War
1992	Recession
1992	Rodney King beating
1993	First Boomer president (Bill Clinton)
1993	Dotcom boom begins
1994	Death of Kurt Cobain
1995	O. J. Simpson trial

In 1991, Douglas Coupland coined the term "Generation X" to describe people born between 1966 and 1980. His book *Generation X: Tales for an Accelerated Culture* was a fictional story about a group of Americans and Canadians who reached adulthood in the late 1980s.[2] He portrayed them as whiny, self-centered slackers, dissatisfied with their lots in life. A year later, Mike Myers and Dana Carvey painted Gen Xers as dim-witted goof-balls in the movie *Wayne's World.* In the basement of Wayne's parents, Wayne Campbell and Garth Algar start a local-access cable TV station dedicated to partying, pursuing "hot babes," and playing air guitar. Their adventures spawned catchphrases that Gen Xers loved to repeat, such as "Party on, Wayne. Party on, Garth," "We're not worthy," "I think I'm gonna hurl," and "Yeah, and monkeys might fly out of my butt."

Of course, this image of moronic slackers didn't fit all Gen Xers. There was Michael Dell, who founded Dell Computers when he was 17 years old. Marissa Mayer, vice president of Search Products and User Experience for Google, who was recently on *Fortune* magazine's list of the 50 most powerful women in business.[3] And there was Jeff Thompson. At the age of 14, he used the $2,500 he had earned from his paper route to start Peripheral Outlet, Inc., now one of the world's leading suppliers of computer parts.[4]

In 1998, *Fortune* ran a cover story entitled "The New Organization Man," which said of Gen Xers: "Young, educated, and fiercely in demand, 'gold collar' workers are getting salaries and perks that would make a Baby-Boomer's thinning hair stand on end. Brats? Perhaps. But hey— they're not the ones who tore up the old employment contract."[5]

Meagan's Thoughts

I read Coupland's book but as a Gen Xer myself, I didn't relate to the central characters who whined about how badly life was treating them. I thought *Wayne's World* was hilarious, but I had no desire to live with my parents, drive a rusty Gremlin, and focus my life on partying. Like most of my friends, I was concentrating on surviving college, socializing, and doing something with my life that made good money and didn't leave me feeling like I'd sold out.

When I graduated, I was offered a job as a sales rep with a major food manufacturer. It was 1993. The country was in a recession and jobs were scarce, so I jumped at the chance to work for a well-established corporation. I got a company car, full benefits, and a salary that was five times what I was making at the part-time retail sales job I had during college. I promised myself that I would succeed.

Two months later, I hated my job. The work wasn't hard, but there seemed to be unspoken rules I didn't understand. For example, my customers, who were all men my father's age, saw me as an intrusion on their day. They wouldn't make appointments with me, so I had to time my visits to catch them when they weren't busy. This wasted enormous amounts of my time and required me to work extra hours, for which I was not paid.

Also, I didn't much care for the people in the food industry. Many seemed angry to be there; they were often grumpy and rude. Once, I asked a receptionist when a store manager would be available. She ignored me and kept on typing. When I complained to the manager about her, he rolled his eyes and said, "Okay, and your point?"

Worst of all, Bill, my direct supervisor, was a sexist jerk. He would say things like "girls should wear their hair long" and "women should stay home and take care of the family." I was raised by liberal parents who preached and practiced equal rights for men and women. I was shocked that people like Bill even existed. I had no idea how, or even *if,* I should respond to his comments.

When he wasn't making idiotic statements about the role of women, he made assumptions about my knowledge and experience that left me floundering. For example, he'd tell me, "You need to be proactive, not reactive." I didn't know what he was talking about, and he wouldn't take the time to explain. It was like I was a British citizen and he expected me to know how to play baseball. I knew what the words meant, but I had no idea how to play the game.

Sixteen years later, I know what proactive and reactive look like in a business environment. As a 23-year-old new to the corporate world, I was clueless.

I know there were many things I could have done differently to improve my experience, but the management didn't go out of its way to help. The training consisted of shadowing another salesperson for a few days and meeting once every two weeks with Bill. I was reasonably successful in this job, but it was not fun.

The final straw occurred when I was out of town, doing some store resets, which had to be done at night. After working for 10 hours straight, I dragged back to my hotel room at 6:00 A.M. to get some sleep before making the two-hour drive home. Before drifting off, I checked my voice mail. There was a message from Bill saying that there was an emergency in the office and that I needed to get in ASAP. I called and got his voice mail, so I left a message reminding him I was out of town, but would be in as soon as I could. I got up, got dressed, checked out of the hotel, and sped back. I arrived bleary eyed, with no makeup and in wrinkled clothes. Bill's big emergency was that the fax machine was jammed and he wanted me to fix it. That ripped it. I gave Bill two weeks' notice on the spot.

In retrospect, I realize there was a big generational difference between Bill and me. Because of his longevity, he truly felt that some tasks were beneath him. A few months earlier, when Bill was helping me with a late-night, last-minute reset, he said, "My wife doesn't understand why I am even here tonight. She can't believe someone with my seniority would even have to do a reset. I told her I agreed."

I was annoyed. At least he got dinner. I had canceled plans with my girlfriends for dinner to do this reset. To a Gen Xer, seniority means nothing. They usually don't perceive tasks as beneath them, nor do they shy away from hard work, but they expect people around them to operate in the same fashion, title or no title. So, although Bill's behavior with the fax machine made perfect sense to him, I thought it was absurd that he wouldn't take care of the problem himself—and I was amazed that he would impose it on me after I had worked all night.

Larry Responds

Hey, Meagan, who said work should be fun?

Everything you say about your experiences with that company falls into the category of "welcome to the real world." You were in a tough industry where margins are thin, so price is everything. It's no surprise the store managers wouldn't make time for you. They were your customers, not the other way around. You *were* an intrusion on their day. As for the rude receptionist and your bigoted boss, again I say, "Welcome to the real world." I'm not saying you should put up with blatant sexism, or anything else that's patently inappropriate, but organizations are full of jerks. As a salesperson, it was your job to either charm them out of it, figure a way around them, or insist that you be treated differently. As for Bill's thing about seniority, your being young made it easy to discount his feelings. When you've put in the years like we Baby Boomers have, you may feel differently. Some jobs might not be beneath you, but it's natural to feel that you've earned the right to let someone else do them. I'm not defending Bill's behavior with the fax machine. That was carrying the concept to the absurd. But the reality is that organizations require differentiation of labor. The CEO doesn't spend her time sweeping the floor. On the other hand, if she spills her coffee and there's no one around to clean it up, she should go get a towel and do it herself.

Anyway, your mother and I were a bit freaked out when you told us you'd resigned. We had been quite relieved when you found a job so soon after college, so this news was not welcome. We were amazed that you were so nonchalant about it. As a Baby Boomer, I've had a few moves in my career, but I always planned for them carefully, making sure that there was another position to take the place of the one I was leaving.

Looking back, I realize your attitude was not uncommon for someone from Generation X. I've since learned that the average employee in his late 20s has already switched jobs five or six times. Unlike Baby Boomers and Traditionals, you Gen Xers think job hopping is okay. I'm working with some thirty-something managers now who look with suspicion at the résumé of a potential new hire if the person has had only one job. For them, if you've been out of school for three years and haven't held more than one position, there must be something wrong with you. A history of moving from one job to another has morphed from an indication of disloyalty or inability to hold a job to a desirable credential indicating a wide breadth of experience.

• •

Signposts for Generation X

Signpost: 1965: Children Become Unfashionable

Compared to their parents, Generation Xers were not born during a baby boom. In 1960, after more than a decade of research, the U.S. Food and Drug Administration (USFDA) approved Envoid-10 for public consumption. Soon referred to as the Pill, it gave women more choices when planning their future. Not just a choice to go to college, but also a choice to work or otherwise train for a skill. Prior to 1960 there were limited job options for women; teacher, secretary, nurse was the triumvirate. Marriage and children was no longer the only choice; women could now take care of themselves.

This is not to say that marriage and pregnancy, wanted or not, were the only reasons women did not go to college before, but the Pill undoubtedly gave more women the opportunity to expand their choices when they graduated high school. In 1965, for the first time in 10 years, the birthrate fell below 4 million,[6] and it continued to decline until 1980. More women pursued higher education than ever before: At the dawn of the 20th century, females held only 19 percent of all undergraduate college degrees, but by 1985 more than half of college students were women and 25 percent of them were older than 29.[7] As for marriage, the percentage of women who married dropped 47 percent between the 1940s and the mid-1970s.[8]

The emerging women's movement reinforced these trends. Inspired by the publication of Betty Friedan's *The Feminine Mystique* in 1963 and by the creation of the National Organization for Women (NOW) in 1966, the movement encouraged women to postpone marriage and family in favor of pursuing careers. The media reflected the trend. *The Mary Tyler Moore Show*, about a single young woman in her 30s making it as an assistant station manager for a local Minneapolis TV news show, was one of the most acclaimed television programs ever produced. *Ms.* magazine replaced *Ladies' Home Journal* as the major source of gender-related information for many female readers. And *Cosmopolitan,* which portrayed sexy singleness as the ideal status for women of all ages, soared to the top of the charts.

Along with the trend to having fewer children—and having them later in life—an antichild sentiment seemed to prevail in the movies. *Rosemary's Baby*, about a woman who gives birth to the Devil's child, began the trend in 1968, followed by *The Exorcist* (in which a 10-year-old is possessed by the devil), *The Omen* (in which a politician is horrified— pun intended—to learn his son is literally the Devil), and *The Little Girl Who Lives Down the Lane,* in which Jodie Foster plays a murderous child prodigy.

Most memorable, however, is Sissy Spacek's portrayal of *Carrie*, a bullied teenager who discovers she can bring death and destruction to her tormentors simply by thinking about it. The 1970s finished with *Halloween*, a highly popular film about a young man (Michael Myers) who wears a mask and murders his fellow teenagers.

You could argue these films were just entertainment, not a reflection of how children were perceived, and it's true that most people did not think of their children as spawns of Satan. Still, these films were a dramatic contrast to the movie portrayal of children in the 1950s, when the worst thing kids did was swap places behind their parents' backs, as Haley Mills did in *The Parent Trap*.

With the introduction of the Pill, the emergence of the women's movement, and the general feeling of society that having children had become *antiquated*, is it any wonder that Generation X is the smallest generation in recent history? To make things worse, by the 1970s, 50 percent of all Baby Boomer marriages had ended in divorce. This meant roughly half of all Gen Xers witnessed the dissolution of their families.

Gen Xers React: The Desire for Family and Roots

It's hard to imagine growing up in a society that values children less without the children feeling it. Paradoxically, Gen Xers appear to value children more. A publication by New York Life Insurance reinforces this point: "For decades, two children per family was the norm. Between 1995 and 2000, however, the rate of women having three or more children jumped from 11.4 percent to 18.4 percent."[9] That's a huge increase. It suggests that Gen Xers may be looking to create the family environment they thought they missed in their own childhoods.

As twenty-somethings, Gen Xers were far more cautious to marry than their Baby Boomer parents. When Generation X women reached their early 30s, 22 percent were still unmarried, compared to 10 percent of Baby Boomers.[10] Their reluctance to marry young didn't, however, mean they abandoned the institution: They only postponed it. In a study of 300 couples, Gen Xers scored higher than other generations in interviews designed to measure their level of commitment to each other.[11] As the New York Life Insurance study showed, they also had more children than their Boomer parents.

Spending time with their families is important to Gen Xers. As a result, managers need to think twice before asking them to work overtime or on weekends. Many were latchkey kids who don't want their own children to suffer the same fate. This doesn't mean they won't put in extra time for you, but it comes at a high cost. They want to see a logical reason for doing so and if they perceive that staying those extra hours could have been avoided by better management they will resent the intrusion on their time and blame you, the manager, for your ineptness.

Signpost: The Disillusioning 1970s

In the 1970s, reaction to the Vietnam War soured the attitudes of many toward government and the establishment. Where World War II brought the country together, Vietnam tore it apart. The United States had not been so divided since the Civil War.

To add to their disillusionment, prices climbed but wages didn't. When OPEC launched an oil embargo against the United States, gasoline became scarce and long lines at the pump became common. Inflation climbed into double digits. Prices rose and wages stagnated, and a new term for our misery was coined: "stagflation." (Stagflation is an economic situation in which inflation and economic stagnation occur simultaneously and remain unchecked for a period of time. The portmanteau stagflation is generally attributed to British politician Iain Macleod, who coined the term in a speech to Parliament in 1965.[12])

Unemployment reached more than 8 percent, and the country plunged into the worst recession since the Great Depression. Union workers—postal employees and railroad workers, coal miners and longshoremen, truckers and Pennsylvania state employees—all went on strike. Richard Nixon resigned.

The depressing decade ended with members of Iran's Islamic Revolution taking 66 American citizens hostage at the U.S. Embassy in Tehran. The crisis dragged on for more than a year until the hostages were released when Ronald Reagan became president.

To say that the 1970s was a decade of disillusionment for Baby Boomers is an understatement. These idealistic flower children, who were starting their careers as the decade began, soon discovered that the world was a much harsher place than they had envisioned in their college discussions about improving humanity's lot. It was in this crucible of disappointment and hard times for their parents that Gen Xers spent their formative years, acquiring many of the signposts that would affect them later in life.

Gen Xers React: Distrust and Disappointment

The 1970s were a crazy time for the Baby Boomer parents of Gen Xers. When they graduated from college, the economy was in the pits, so their careers got a slow start. They struggled with the economic backlash of Watergate, the oil embargo, stagflation, and the hostage crisis. The sexual revolution was in full swing, so many were experimenting with "open marriage," communes, and other creative living arrangements. Not surprisingly, the divorce rate climbed past 50 percent and families dissolved. All the while, their Xer children watched from the sidelines. So it's no big surprise that as these children have matured, they've been described as cynical and disillusioned. If the mantra of Baby Boomers is "We are all brothers and sisters on one big happy team," the mantra of Generation X is "Take care of yourself because no one else will." Of course, not all of them turned out so bitter. Meagan is a Gen Xer, and she survived the 1970s with her positive attitude intact—mostly. She describes herself as a happy pragmatist rather than a disillusioned cynic.

Meagan Remembers the 1970s

Two memories stand out from the 1970s for me. When I was four, my dad was struggling to find work. He said we had to be careful with our money because the economy was so bad. I remember going to the gas station with him on Saturdays and waiting forever to get gas. He'd bring a game so we could play while we waited. I remember him saying that he wished he had more than $4.00, so we could fill up and make the trip worth it. That memory sometimes crosses my mind when I'm tempted to buy something I probably shouldn't because it's too expensive. Of course, that doesn't always keep me from giving in to temptation.

The other memory is from when I was nine. I was concerned when I heard that the U.S. hostages in Iran wouldn't be home for Christmas. I worried about who would arrange to give them their gifts if they were not with their families.

Other than those two recollections, my memories had nothing to do with turbulence of the times and were mostly happy, but I was lucky. I had parents who wanted to be together and weren't alcoholics, drug users, or crazy. Many of my friends weren't so lucky. Three ran away from home before they were 15. Another had an abortion at age 14. Two had to go to drug rehab, and one of them ended up dying from an overdose. So for me, the 1970s were okay, but I wasn't blind to the fact that we were living in troubling times, and many of my friends were struggling.

Signpost: *Sesame Street* Rules

The innovative weekday television show *Sesame Street* premiered on PBS in 1969. Baby Boomers loved it because it entertained and educated their kids. Parents didn't feel guilty that their children were watching mindless cartoons. The kids loved it because it was interesting, engaging, and *fun*. The learning was incidental. The show's producer, Joan Cooney, wanted to package education so it "went down more like ice cream than spinach,"[13] and the effort paid off: An estimated 77 million children have watched *Sesame Street*.[14]

The most notable difference between *Sesame Street* and other children's TV shows, previous or current, is its pace. Shows like *Romper Room, Howdy Doody,* and *Captain Kangaroo* flowed as slowly as a regular TV sitcom. *Mister Rogers' Neighborhood* oozed out of the television like molasses on a cold morning. *Sesame Street* came at you like a machine gun: a one-minute skit in which Oscar the Grouch gave a reading lesson followed by a three-minute interaction with the adults on the show, followed by a 10-second cartoon. It was geared for the short attention span of three-year-olds, and it worked.

Twelve years later, MTV employed similar pacing with the same group, now teenagers. It showed rock music videos 24/7 interspersed with comments from hosting VDJs (video disc jockeys). The videos typically flashed images of the artists in rapid succession, often in sexually suggestive scenes, with loud rock music playing in the background. One Gen Xer told us that watching MTV was like watching *Sesame Street,* only the content had morphed from numbers, letters, and phonics to sex, drugs, and rock 'n' roll. What's not to like about that?

Gen Xers React: Engage Me!

Since learning is the "job" of a child, *Sesame Street* and its followers, *The Electric Company* and MTV, convinced Generation X children that learning—their job—should be fun and fast paced. Translated to the workplace, Gen Xers place a high value on fast-paced action and having fun. This doesn't mean Gen Xers expect work to be all giggles and parties, but it does mean they expect work to be engaging. If it isn't, they tend to get bored quickly.

Most of the workers at New Belgium Brewery, the maker of Fat Tire Beer, are Gen Xers. These workers are engaged because they are part owners in the business, entitled to a portion of the profits based on how the business performs. Once a month, CEO Kim Jordan shares all the financials with the employees in a company-wide meeting at their headquarters in Ft. Collins, Colorado. As for the fun, New Belgium hosts regular parties, celebrations, barbeques, and picnics where the members of the mostly Gen X workforce are encouraged to bring their families. Once a year, they sponsor a daylong bicycle fest, called Tour de Fat, where everyone dresses in outlandish costumes and engages in bicycle parades at the brewery. They also take the Tour de Fat to cities across the country as a way to promote Fat Tire Beer.

A word of caution: Words like "fun" can mean different things to different generations. We interviewed Derek, a Generation X technology sales representative, who described his team leader James's attempt at "fun":

> James was into having the team meet to discuss sales strategy at his favorite bar on Friday nights after work. I wanted to be seen as a team player, so I usually went, but I resented the intrusion on my time. Working out is important to me and going to these "meetings" meant sacrificing my gym time.
>
> To make matters worse, James's bar was a dump: dark, filled with smoke, and one day short of the wrecking ball. We'd sit there, coughing from the bad air, while we watched James devour the free meatballs. It was disgusting. If he wanted to take our personal time to conduct business, he should, at the very least, have asked us where we wanted to meet—or if we needed to meet at all.

Signpost: The Decadent 1980s

In Chapter 2, we mentioned this as a signpost for the Boomer generation. The economy improved, and Boomers shifted their focus from idealism and surviving the turmoil of the 1970s to consumerism and the drive to succeed. This shift, of course, affected their Generation X children, who were just entering their impressionable adolescent and teen years.

With the prosperity of the Reagan years, many watched their parents move from the city apartment to the suburban trilevel and trade the VW in for a Beamer. They lived the good life for a few years until Black Monday, October 19, 1987, when stock markets around the world crashed, shedding an unprecedented amount of value in a short time.

Gen Xers React: Getting the Good Life

Having lived most of their formative years in "the Decadent 1980s," Generation Xers have a taste for the "good life" and are willing to work for it. The members of the 1993 freshman class of the University of California were asked if they wanted "to be better off financially," and 74.5 percent responded, "Yes." In a *Reader's Digest* survey of 1,050 Americans, 74 percent of Gen Xers agreed with the statement: "Hard work is the key to getting ahead."[15]

Signpost: Latchkey Kids

To support the rampant consumerism of the 1980s, many families chose to have both parents work. Close to 50 percent of Generation X had mothers who worked outside the home.[16] Consequently, nearly half of Generation X children had no one to greet them when they came home from school. It's estimated that 40 percent of Generation X children were what came to be known as latchkey children, that is, kids given a key to their houses and expected to remain at home alone.

As mentioned in Chapter 1, the result is that many Gen Xers have a highly developed sense of independence, reflected in the entertainment they chose as teenagers. Gen Xers loved *Beavis and Butt-Head*, a television cartoon series about two dim-witted MTV fans who constantly rattled the cages of the adults around them. Gen Xers' favorite movies included *Fast Times at Ridgemont High*, *The Breakfast Club*, and *Ferris Bueller's Day Off*, all showcasing Generation Xers being on their own and smart enough to take care of themselves.

Successful marketers targeted this independence as well. According to *Advertising Age*,[17] the U.S. Army's 20-year-old tagline, "Be all you can be," was the number two jingle of the century, but by the late 1990s, it was failing to get sufficient numbers of Gen Xers to enlist. Once the Army replaced it with the tagline, "Army of One," the number of daily hits to the Army's Web site increased from 7,300 to 30,000 and the military reported being on track to meet its recruitment goals.

Gen Xers React: Independent Spirits

Gen Xers tend to be highly independent workers. A common Gen X attitude is, "Tell me what you want done, give me the tools I need to do it, train me to use them, and then leave me alone!" They tend not to like to work in teams but will do so if they see the need. They have little patience with rules that don't make sense to them.

In the early 2000s, it was Gen Xers who pushed corporations to allow telecommuting, working from home, and flextime. Baby Boomer and Traditional managers who resisted were often bombarded with Generation X's trademark question: "Why?"

The best course is often to allow Gen Xers to work independently if possible. Don't get distressed if they're less than enthusiastic about working in teams. That doesn't mean they should be able to opt out of working with others if the job requires it. Just don't let their lack of "Kumbaya" spirit get you down.

Generation Xers have little patience with the concept of "paying your dues." During their adolescence and teen years, with their parents often absent, they figured out how to solve their own problems and find their own way. Requiring them to put in time before they can be considered for promotion seems like a waste of time and talent to many Gen Xers. "If I can do the job, I should get the promotion, regardless of my seniority," is a common Gen Xer mantra.

· ·

Meagan Reflects

I loved being a latchkey kid because my time was my own. I was nine years old, and every weekday afternoon from four to six-thirty I had total freedom to decide what I would do. I could watch TV, talk on the phone, do my homework, or play with the dogs. It was all up to me— and I usually did all of them at the same time.

The fly in the ointment was the list of tasks that management (Mom and Dad) left on the kitchen counter for me to complete every day. The rules were simple: Finish the assignments to an acceptable level of quality (as demonstrated during orientation) and do them before management returned home. I could decide when to do the tasks, in what order, and how many breaks I could take. And if I had a problem, it was up to me to deal with it.

I never had the kinds of problems Macaulay Culkin faced in the 1990 movie *Home Alone* (foiling the plans of a couple of bumbling burglars trying to break into his house), but I had my share. For example, when I was nine and home alone, I dropped a bowl of ice cream. It shattered and ice cream went everywhere. While I fetched a broom and mop to clean up the mess, our dog, Pepper, licked up the ice cream and cut her tongue wide open. Then she proceeded to run around the house with her tongue hanging out, flinging blood everywhere. I called my dad, but he was in a meeting, and my mother was attending a college class. This was long before cell phones, so I had to solve the problem myself. Terrified that Pepper would bleed to death, I figured I'd better get her to the vet. I knew I couldn't take her on the bus so I called a cab and paid for it with money from my piggy bank. Pepper got treated. Problem solved.

• •

Signpost: The 1990–1991 Recession: Parents Laid Off

July 1990 marked the beginning of a mild and short-lived economic downturn. For a variety of reasons, however, the labor market continued to decline long after the recession was over.[18] White-collar professionals and middle managers were hit especially hard.

By the end of 1993, IBM, known for guaranteeing employees a "job for life," had shed 100,000 jobs. General Motors announced the closing of 21 plants. Consumer products giant Procter & Gamble began eliminating 13,000 jobs. Xerox, USAir, Martin Marietta, and many more announced impending layoffs. Generation X, many of whom were teenagers or in their early 20s at the time, watched as their parents were furloughed in droves, often after many years of loyal service.

Gen Xers React: No Automatic Loyalty

Generation Xers are skeptical of loyalty to their employers. Given what happened to their parents or their friends' parents, they tend to respond cynically to talk about company loyalty, team spirit, and being one big, happy family. They think, "Yeah, we're one big, happy family until the company is sold, or the economy tanks. Then it's every man and woman for themselves."

Given the volatility of the economy, this is probably a healthy attitude for anyone to adopt. It means, however, that Gen Xers may only stay with an organization until they've learned all they can or until something better comes along. According to a 2005 study of more than 1,500 Gen Xers,

77 percent said they'd quit their jobs if offered "increased intellectual stimulation" elsewhere.[19]

Despite Gen Xers' willingness to commit to home and family, they often draw the line at "marrying the company." But that doesn't mean they won't commit to working hard while there. A Catalyst Study found that over 80 percent of Gen Xers care deeply about the fate of their companies and are willing to put in more effort than is expected of them.[20] At the same time, they tend to be unwilling to make a lifetime commitment to the organization because they have a realistic view of the organization's inability to make a lifetime commitment to them.

Since Gen Xers are constantly preparing for the next job, they need to see value in what they are doing in this one. They have little patience for wasting time on cumbersome policies and procedures. Assigning a Gen Xer to a job he considers unworthy of his attention is a great way to encourage him to leave sooner.

Likewise, a Gen Xer tends to apply the amount of effort she feels the job deserves. If she thinks that what she is doing is important, that she is learning something from doing it, or that it's fun to do, she will be motivated to do it well. If the job is routine and only requires an adequate amount of effort, that's what she will give it. If she thinks the job is stupid, she'll either question why you're making her do it or she'll ignore it altogether.

The lesson here is not to give a Gen Xer a job, but to give her or him an experience that's challenging, exciting, and an opportunity to grow. You'll get better results and they'll feel more loyalty toward you.

Given the independent nature of most Gen Xers, it's no wonder they prefer to be judged on their own merits rather than on the performance of their coworkers, team, or company. As children, they spent lots of time "home alone." They watched TV alone, they played video games alone, and they were drawn to sports that emphasized solo rather than team performance.

Sports-loving Baby Boomers tend to be drawn to team sports like football, basketball, baseball, hockey, and soccer. Gen Xers, on the other hand, are drawn to sports that emphasize individual performance. It's no coincidence that the popular X Games, which featured the solo sport of skateboarding, were first broadcast on ESPN in 1993, the year most Gen Xers were in their teens and early 20s. Those games have now morphed into the Extreme Games and include bungee jumping, Eco-Challenge, inline skating, skateboarding, skysurfing, sport climbing, street luge, and biking—all individual sports.

- -

Meagan Reflects

You could not find a more typical Baby Boomer story than that of my parents. I have seen pictures of them from the 1960s and early 1970s. They look as ridiculous as all their peers. Shaggy hair, wire-rimmed glasses, sideburns, ponchos—it's incredible.

I was an only child. My parents, in their free-thinking ways, took me to all their social activities and grown-up functions. Unlike the Traditional Generation, who expected their children to be seen and not heard, my parents expected me to express myself in front of adults, make my wishes known, and ask for what I wanted. I know they didn't think I was a devil-child, but I am fairly certain their friends did.

As a child, I was expected to entertain myself. All of this was fine by me. I loved the combination of attention but anonymity. It satisfied my needs and provided me with an incredible sense of freedom and entertainment. To this day, I am most content in situations that imitate this model. In school, and now in work, I was and am drawn to projects and careers that reward individual thinking and allow me to work independently.

Unconsciously I have created a similar environment in my own company. We are a small group of Gen Xers and Gen Yers. Everyone works on his own from home. We are in frequent contact via phone, email, and tweeting. As a group, we have a conference call about every two weeks and a face-to-face meeting once a quarter. Nobody has a title; you can call yourself whatever you want. It's a bit of a joke because sometimes people change their title depending on their mood. Everyone knows what the company's goals are and what she needs to do to reach those goals. People can work when they want to work and for as long as they need to work to meet their goals. It's Gen X Utopia.

- -

Companies on the Cutting X

Companies that are successfully attracting and retaining Generation X employees tend to offer benefits, working conditions, and policies that appeal to Gen Xers' sense of independence and their desire to balance work and home. For example:

- ➢ SAS Institute, a privately held software company in North Carolina, has the best on-site childcare in the state. SAS encourages family life balance by offering unlimited sick days and elder care.[21]

- ➢ NetApp,[22] founded in 1992, is a $3.3 billion company that provides storage and data management solutions for businesses. NetApps attracts and retains Gen Xers with benefits like:

    - ⬦ Casual dress and flexible hours (when possible)
    - ⬦ Time off from work for employees to do volunteer work
    - ⬦ Adoption Assistance Plan that reimburses the costs of adopting children

- ➢ Plante & Moran, the twelfth largest accounting firm in the United States, advertises on the recruitment page of its Web site that it is "100% Jerk Free."[23]

- ➢ W.L. Gore & Associates makes Gore-Tex fabrics, Elixir guitar strings, and Glide dental floss. Everyone, no matter who you are at Gore, has the same title of "Associate." Gore uses a "lattice" structure that allows associates to choose projects, make decisions, and tap into the resources and information they need.[24]

- ➢ Criner Construction is a 10-person home remodeling company located in Yorktown, Virginia. The company is divided into two-person teams of carpenters who are totally responsible for their assigned projects from planning to execution. Every month, owner Robert Criner publishes the performance numbers of the teams, along with a summary of the company's financial progress. At the end of the year, he brings everyone into a meeting room where he puts the employees' portion of the company's profit sharing on the table, *in cash,* and tells them to divide it up as they see fit. In 2008, this amounted to $30,000. For some reason, these people love their jobs.

- ➢ Genentech is the penultimate Generation X company. It was founded by DNA expert Dr. Herb Boyer and venture capitalist Bob Swanson one night in a bar in 1976. The two men sketched out their dream of a futuristic biotech company on the back of an envelope. Genentech now boasts 11,000 employees and leads the search for cures for diseases.

Sixty percent of Genentech's employees are Generation X, which is double the national average.[25] If you add in the Generation Yers working there, as of this writing, 75 percent of Genentech employees are under the age of 44.

Genentech likes to work hard and play hard. The employees have monthly parties called Ho-Hos (nobody knows where the name "Ho-Hos" came from). When celebrating the 100th batch of a new drug, they have cake and champagne on the patio. CEO Arthur Levinson arrived for a lab photo dressed up in a hunter's costume. The point was that a scientist had to have a hunter's instincts when hunting for the cause and cure for cancer.[26]

The culture at Genentech is called "casual intensity." You can walk into a lab filled with scientists performing potentially life-saving experiments and hear rock 'n' roll blasting over the sound system. According to Levinson, what captures the attention of their Gen Xers goes beyond the parties, music, and free espresso (offered in the cafeteria): It's Genentech's mission:[27]

. . . to be the leading biotechnology company, using human genetic information to discover, develop, manufacture and commercialize medicines to treat people with serious or life-threatening medical conditions. The secret of Genentech's commercial success is its unique corporate culture.

Levinson protects Genentech's mission, focus, and culture from "evil ghosts" like bureaucracy, idle talks, bloated discourses, and mind-numbing meetings. To keep the focus on the mission, Genentech hangs large posters of the stories of its patients on the walls. When a patient dies, they take the picture off the wall with a small ceremony. Everyone at Genentech feels it; it is always a sad day.

· ·

Meagan Shares Her Gen X Opinion

When I was in my mid-20s, the company for which I was working held a conference at the Coronado Hotel in San Diego. I was happy to go but surprised to learn I'd have to share a room with a manager from another team whom I had never met. As a Gen Xer, I thought this was ridiculous. If the issue was expense, I would have rather stayed at a cheaper hotel and had my own room.

The meeting was four days long. I know that part of the reason the company wanted us to share a room was so we could bond, but every night there was a dinner or a cocktail function that was mandatory. That gave us plenty of time to meet, greet, and connect with people of every position in the company. I found sharing a room an intrusion on my privacy. Not being able to have some alone downtime after a full day of meetings was exhausting, not bonding. I felt like I was working even while I was sleeping!

The last day was a "free" day. It consisted of a choice between playing golf or going to Sea World. I do not golf, so I went to Sea World. There were about 20 of us trooping around there under my boss's watchful eye. Since there were several layers of management with us, we reps did not feel comfortable discussing anything but work. The entire day was spent watching Shamu and talking about market share. At one point, my boss (a Baby Boomer) smiled at me and said, "Beats working, doesn't it?"

I thought, "This *is* working! We just happen to be watching a killer whale perform tricks while we do it."

I'm guessing some of you Baby Boomers reading this think I am being whiny and nonappreciative. Yeah, probably. But here is the generational difference. I have no problem working long hours at a meeting. In fact, I love the engagement and the interplay. And I realize that part of working requires you to schmooze at after-dinner events. But the team part of teamwork for us Gen Xers does not mean working all the time. My personal life is important to me. If the job is rewarding, and we can balance it with our personal lives, we Gen Xers will work extremely hard.

And as much as we like to be lone wolves, we can work and play well with others when we need to. Within my own company, I arrange "team-building" activities outside of work hours. We decide what these *fun* endeavors will be together. Everyone throws in his or her idea, and we take a vote. During the outing, we don't talk about work, but everything else is on the table. It has become a great way to really get to know each other.

Recently I took one of our Gen Y employees on a business trip with me. My experience with my previous company taught me to make sure everyone gets her own quarters. The following morning, I asked her how she liked her room. She said it was lonely. I was surprised by her answer. She explained to me this was the first time she had traveled for business and had her own hotel room. She told me she was happy she could access her Facebook account to keep her company!

What *are* we going to do with these young people today?

The Bottom Line

Despite the derogatory descriptors assigned to them early in life, Generation Xers have turned out to be hardworking, responsible, family-focused adults. Working in teams is not beyond their capabilities, but they tend to prefer flying solo. They have little patience for policies, procedures, and rules that don't make sense, and they are likely to ignore them when they can't be changed.

Gen Xers often distrust institutional intentions, relying instead on themselves for their personal and professional development. Consequently, unlike their Traditional and Baby Boomer predecessors, they place their loyalties with themselves rather than with the organizations for which they work.

If you manage Gen Xers, give them the training and resources they need to do their jobs, be clear what results you expect from them, and then get out of their way and let them perform. Treat them more like peers than subordinates; Gen Xers have little use for authority if it's just for authority's sake. Mentor and coach them to help them develop and they will respect you. Boss them around and insist they follow rules they think are stupid and they will mock you behind your back or leave.

Managing Generation X

"Children begin by loving their parents; as they grow older they judge them; sometimes, they forgive them"
—Oscar Wilde

In the mid-1990s, corporate America feared Generation X and scratched their graying beards over how to corral them and make them perform. Now, as Gen Xers reach their late 30s and early 40s, they have turned their attention from being the self-centered, gold-collar, corporate prima donnas they were portrayed to be and focus on managing the responsibilities of home and family. They've become adults—but they haven't been completely tamed. Take Tarre, for example.

Tarre is a Gen X dental hygienist and mother of two whom we interviewed for this book. She works in a group practice with two dentists and seven hygienists. She enjoys her work and likes the variety of patients she sees.

During an exam, one of the older dentists (a Traditional) told the patient that he was going to fill a cavity. Tarre thought this was a mistake. The decay was too advanced for a simple fill. Tarre quickly spoke up in front of the patient and told the doctor what she thought.

The dentist asked Tarre to step into the hall, where he informed her that if he wanted her opinion he would ask for it and that she should never disrespect him in front of a patient again. With ears burning, Tarre said, "Okay." A week later, she was home on her day off when the office manager called to see if she could come in to replace a hygienist who'd called in sick. Tarre declined.

"Normally," she told us, "I would have been happy to help out. I know what it is like to be short staffed on busy days. But since the episode with the dentist, when all I was doing was speaking up for what I thought was best for the patient, I didn't feel like being a 'team player.'"

Typically, Gen Xers have little respect for organizational protocol, especially if they see no reason for it, so for Tarre, her response to the dentist is no big surprise. We're just surprised she was so passive-aggressive about it. Many Gen Xers we know, including the coauthor of this book, would have told him what he could do with his job and walked out.

If you are a Traditional or Baby Boomer with a strong sense of pro-priety, you may be thinking the dentist was right: "Who does Tarre think she is? When she goes to dental school and completes an internship and gets 20 years of experience under her belt, maybe she would be qualified to give the dentist advice. But even then, not in front of the patient." And you'd be right—from a Traditional or Boomer's perspective. We're not suggesting that he shouldn't ask Tarre to use better judgment when voic-ing her opinion; however, assuming Tarre is a valuable asset to the prac-tice, and he wants to keep her, he might adjust his management approach to fit Tarre's Gen X attitudes—to ask rather than tell her to not express her opinions in front of a patient.

These attitudes include:

> Little respect for title, rank, or position. Great respect for accom-plishment, knowledge, and effectiveness.

> The desire to make individual contributions. Gen Xers can be good team players, but they don't buy into the hackneyed phrase, "There's no 'I' in team." Gen Xers know there is: It's them.

> The expectation that their input will be valued and rewarded.

> The desire to be pampered. All of us like a little special attention, but these folks are the "gold-collar" generation. They're used to it. Health food in the cafeteria, an on-site workout room, day care facilities, and organized sports teams are a few of the perks large companies have established for their Gen Xers. New Bel-gium Brewing Company has a coffee bar complete with one of the most expensive espresso machines available, imported from Italy.

> ▷ Focus on the family. Unlike Boomers, who often put work first and family second, Gen Xers want a balance between the two. Not that they won't stay late or go the extra mile, but there had better be a good reason for it.
>
> ▷ Little patience with boredom. Generation X was the first *Sesame Street*/video game generation. They're used to being engaged in activities that are fast paced and interesting.
>
> ▷ Little or no automatic loyalty. Given what happened to their Baby Boomer parents during the downsizing of the early 1990s, Gen Xers tend to place their loyalties with themselves.

Anyone managing Tarre and other members of Generation X would be wise to have some strategic goals in mind if they want to keep her:

1. Keep her interested and engaged.
2. Derive the full benefit of her insights and ideas.
3. Create a career path for her to progress within the organization.

Tips for Managing Xers

Generation X adults were shaped by the signposts of the mid-1960s to the mid-1990s. They grew up in a different environment from that of their Baby Boomer parents, one in which having children was not as fashionable, staying at home to raise them not as common, and staying together as a family not a given. They were young children during the stagflation of the 1970s and young adults when the grown-ups around them were being laid off in the early 1990s. They grew up wary, independent, and adamant about what they wanted out of work and life.

Those who successfully manage Gen Xers recognize these characteristics and act to support them. Here's how they do it.

1. Give Them Individual Recognition

In addition to team recognition, make sure that Gen Xers are spotlighted individually for jobs well done. To the degree you can, put them in working situations where they can shine, even if it's in a team environment.

Bernice, who is a Baby Boomer, leads a marketing team for a major credit card company. Most of the team's members are Gen Xers. She tells us that she makes it a point to reward her teammates in a way that is significant to them.

"It is very simple," says Bernice. "Whenever one of the members has a good idea or has helped us out of a jam, I send a brief email to everyone outlining what the Gen Xer has done. The team is stronger for the efforts of the Gen Xer and the Gen Xer is happier for being recognized. Besides, I am not foolish. That Gen Xer could be my boss next year."

You may be thinking, "Yeah, Bernice, you're just sucking up to them to get what you want." Our response to that is, "Of course she is, and there's nothing wrong with it, as long as it's a fair and honest description of what the person actually did."

2. Create Collegial Teams

Although Gen Xers tend to seek individual recognition, it doesn't mean they can't or won't work well in teams. They tend to look for support among small groups within their teams or coworkers. Their relationships tend to be based more on professional, mutual respect than on the fact that they're all on the same team.

For example, we spoke with Sam, who is a Gen X chemist for a genetics research company. Since he graduated in 1993, Sam has worked in seven different labs for seven different companies. He has been with his current employer for about three years. Sam says what he likes most about his job are the other technicians with whom he works.

"There were other labs that had better technology, and some had a better salary schedule, but there was always something missing," said Sam. "I never really felt connected with the other researchers. Part of the problem was age. I was younger and didn't feel like I had anything in common with older scientists. Looking back, I probably should have tried harder to understand where they were coming from."

Sam added, "The group I am with now is terrific. We have a good time, get important work done, and are always learning from each other. The fact that I feel like I am working with a group of allies is especially refreshing when deadlines are approaching and stress levels are high."

Rather than a melting pot of people, to a Gen Xer, a successful team is a group of driven people, each with a talent that contributes to achieving the goal. The team decides on the plan, and the members complete the tasks. Team members have the freedom and the space to go about getting the job done as they see fit, as long as the desired results are achieved. They communicate with each other as needed by email, texting, videoconferencing, or discussion over the cubicle wall. At the end, they come together and put the pieces of their project together like a jigsaw puzzle. It is this weblike structure that creates a satisfactory team experience for the Gen Xer. No group hugs or singing "Kumbaya," just individuals working with each other to accomplish a goal.

3. Establish a Meritocracy

Merriam-Webster's online dictionary defines "meritocracy" as "a system in which the talented are chosen and moved ahead on the basis of their achievement." Notice that there's no mention of whom they know, how they schmooze, or how long they've been with the company.

Intel Corporation makes "meritocracy" a part of its official policy. This is an excerpt from its policy manual that sounds as if it was written specifically for a Generation X–rich environment:

> Intel's very challenging and fast-paced work environment has been integral to its continued success in the highly competitive and evolving high-tech industry. While maintaining a work culture that ensures Intel's success, Intel also strives to treat each employee fairly and with dignity. Consistent with this principle, Intel seeks to:
>
> - Reward individual performance through meritocracy-based compensation practices
> - Create opportunities for advancement and growth, and an environment that allows employees to continuously improve and expand their skills
> - Provide market-competitive compensation and a pay structure that allows employees to share in Intel's success
> - Promote open communication and prompt resolution of employee issues
> - Provide a safe and secure work environment for all employees.[1]

Gen Xers have little patience with organizational politics, especially patronage. Nothing will turn a Gen Xer off faster than seeing someone receive a promotion that wasn't based on merit, but on whom he knows. The old saying, "It's who you know, not what you know, that counts," drives Gen X cynicism. The better course, obviously, is to award promotions, raises, and other discretionary perks on merit alone.

This is easier said than done.

One of our clients, the CEO of a medium-sized manufacturing company, recently needed to replace his retiring sales manager. He was considering two Gen X candidates for an internal promotion. One was the top salesperson, with an abrasive personality. The other had lower sales but was universally liked by everyone. Strictly following the principles of meritocracy, the first choice would be the one with the higher sales, but that discounts the value the other's personality brings to the mix. Either way, there are probably going to be more than just hurt feelings for the one who doesn't get it.

To minimize the negative consequences of this conundrum, the manager needs to make it clear that the merit criteria go beyond sales figures. If he doesn't, he risks alienating the one he disappoints, as well as all the other Gen Xers who weren't considered for the promotion but were watching the process.

4. Support Their Lifestyle

After watching their parents work 14-hour days at jobs they didn't like and from which they were callously laid off, Gen Xers realized that there is more to life than a paycheck. For Gen Xers, doing what they enjoy tends to trump bringing home more money.

Consider Margaret, a Gen X grade school art teacher. An artist herself, Margaret studied art in school but never thought she could make a living at it. When she was 22, a chance meeting with a friend's dad, who was an art teacher, changed her mind. She told us, "The way he described his day, working with the kids, creating art, really sounded good to me. I thought to myself, 'This is what I want my workdays to look like.'"

Margaret went back to school, earned her teaching certificate, and within a month was offered two positions. One looked good and paid well, but the school was a 45-minute drive from her house. She knew the drive would eat up much of her personal time and not leave room for any of her after-work art projects.

The other offer came from a brand new school only two miles away. The position paid significantly less but she would have a large art room with lots of windows, two sinks, and a kiln, none of which the other school had. Margaret accepted the position at the closer school and has been the art teacher there for more than eight years.

A lot of Gen Xers would handle this situation the same way. Money is an important consideration but it's not the only consideration and, sometimes, it's not even a consideration at all. You will be better able to hire and retain Gen Xers by supporting their need for a well-rounded lifestyle.

5. Provide Schedule Flexibility

"It's not what I do at work that defines me," said Sheila, a Gen X restaurant data analyst. "It's the stuff that I do outside of work that makes up who I am."

Many of the strengths Gen Xer's possess, like independence, willingness to take responsibility, and having a can-do attitude, can be traced to their signposts as latchkey children. Ironically, most of them don't want their own children to suffer the same fate. Being there for their kids is as important as having a fulfilling job, which means flextime, telecommuting, working from home, job splitting, or working part-time—things that have enormous appeal to them. And it's not just the moms: According to scouting.com, between 2006 and 2009, the number of stay-at-home dads in the United States tripled.[2]

It's estimated that more than one in four Gen Xers presently have some kind of flexible work schedule. They pushed for telecommuting from home when they entered the workforce in the 1990s and now it's a common practice in many industries.

Aflac offers a 4-by-10 workweek, where employees can put in four 10-hour days and take off three days each week. They also offer a 3-by-12 workweek, where employees work three 12-hour days and have four days off per week.[3]

ARUP Laboratories offers a "Seven-On/Seven-Off" schedule in its technical and support sections. Under this arrangement, employees work seven 10-hour days in a row and then have seven straight days off. Although employees work a total of 70 hours under this plan, they are paid for 80 hours. Because they do not work 26 weeks of the year, they are not offered any extra paid time off.[4]

Texas Instruments allows employees, on a case-by-case basis, to adjust their work schedules to meet their personal needs. For instance, if a worker has a sick child, he might opt to work from home that day. If another worker has a doctor's appointment, she can come in late and work late. If still another worker has a late-night conference call with an overseas office, she can come in late the following day.[5]

Adobe Systems encourages employees who don't need to be present in the building to work from home. According to Todd Davidson, director of business development, the company believes in giving people the greatest amount of flexibility possible to get their jobs done. The practice also provides a laboratory for testing Adobe's collaborative software products. As Davidson puts it, "Adobe believes in eating its own dog food."

Even government is getting in on the act. In 2003, the state of Arizona, by order of then-governor Janet Napolitano, declared a goal of having 20 percent of its employees telecommute.

For the Gen Xers who have become today's soccer moms and dads, these are the perfect arrangements for their busy schedules. Given their desire to focus on family first and the job second, offering them flexible options is key to retaining them, and if they can't get schedule flexibility from you, they will look for it from another employer.

6. Help Them Prepare for Their Next Job

From their perspective, Gen Xers believe that job security rests in their ability to find another job. They have little faith in being with the same company 20 years from now because they saw such faith by their Baby Boomer parents betrayed by reengineering and downsizing in the early 1990s. In their minds, every job is a temporary assignment; they are more like independent contractors than employees.

It is tempting to not invest in them developmentally. After all, why spend money to train them if they're just going to leave anyway? Ironically, the opposite often occurs.

We've interviewed many Gen Xers who have left jobs *because* there was little or no training. One nursing home manager told us that when she instituted a CNA (Certified Nursing Assistant) certification training program, her turnover dropped from 110 percent per year to 76 percent. When she added advanced classes in resident care that would help prepare CNAs for admission to nursing school, the turnover dropped to 27 percent.

Her experience was confirmed by a University of Pittsburgh study, published in *The Gerontologist*, which clearly showed that training, rewards, and workload are the major considerations for nursing home employees who are deciding whether to stay or leave.[6] Simply put, if they feel like they're getting adequate training, adequate rewards, and a reasonable workload, they're more likely to stay. Notice that training was listed first.

Or consider USAA, a financial services company based in San Antonio, Texas, that provides insurance, banking, and investment services to members of the U.S. military and their families. The company ranks 189th on the Fortune 500 list, with revenues of just under $12 billion. Its automated call-distribution system, the largest in the world, handles more than 16 million transactions a day. At USAA, training is an important component in achieving its top-rated customer services scores (J.D. Power and Associates and Zogby polls of American consumers consistently rank USAA as the best customer service company—not just insurance company, bank, etc., but the best company for customer service). New hires receive an extensive orientation, including a class on the military lifestyle. Those working in the insurance department receive 10 weeks of training that prepares them to receive their required licenses. The company also pays for employees to receive undergraduate and graduate degrees. USAA's total employee turnover varies between 4 and 8 percent, which is considerably lower than the industry average, which is often upward of 25 percent.[7]

In addition, consider Quicken Loans, an online mortgage company that sidestepped much of the mortgage crisis during 2008 by sticking to mainstream home loans. Quicken was on *Fortune* magazine's 2009 list of the top 100 companies to work for. It offers its employees 250 hours of training every year.[8] Chairman and founder Dan Gilbert personally describes the company's core principles and its dedication to customer service to new employees during the first day of orientation.

7. Vary Their Experiences

Since Gen Xers' long-range career goals are always lurking in the backs of their minds, the more experiences they can acquire during their tenure with you, the more attractive their jobs will be. Consequently, opportunities to manage multiple projects, work on cross-functional teams, participate in job sharing, and be involved with volunteer projects are major motivators for Gen Xers. With each new assignment, they expand their growth portfolios for future opportunities.

Roxanne is a good example. She is a communications director for a dental supply company. Recently, Roxanne was asked to travel out of town with the sales reps about once a week. The added responsibility did not come with extra pay. Because of the economic slowdown, the company had been forced to cut back and lay some people off. Roxanne was taking over part of a position that would not be refilled for some time.

When we asked her if she resented the added duties, she replied, "No. I'm sorry we had to let some people go, but the change in structure gives me an opportunity I didn't have before. I get to learn a part of the business that previously was foreign to me. I don't imagine I will be participating with the sales team years from now but having this chance will open doors I was not aware of."

Ironically, like job training, job variation and cross-training raise the odds Gen Xers will stay. When they get to do lots of interesting things, the chances they will get bored decline and the odds they will feel more invested in the organization rise.

8. Apply Donald Trump Training (aka White Knuckle Terror)

Preferring to work alone, Gen Xers expect to be trusted to do their jobs without having to run to their managers for decisions or permission to use their judgment to solve problems.

The owner of a small manufacturing company we know is looking forward to retirement next year. He's grooming a Gen Xer to take over. To facilitate this process, he uses what he calls the "Donald Trump Apprentice" approach, based on Trump's television show, *The Apprentice*, where he assigns apprentices tasks and then lets them sink or swim. Our friend meets with this protégé every Friday to discuss the upcoming week, then heads for the golf course and doesn't come back until the next Friday. The Gen Xer is to call him *only* if the place burns down or someone dies. Otherwise, she's on her own.

Every Friday, he applauds her for the things she did well and holds her brutally accountable for her mistakes. In a speech we attended years ago, business guru Tom Peters called this the "White Knuckle" approach to leadership training. He said, "You don't really have a grasp of what leadership is like until you experience the white-knuckled terror of being totally responsible for what you are leading." Our experience has shown that Gen Xers embrace this approach to their own development with gusto.

By the way, the last time we checked, this project was going so well that our friend was planning to extend his golfing hiatuses to a month.

9. Get Rid of Stupid Rules

In spending lots of time alone as children, Gen Xers were forced to create their own rules. As a result, they have little tolerance for rules that make no sense to them. We know a manager who pulled his team of Gen Xers into a room, put a copy of the three-inch-thick policy and procedure manual on the table, and ordered them to figure out how to cut its weight and volume by half. Four hours later, they'd trimmed the book by 60 percent. He said his team was delighted and one member told him, "This is the most fun I've had at work since I started here."

Gen Xers have little tolerance for what they perceive to be stupid. George, a Gen Xer, supervises the warehouse of a shipping company. "I like my job because the objectives are clear and we run our own show," he told us. "Shipments come in and we get them sorted and shipped out. As long as nobody loses a finger and we don't make any mistakes, I know we are doing a good job. I have a great group of people working for me. We work hard and play hard. Once a quarter, I take everyone out on a Friday night pub crawl as a reward for their dedication."

George continued, "The company recently sent in a consultant to analyze our procedures. I had to spend over half my day sitting with the guy, explaining our business to him. This was an incredible waste of my time, my crew's time, and the company's money. As I sat with the consultant, all I could think was, 'I can't get reimbursed for the quarterly pub crawl because of budget constraints, but they can afford to pay this guy big bucks to sit here wasting my time.'"

When we heard George tell this story, we had mixed feelings. It does seem silly that he can't get reimbursed for the pub crawl, especially since the crew does such a good job. On the other hand, the budget may be so tight that the company can't afford it. Being members of the breed ourselves, we know consultants are not cheap, but if he does his job, the suggestions the consultant will offer will far offset the money the company spent on his services. It seems that George's boss needed to clarify why the company can afford to hire the consultant when things are so tight that they can't afford to buy the crew a night out. It's all a matter of perception.

Our advice is to anticipate some of your decisions might appear stupid to your Gen Xers, so explain the reasons for making them. Of course, that's after you've thought long and hard about whether they *really are stupid*.

Similarly, look at all the paperwork you do, and ask if all of it is really necessary. Start a "Save-a-Tree" campaign. Look at the forms and documentation Gen Xers must complete. Try streamlining the questionnaires, charts, and data sheets. Can one page be created or can a standardized form be used? Gen Xers will appreciate the effort, especially if you ask them to participate in figuring out how to do it.

In addition, if you ask them to come in early, stay late, or work their days off, be prepared to explain why. If the reason doesn't make sense to them, expect an argument or a downright refusal. Gen Xers will go the extra mile when it's needed, but the reason to do so must be powerful if you expect them to give up attending their kid's softball game that night.

10. Coach Office Politics

Gen Xers tend to lack the intuitiveness Baby Boomers possess when it comes to office politics. Tarre, the dental hygienist, is a good example. She may have been right, but her approach with the Traditional dentist so offended him that being right didn't matter. Imagine if she'd waited until he left the room, took him aside, and said something like, "Dr. Smith, I'm the hygienist here, so I'm not trying to tell you what you should do, but I'm wondering if you would like me to say something when I have an opinion about a patient's treatment?" If he'd said no, so be it. If he'd said yes, at least she'd have gotten permission to speak up. Either way, she wouldn't have set him up to be embarrassed in front of the patient.

For most politically savvy Baby Boomers, this may seem like a no-brainer, but many Gen Xers lack such insights. They place a high value on calling it like it is and expressing their opinions candidly, sometimes to their own demise. According to Ron Zemke, Claire Raines, and Bob Filipczak, authors of *Generations at Work,* only 20 percent of Gen Xers are politically savvy when it comes to navigating the jungle of corporate bureaucracy.[9]

11. Challenge Them

Gen Xers are happy working in an MTV/*Sesame Street,* come-at-you-fast style, which means they like activities that require intense bursts of energy and challenge them to think quickly. According to J. Leslie McKeown, author of *Retaining Top Employees*, Gen Xers work well with ambiguous assignments as long as the objectives and deadlines are clear.[10]

They're also willing to work hard when they see the point of doing so and the benefits of the job justify the effort. For example, Alex, a Gen Xer we know, is senior vice president of sales and marketing for a consumer electronics company. He has a group of mostly Gen X salespeople, who spend much of their time traveling. Alex keeps in touch with everyone through email and PDAs. All his salespeople manage their own time. They are well paid and enjoy great benefits and bonuses. As long as they get the job done, they can decide when to take off, when to relax, and when to work.

Alex expects his employees to pick up the slack when the situation calls for it or in an emergency. If a customer needs attention during off hours, he wants his people to answer the phone and take care of the problem. For Alex, occasionally sacrificing personal time for work is the price everyone on the team pays for being able to manage his or her own time and schedule. Something must be right about this approach because even in a tough economy, Alex's Gen X team outshines all competitors' sales teams.

12. Keep Things Moving

Ready. Lights. Action. Gen Xers tend to like a fast pace and will become frustrated when they feel things are lagging. They often turn their noses up at team meetings because they consider them bottlenecks that delay, rather than accelerate, decision making. One of our clients put a big red action button (think of the Staples Easy Button) on the conference table. If it looks like a meeting is starting to drag and go off course, anyone can hit the action button, which rings a loud bell, getting everyone back on task.

To make meetings more productive and more inviting to fast-paced Gen Xers, we suggest the following eight-step meeting strategy:

1. **Determine the purpose**. Gen Xers are quick to judge something as stupid if it wastes their time. Holding a meeting every Friday afternoon just because it's Friday is stupid to a Gen Xer. Having a clear purpose for the meeting that contributes to her success on the job is smart.

2. **Consider alternatives to meetings**. Can the purpose be accomplished equally well through a less time-consuming method, such as email, Twitter, or Facebook or through audio- or videoconferencing? If the purpose is simply to keep everyone informed, maybe so. If it's to discuss a complicated matter, generate enthusiasm for a new plan, or brainstorm solutions to a problem, maybe not. The bottom line is not to hold meetings just for the sake of holding meetings. It will drive your Gen Xers crazy.

3. **Create an agenda**. Be sure to identify who, what, and when. In other words, each item on the agenda should describe who's responsible for presenting the issue, what they expect to accomplish (decision, solution, information dissemination, etc.), and how long they expect to take (e.g., 2:00 P.M.–2:15 P.M.).

4. **Start on time**. How often have you arrived at a meeting at the scheduled time only to have it start 15 minutes late? The problem with starting meetings late is that they then tend to run late. It also insults the people who made an effort to get there on time and rewards the people who were tardy. Finally, it teaches those who are concerned about their time (like many Gen Xers) to arrive late on purpose.

If you want your meetings to start on time, *start them on time*, even if people are missing. As people learn that a 2:00 P.M. meeting really starts at 2:00 P.M., they will begin to get there on time. Either way, proceed without them.

5. **End on time**. How often have you attended a meeting that was scheduled to end at 3:00 P.M., only to have it drag on to 4:00 P.M. or 5:00 P.M. or later? There is only one reason meetings don't end on time: It's because they don't end on time. If you want your meetings to end on time, *end them on time.*

If you stick to the ending time, a magic thing will begin to occur. As the ending time approaches, people will start talking faster. They will come to the point quicker and digress less. It follows the famous Parkinson's Law, which says, "Work expands so as to fill the time available for its completion."[11]

6. **Stick to the agenda**. This will help keep the meeting from getting off track.

7. **Assign responsibilities**. Gen Xers like to know what they are responsible for. If a meeting ends and there isn't clarity about who's going to do what by when, Gen Xers will often assume it's someone else's responsibility. When they're asked later why they didn't produce, they will blame you for not clarifying what they were supposed to do.

8. **Take notes and distribute minutes with assigned responsibilities clearly defined**. That way, when the Gen Xers get the email with the minutes, they know what they're supposed to handle and they can act accordingly. Remember, Gen Xers tend to be individual players who don't like to worry about what the other people on the team are doing.

13. Reward Winners with Your Time

When we conduct leadership seminars, we ask the audience to divide their employees into three categories:

1. **Eagles:** Those are the ones who soar. They go the extra mile at every turn. They come in early, work hard, are accountable for their performance, consistently go the extra mile, and always do it with a smile.
2. **Sparrows:** They come to work, do their jobs, and go home.
3. **Turkeys:** They come to work late, do very little, go home early, and complain about everything.

These are overgeneralizations, but they help us make a point. When we ask the audience to tell us with which group they spend the most time interacting, invariably it's the Turkeys. Ironically, the Turkeys are usually the ones who offer the lowest chance of a return on a manager's investment of time. At the very best, with a lot of coaching, cajoling, and counseling, a Turkey may start behaving like a Sparrow, but the chances he will ever become an Eagle are slim.

On the other hand, if you spend 70 percent of your interaction time coaching your Eagles to fly higher, 25 percent of your time helping your Sparrows become Eagles, and 5 percent of your time urging your Turkeys to get their acts together, the return on your time investment can be enormous.

This concept has particular application for Gen Xers. We've made the point throughout this and the previous chapter that they are independent and like to work alone. That doesn't mean, however, that they don't value input that will boost their career prospects. We suggest that you analyze the time you spend with the three groups and make a special effort to spend more time with your Gen X Eagles and Sparrows and less time with the Turkeys. Your Eagles and Sparrows will fly higher and your Gen Xers will respect you for how you invest your time.

14. Reward Action

Given their latchkey-driven independence, Gen Xers are used to taking charge of situations and getting done what needs to be done. They also respect that quality in others. Make a special effort to recognize and praise those who take action. Rewards can be as simple as praise or acknowledgment of a project moving forward. This not only recognizes the Gen Xer for her individual efforts but also creates a clear message to other Gen Xers that taking action, versus getting ready to get ready, is a quality that you value.

15. Offer Sabbaticals

Baby Boomers have spent their lives living to work. They've dedicated themselves to their jobs and their careers, often to the detriment of their families. Gen Xers, on the other hand, work to live. Their careers are important to them but would never come before their families and their personal lives.

Progressive companies interested in catering to their Gen Xers often offer sabbaticals. Intel Corporation provides eligible employees with an eight-week sabbatical, with full salary and benefits, after each seven years of full-time service.[12] In fact, of *Fortune* magazine's 2009 100 Best Companies to Work For list, 25 offer full-paid sabbaticals.[13]

They don't have to be fully paid. Accenture is a high-performance business consulting firm that was recently named to *Working Mother* magazine's 100 Best Companies for Working Mothers for the sixth consecutive year. Accenture created the Future Leave program, which offers employees a short-term (up to three months), unpaid break from work to spend time on personal priorities. Employees can choose to have a portion of their paycheck held in a savings account for this sabbatical, which can be taken every three years.[14]

At Adobe Systems, every five years, employees get a three-week, full-paid sabbatical in addition to the standard 24 vacation days and 6 holidays they get every year.

For Gen Xers who want to develop their lives outside work, sabbaticals can be a powerful motivator as well as an incentive to stick around until they become eligible for this benefit.

16. Beware of Hovering

No one likes to feel like they're being micromanaged, but given their signpost of latchkey independence, Gen Xers are especially sensitive to it. Take Susan, a Gen Xer we interviewed. Susan works as a lease agent for a property management company. She likes her job because she works with a variety of people, no two days are the same, and her coworkers keep her on her toes. Susan told us that what bugs her about her Baby Boomer boss is her tendency to meddle in Susan's efforts to get her job done.

For example, Susan told us, "I had decided to take a break. We had just finished hashing out a bonus plan for the new hires, and I had a few minutes before meeting with a client. I sat down in the break room and just stared off into space. It felt great to just take three minutes and 'veg.' Tina, my Baby Boomer boss, came into the break room, purposely stood in my line of vision, and said, 'What are you doing? Don't forget you have a client coming in at 2:00.' I was so annoyed I wanted to strangle her. Later I thought about it and I am sure Tina thought she was being helpful, but at the time she was butting into my time and micromanaging me."

In Chapter 12, we'll discuss how, when, and to what extent you should manage each generation, including when it's appropriate to micromanage someone. As a rule of thumb, however, it is wise to avoid the practice with Generation X. They tend to be prickly about it.

17. Provide Feedback

In Chapter 4, we described the Gen X attitude toward supervision as, "Tell me what you want done, give me the tools I need to do it, train me to use them, and then leave me alone!" We omitted the final step in that process, however, which is: "When I'm done, tell me what you think."

All the emphasis on Generation X being independent does not mean they don't want feedback. We think of Gen Yers and Linksters as the video game generations, but it was Generation X that first embraced games like Pong, Donkey Kong, and Pacman when they were teenagers—all individual activities that provided instant feedback.

They want to know how they are doing and they want to know it immediately. And being the raging individualists their signposts inclined them to be, they want to know how they are doing first and how the team is doing second.

They also tend to prefer systems that allow them to monitor their own progress toward clearly defined goals. A Gen X salesperson who can monitor her own sales numbers and gauge her progress toward making a bonus tends to be a very motivated salesperson. A Gen X nurse who can compile his own patient satisfaction ratings and know how they will affect his performance review will make greater efforts to please his patients. A

Gen X scientist who can monitor her own progress toward the discovery of a new drug will be happier than one who doesn't have access to that information.

Not all work situations lend themselves to self-monitored feedback systems. In those cases, the Gen Xer's supervisor must provide the information. Here are some guidelines for giving feedback:

1. **Do it often.** The annual performance review just doesn't cut it for someone who wants instant feedback. We suggest a minimum of monthly feedback sessions that include positive comments about what the person is doing well and constructive suggestions for what needs to be improved. In between, praise often and let him know when he's off course.

2. **Keep it matter-of-fact.** Refrain from subjective statements. Gen Xers tend to be commonsensical when it comes to work-related information. The Gen Xer wants to hear what you have to say, take action, and move on. It's an offshoot of, "Tell me what you want done, give me the tools I need to do it, train me to use them, and then leave me alone!"

> **Subjective:** Jan, you've got a terrific attitude.
>
> **Objective:** Jan, I really appreciate the way you've jumped on this project and turned it around. The progress numbers have shown a considerable increase.
>
> **Subjective:** Bill, you seem to not care as much about this project as you used to.
>
> **Objective:** Bill, you've missed two deadlines, and I'm concerned about this project. What's going on?
>
> **Subjective:** Lisa, you need to be more excited about your assignments. Your lack of enthusiasm is bringing everyone down.
>
> **Objective:** Lisa, when you roll your eyes and say this project sucks in the middle of a meeting, it really brings the rest of us down. I'd prefer that you keep those kinds of downer statements to yourself.
>
> **Subjective:** Neal, you've got great talent in working with customers. Way to go.
>
> **Objective:** Neal, the way you resolved that problem for Mr. Jones was brilliant. I especially liked the way you showed him how even

though it was going to cost him more money in the short run in the long run he would save a bunch. Nice job.

3. **Make it immediate or slightly delayed.** When giving positive feedback, give it as quickly as possible. If you wait 30 days to congratulate a Gen Xer on a big achievement, the Gen Xer will probably wonder where your head has been.

Positive feedback can be done in person or through technology. It should include letting others know what the Gen Xer accomplished. Positive feedback needs a certain amount of ceremony attached to it, depending on how big the achievement is. If the Gen Xer completed an important project before the deadline and under budget, that probably deserves a little pomp and circumstance.

There should be a cooling-off period before giving negative feedback. As the sender of the feedback, you want to be coming from a rational place so your communication is clear. The cooling-off period allows you to gather your thoughts and present the information rationally. Do not, however, let the cooling-off period become a long delay or an excuse not to give the Gen Xer the feedback. If you wait too long, the Gen Xer will feel you have been storing stuff up and unable to get over things and wonder why you didn't say something in the first place. Waiting more than 48 hours is probably letting it go too long.

Unfavorable feedback should be done face-to-face and in private. The use of technology to spread the word about positive achievements is fine, but it doesn't work for negative feedback. There are too many chances for miscommunication when using email or voicemail and it opens the door for your Gen Xer to distrust you.

4. **Make it constructive.** Constructive feedback is feedback that is definitive and explicit. The feedback is focused on the issue and based on what has been observed, not gossip.

Constructive feedback can be congratulatory for a job well done or it can be corrective for an issue that needs fixing.

Example: "David, the sales presentation you gave today was spot-on. The PowerPoint slides were clear, you used terminology that everyone could understand, and the graphs were easy to read. You answered everyone's questions thoroughly, especially when Mr. Smith asked about delivery times. The effort you put into this was obvious."

Example: "David, the sales presentation you gave today could have been better. The slides weren't clear, you used terminology that our client had trouble understanding, and the graphs were too small to see. I was surprised when you struggled to answer people's questions, especially when Mr. Smith asked about delivery times. As the account manager, you should be able to answer these kinds of questions. I know you'll do better next time."

5. **Convey high expectations.** The last sentence above illustrates an application of the Pygmalion Effect. A character from Greek mythology, Pygmalion was the King of Cyprus who sculpted a statue of a beautiful woman. He fell in love with the statue so intensely that Aphrodite, the Goddess of Love, decided to do Pygmalion a favor and bring the statue to life as a real woman named Galatea. (This story is kind of like Pinocchio, but with erotic overtones.)

George Bernard Shaw used the name and concept for his play *Pygmalion,* which was later adapted into the musical *My Fair Lady.* In the play, Professor Henry Higgins bets a colleague that by providing the right training and encouragement to Liza Doolittle, a Cockney flower girl from the streets of London, he can pass her off as a refined lady of London society.

In their book, *Pygmalion in the Classroom*, Robert Rosenthal and Lenore Jacobson demonstrated that when students are expected to do better, they tend to do better, and when they are expected to do worse, they tend to do worse.[15] This became the basis of what is commonly known as the Pygmalion Effect or the "principle of the self-fulfilling prophecy." It says that people tend to rise to the level of expectations placed upon them.

It makes sense then that if you are going to give an employee feedback that is corrective you also want to convey that you have great expectations that he will master the problem and prosper. To expect otherwise is to lower the odds that he will succeed.

18. Allow Them to Be Themselves

Give the Gen Xer as much personal freedom as the industry or organization will tolerate. Gen Xers value their individual style and the more they can bring that style into the workforce, the less resentful they will feel when you ask them to give up personal time. This may include having a flexible dress code, being able to listen to music while they work, and even bringing their pets to work.

Alex, the Gen X senior VP we mentioned earlier, has created a casual corporate culture. When he started with the company 10 years ago, most people wore slacks, closed-toe shoes, and button-down shirts. Alex moved the environment from business casual to casual. Now salespeople in the office wear jeans, shorts, and even flip-flops. (Of course, when they visit customers, they dress as the customer does.) The company has become so well known for its casual atmosphere that it gives out flip-flops with the company logo on them to customers who visit the office.

"The casual dress does not mean we take work casually," says Alex. "We even like to throw people for a loop once in a while and show up in suits. Our customers are amazed when we wear a tie. We work very hard but have a good time while we do it. As long as we do what needs to be done, we have lots of freedom in how we do it."

19. Have Fun

The more fun Gen Xers have with their work, the more they are willing to compromise on other issues. Fun is a key part of the work-life balance. It doesn't mean that the work is easy but that the work can be accomplished with an attitude of relaxed intensity. Many Gen Xers we have interviewed have told us, "Once the job is no longer fun, it is time to leave."

Zappos.com, an online shoe retailer, makes a special effort to cultivate fun in its work environment. It avoids serious titles, instead using titles like Lead Party Maker. Each cube area reflects its own theme, from rain forests with hanging monkeys to Elvis fans, cheerleaders with pompoms, and a spooky area called Area 52.[16] Zappos.com employees regularly give tours to visitors to showcase all the unique personalities represented. It has a napping room and spontaneous parades that break out and wind their way through the office cubes like a conga line. Zappos .com believes that employees will be happier if they can be themselves and let their personalities shine through.

Whether you initiate this crusade for fun by getting everyone tickets for a sporting event, holding potluck munchie days at the office, sponsoring a hiking or cycling outing, treating everyone to a spa day, or renting a limo and having a pub crawl, it's important to ask your Gen Xers what they would like to do. Remember James in Chapter 4: Don't force Gen Xers to "have fun" doing something they hate.

Generation X Managers

More and more Baby Boomers and Traditionals are being managed by Generation X. Gen Xers have already spent over 10 years in the workforce; by 2019 they will be taking over where Baby Boomers have left off.

So far, Generation X has been successful. They are managing people the way they wanted to be managed and people tend to like working for them. In a survey conducted by Talent2, 67 percent of employees claim working for a Gen Xer is preferable to working for a Boomer.[17]

One of the reasons Gen X bosses are so popular is that they often practice what they preach when it comes to life balance. Chere, a Gen X program manager, told us, "A vacation is a vacation. An employee takes a vacation to get away from work, not work from a different location. When I was promoted, I pushed for a no cell phone policy when people went on vacation. We want people to return refreshed, not run-down."

Generation X thinks it's doing a good job, too. Gen Xers are confident managers and proponents of a flexible workplace.[18] They want a life outside work and they respect the fact their employees want it, too.

The Bottom Line

Generation X has a slightly different take on work than the Baby Boomers and Traditionals who preceded them. They are not loyal for loyalty's sake—but they can be very loyal if the company meets their needs. They will not work long hours just because the company wants them to—but they will work long hours if they understand the need and can expect a balance of time off for their efforts. They prefer working on their own to working in a team—but they are team players if the other members of the team do their part to meet a goal. They won't schmooze their way to a better job—but they will seek better jobs on the basis of their abilities. They get bored easily—but they will be engaged if you challenge them, remain flexible, keep things moving, and recognize their achievements.

Attracting and retaining Gen Xers helps make your company better by making you more aware of employee needs, more open to different ways of doing things, and more agile and adaptable.

And it sets you up for an influx of Gen X managers who value independence, balance, variety, challenging work, and merit-based promotions—all qualities any organization would love to have.

CHAPTER 6

The Next Elephant in the Python: Signposts for Generation Y

"I want to be able to look back and say, 'I've done everything I can, and I was successful.' I don't want to look back and say I should have done this or that. I'd like to change things for the younger generation of swimmers coming along."
—Michael Phelps, Generation Y Olympic Champion

"Call me an idealist, but I want to make the world a better place to live. I only buy from planet-friendly companies. I drive a super-fuel-efficient car. I don't eat meat and try to only eat organic food. I do volunteer work for a dance company and I work part-time for Starbucks, whose philosophy matches mine. If it didn't, I'd quit."
—Kelsey Wolf, Generation Y daughter of Dyan and Shap Wolf

Critical Events in the Lives of Generation Y

1983 First functional laptop
1987 Baby Jessica
1989 *Exxon Valdez* spill
1989 Berlin wall comes down
1989 United States invades Panama
1990 Persian Gulf War

1991 Rodney King beating
1993 Waco massacre
1994 Tonya Harding–Nancy Kerrigan encounter
1995 Oklahoma City bombing
1995 O.J. Simpson acquitted
1998 President Clinton lies about Monica Lewinski and is impeached
1999 Columbine massacre
2001 9/11
2001 War on Terror declared
2001 Anthrax
2003 Space Shuttle *Columbia* explodes, killing seven
2003 Invasion of Iraq

By the 1980s, Baby Boomers who had postponed having children in the 1960s and 1970s were reaching their mid-30s and realizing that if they were going to start families, they needed to do it quickly. Their biological clocks were ticking. In addition, with divorce rates hovering around 50 percent, many Boomers who already had children were remarrying and starting second families. Together, they spawned Generation Y.

Born between 1980 and 1995, Generation Y boasts 70.4 million members, representing 26 percent of the American population. They are also called the Echo Boom Generation because, like an echo from the past, they replicate the bulge in the birthrate caused by their Baby Boomer parents between 1946 and 1965.

Signposts for Generation Y

Signpost: Helicopter Parents

It was 1986. Two of our Baby Boomer friends, Shap and Dyan Wolf, had just had a baby. They were ex-hippies in their mid-30s who had gone on to professional lives—he a social science researcher for a university and she a city personnel officer. They had become firmly ensconced in the Yuppie lifestyle—owning their own home, driving nice cars, and eating at good restaurants—but they still described themselves as "free spirits" and never missed a Grateful Dead concert. After 13 years of marriage, they decided it was time to have a child. When they announced Dyan's pregnancy, they told us that they were determined to do this kid thing right.

And they did. Dyan breast-fed Kelsey and gave her only organic baby food. They read to her, held her, coddled her, and rocked her constantly.

They bought her only educational toys. They converted their living room into a replica of Romper Room. They took her to Gymboree regularly and enrolled her in an experimental preschool run by Shap's university. Later, they got her into a magnet high school for the arts. They arranged playdates with her schoolmates. They equipped their house and car with all the latest child safety features, including a car seat that would protect her if they happened to drive over Niagara Falls. And, of course, they had a BABY ON BOARD sticker in their car's back window.

Dyan and Shap were typical of Boomer parents in the 1980s and 1990s. They were older than others in their generation who had given birth to Generation X. They'd sown their wild oats, gotten their careers going, and achieved financial security. They had the maturity, the desire, and the money to "do it right."

Similarly, for the Boomer couples who were creating second families, it was often a matter of wanting to correct the mistakes of the past, to be better parents than they had been the first time around.

These Baby Boomers committed themselves to raising great children, and in most cases they did. The term "latchkey kid" was replaced with phrases like "stay-at-home dad," "soccer mom," and "helicopter parents." Like helicopters, they hovered over their children's every move. They often arranged playdates with friends, scheduled extracurricular activities, helped their children with their homework (sometimes doing it for them), and made sure the kids wanted for nothing. The parents of Generation X often left their children to fend for themselves while the parents pursued their careers. The parents of Generation Y, on the other hand, often catered to their children in any way they could, whether it was attending piano recitals, going to soccer games, running interference with difficult teachers, or even getting involved in their children's college admissions and job interviews.

Much of this involvement was driven by parents who wanted to give their children every possible competitive advantage. They searched for the best nursery schools, kindergartens, high schools, and college preparatory schools. In urban centers like New York, Los Angeles, and Chicago, the competition could be fierce. The *Chicago Tribune* ran this report in 2008:

As the gentrification of a handful of Chicago neighborhoods pushes on, the competition for spots in the city's most coveted schools—public, private and parochial—has reached new levels as young, well-off parents move in. Statistically, it's more difficult, for example, to get into Drummond Montessori, a public magnet school in Bucktown, than it is to get into Harvard University. About 995 children applied for the 36 openings at Drummond next school year, a four percent acceptance rate. Harvard accepted about nine percent of its applicants last year. At Sacred Heart, an independent Catholic school in Rogers Park, the competition is so fierce, parents are applying now for "early admission" for 2009–10. And at the private British School, which just last month opened a $25 million, five-story schoolhouse in Lincoln Park, the preschool and kindergarten classes for next year already are full, with a waiting list. Annual tuition: about $18,000. "It's crazy," offered Lakeview resident Todd Winer, who has applied to ten schools for his kindergarten-age son. "I feel like I have a better shot at winning the lottery than getting into a school we want."[1]

This involvement could go to absurd lengths. We know a couple who made weekly appointments with their two children's teachers to discuss their progress. They insisted the teachers email them all test scores. Each fall, they signed their kids up for soccer, school plays, dance lessons, piano lessons, competitive swimming, baseball, and karate lessons. The husband was a stay-at-home dad, responsible for chauffeuring the kids to all these activities. To keep it all straight, they all carried PDAs so they could coordinate their schedules.

In most cases, this kind of involvement is probably better than leaving your kids to fend for themselves, as many Boomer parents did with their Gen X children, but it can take its toll.

University of Michigan child psychologist Michelle Kees, PhD, points out that with the explosion of extracurricular activities available to children in the past 15 years, there's been a significant risk of overscheduling them. In a University of Michigan Health System bulletin, she goes on to say, "Children who are over-scheduled can have a higher incidence of anxiety, especially performance anxiety. They often wonder how they're doing in a certain activity and strive for perfection or overachievement. We often see that these children are showing some signs of depression, such as withdrawal from friends and family, and feeling badly about themselves when they don't quite measure up."[2]

It's not just the parents who are guilty of overscheduling their kids. The sponsoring organizations and schools do their share. Larry has two nephews, Meagan's cousins, who are now in college. When they were 11 and 13, they were involved in a plethora of sports and extracurricular activities, including playing on an organized baseball team. They invited us to one of their games, which took place on a school night in May. It was held at a huge park with four diamonds, bleachers, lights, concession stands, electronic scoreboards, and manicured green fields. When we arrived, games were in progress on all four diamonds. The first round was scheduled for 4:00 to 6:00 P.M., the second from 6:00 to 8:00, and the third from 8:00 to 10:00. Our nephews' game was in the last slot. Of course, the previous two games went past their end times, so our nephews' game didn't start until 9:10 P.M. It ended at 11:30 P.M. On a school night! According to our nephews' mother, these games are played four nights a week. When do these kids do their homework or hang out with their friends?

Some helicopter parents go so far as to shield their children from the consequences of their actions. If Johnny hasn't done his homework, they'll do it for him. If Janie needs a ride to a friend's house, they'll drop everything and take her. It's as if they feel responsible for their children's happiness and success. Grade school teachers have told us about parents who call to complain if their child fails a test. Ironically, most will try to negotiate a higher grade rather than commit to helping the child overcome the problem. One teacher told us, "It's a dilemma. You want parents to be involved in their kids' schooling, but these people seem to care more about the kids' grades than whether or not they learn anything."

Helicopter parents often refuse to let their children learn that life requires some "heavy lifting." They buy them cars when they're teenagers, give them money so they don't have to work, and even fill out their college applications for them. Then they wonder why their kids won't take responsibility for themselves.

A Gen Yer Comments

My parents didn't spoil me, but lots of my friends got help from their parents that I thought was 'over the top.' For example, my friend Cody failed math his senior year and couldn't graduate unless he took a summer make-up class. Because he hates math so much, his mother knew he wouldn't get around to signing up for the class himself, much less completing it. So she hired a guy from the local junior college to take the class for him! Can you believe it? I think that was totally disgusting.

Even so, most of my friends got more help from their parents than my brother or I did from our mom—spending money, cars, car insurance, clothes, trips—you name it. But that was because our mom was a single mother raising us by herself, so there wasn't a lot of money and time to spoil us. As a result, I think we're better off.

Jasmine Truax

• •

This involvement doesn't stop with graduation from high school or college. Job recruiters tell us that they have seen Gen Y prospects delay accepting job offers until they clear it with their parents. We know of employers who have been asked by potential Gen Y hires to allow their parents to sit in on job interviews. One manager told us he received a call from the father of one of his young employees complaining about the unfairness of his daughter's performance review.

According to Dr. Nancy Weisman, a licensed clinical psychologist in Marietta, Georgia, "Kids need to know they aren't going to be rescued."[3] Many helicopter parents won't allow their children that experience.

Of course, not all parents of Generation Y are as extreme as the helicopter parents we've just described. And like Jasmine's mom, many did not have the means to be as overindulgent. But from our research and inquiries, we think we can safely conclude that there was a kinder, gentler, more indulgent approach to raising Generation Y than there was to raising Generation X or the Baby Boom Generation.

A Baby Boomer recently described the difference in her parenting style between her first two children and her third. "I have two children from my first marriage. Both are Gen Xers in their 30s. When they were young, my husband and I were building a business and were working long, crazy hours, so I relied on the fact that they had each other for the few hours after school before my husband and I got there. Then he and I divorced, and I remarried.

"My current husband and I had one daughter together, who is a Gen Yer. We both work but, luckily, we aren't working the kind of hours my first husband and I did. My new husband goes into the office an hour early every day so he can work from home in the late afternoon. That way, he's there when our daughter gets home from school. She is active in softball and geography club. We make it a priority to attend all her softball games and the geography competitions. My first two children were involved in after-school activities as well, but we rarely had time to attend—something I've always felt guilty about.

"When our daughter turned 16, we bought her a car. My first two children chided me because I didn't do the same for them but there was no way I could have afforded it. Besides, when they were kids I felt like it was safe to allow them to take the bus. Maybe it's because I am older and more aware of the danger, but I just don't feel comfortable with my youngest doing that. My older children tease me that I spoil her and she complains that I allowed them to do things I won't allow her to do. I wonder if I'll ever get it right."

. . . .

A Gen Yer Comments

I did have lots of friends who had a stay-at-home parent, but both of mine had to work, so I did the Kid-Zone After School Program, which my school offered. They watched me from the end of classes every day until my mom picked me up at about 6:00 P.M. She was always the last parent to arrive, but I never felt neglected. I don't think my parents overindulged me. They helped me with my homework but never did it for me. They had high expectations of me and would discipline me if I did something wrong. Of course, that was pretty rare because I was a really good kid. My friends used to accuse me of being 14 going on 41 because I was mature for my age (mentally, not physically). Maybe it's because I was an only child, raised by interested parents.

I did relate, however, to the article about the people in Chicago competing to get their kids into the best prep schools. Not only did my parents get me into the experimental kindergarten at the university, but three years before I graduated from grade school, they made sure I got on the waiting list for the magnet high school. Consequently, I got in and had an extraordinary high school experience: small classes, professional arts instructors, tons of performance opportunities, and only 43 people in my graduating class.

As for the overscheduling that Meagan and Larry talk about, I was definitely overscheduled, but it was of my own choosing. I was crazy about dance (that's why I wanted to go to the Arts School), so all through high school, I was involved in after-school rehearsals, set productions, program marketing, and actual performances. I'm presently finishing up my college degree while working at Starbucks and doing volunteer work for a local dance company. It's a lot. And many of my friends think I don't take enough time to relax and goof off, but that's my nature.

At 23, I'm still very close to my parents. I talk to my mom every day and see them both at least once a week. My boyfriend, who's my same age, is similarly as close to his parents and just as driven with his work and hobbies.

Kelsey Wolf, daughter of Dyan and Shap Wolf

△　　△　　△

A Gen Yer Comments

This pressure to get involved in extra stuff also comes from peers. When one person is involved in many activities and praised by the surrounding peers and adults, it causes everyone else to feel they must perform at that level. It's a race for popularity, scholarships, and acceptance. Grades aren't good enough anymore. Almost everyone who applies to a relatively good school has a 4.0 grade point average. It's the extracurricular activities, volunteer work, and personal stories that get you accepted . . . let alone get the scholarships to afford to go in the first place.

As for parents overprotecting their kids, I have a friend who up until she was 18 years old had never filled up her gas tank on her own. Not only did her parents pay for her gas, but her father also drove her truck to the gas station to fill it for her. So, when her parents were out of town and she needed to drive somewhere, she called her boyfriend to come help her fill her tank. My parents were never that bad.

Hannah Kuenn

Gen Yers React: We Need Feedback and Big-Picture Education

The upside to all this parental nurturing is that these kids are often better educated and better grounded than previous generations. Having lived a childhood where their value was continually celebrated, self-esteem is not a problem; they often have lots of it. The downside is that the members of Generation Y often expect their managers to have a strong interest in them as people. They expect to be applauded and praised when they perform well, just like their moms and dads did when they scored a hockey goal or danced in a recital. And they expect to be gently corrected when they need it, again, just like their moms and dads did.

A Gen Yer Comments

Gen Yers would also like to know what their value is to the company, what they contribute, what they need to do to move up and get promoted. They want to learn new things, figure out what they want to do, and earn more money. When you are young, you are at the bottom of the ladder and you have to work your way up. Most Yers like a bit of freedom on the job so they can improve and learn to adapt to their own abilities to different situations. The job becomes frustrating when, as a new hire you are treated as if you know how everything operates beforehand, and then you get into hot water for not following an unspecified procedure. Unless it's pointed out for you, you often don't grasp the bigger picture, and then get accused of not showing initiative or taking responsibility.

Shea Robins

Take Heather, our twentysomething Gen Y office assistant, for example. From day one, she seemed motivated to do a good job. With some training, she was able to master the duties of filing, billing, banking, running errands, and random tasks "as assigned." She was pleasant to be around, great with customers on the phone, and never called in sick. Her one fly in the ointment when she started was not taking the initiative to do what needed to be done unless she was told to do it.

For example, since we both travel a lot, we give most of Heather's random assignments to her via email or texting. One day a client called to complain that he hadn't received a proposal Larry had promised him three weeks earlier. Larry remembered emailing the proposal to Heather from the road with instructions to add some numbers and send it to the client. He asked Heather what had happened and she said she hadn't received the email. When they pinpointed the date it was sent, Heather remembered that her email hadn't been working for a few days that week.

When it happened, she figured out what was wrong and finally fixed it, but all the pending emails were lost. We were glad she took the initiative to fix the email problem on her own, but we were upset that she hadn't let anyone know her email was down. For three days, we kept sending her assignments that she never received and therefore went undone.

In retrospect, we realize it was our fault. Knowing she's a Gen Yer and new to the workforce, we should have been clearer about her overall responsibilities. If we had helped her understand that her job went beyond doing just what she was asked to do, that she was responsible for the outcome, this problem might have been avoided. A lot more follow-up on our part would have been helpful as well. Over the years we've done a better job of explaining the big picture to her, then following up with her. Consequently, she's grown into a terrific assistant.

- -

A Gen Yer Comments

I work for a cosmetic store as a salesperson. Unlike a lot of my Generation Y friends, I do a good job. I come to work every day, my sales are good, and my customers like me. I've even had some write letters to the store manager saying so. Part of why they like me, I think, is because I'm really into the stuff the store sells, so when I'm helping a customer try out a new product, we really get into talking about it. I also take notes on what the customers like so I can call them when a new product comes in that I think they'll be interested in.

"On the other hand, it seems like my manager only notices when I leave a mop bucket out or make some small mistake that in the long run does not compare with what I contribute to make the store successful. Why can't they just focus on what I do well, rather than crab about a few small mistakes?

And another thing. It drives me crazy that they flip-flop on the rules. Take texting. Supposedly texting from the back room is allowed but then sometimes you can get spoken to about it, gently "shaped" (a word HR used to mean "balled out"). Sometimes you even get written up (another HR term). Other times, texting from the back room is allowed and nobody says anything.

Jasmine Truax

- -

Signpost: Columbine High School

On April 20, 1999, Eric Harris and Dylan Klebold went on a shooting and bombing rampage at Columbine High School near Littleton, Colorado, killing 13 people and injuring 24 others before committing suicide.

The news of the massacre shocked the nation, but it had a special impact on Generation Y because the perpetrators and victims were Gen Yers. Most may not have related directly to the killers, but all were familiar with their issues. For example, many of the news stories described Harris and Klebold as disaffected loners. What teenager hasn't felt disaffected and lonely? It was said Harris and Klebold had been bullied and were seeking revenge. (The record now shows this to be untrue.) But what teenager has not felt bullied and then fantasized about getting even? For many Generation Yers, Columbine was personal.

It was also threatening. In the cases of the John Kennedy, Martin Luther King, Jr., and Bobby Kennedy assassinations, which served as signposts for the Baby Boomer Generation, the victims were celebrities. You can rationalize that for such violence to happen to you you'd need to be a celebrity, so you're safe. Columbine showed Generation Y that the victims and the perpetrators of such an atrocity could be friends and classmates. It could happen to them.

Columbine became a metaphor for a number of tragedies to which Generation Y was exposed in its formative years: the 1995 Oklahoma City bombing, 1996 Olympics bombing in Atlanta, 2001 attack on the World Trade Center and the Pentagon, Hurricane Katrina in 2005, and the 2007 Virginia Tech shooting. Gen Yers learned that the world can be a scary place.

At the same time, Generation Y grew up in a cocoon of safety provided by their doting, sometimes overprotective, parents.

. . . .

A Gen Yer Comments

I wasn't all that freaked out about Columbine. It was just some wacko kids that had nothing to do with me. What was weird was the aftermath. There were these lock-down drills where we practiced what we'd do if someone went berserk in the class with a gun. We were supposed to hide under our desks, which seemed kind of pointless if someone really wanted to shoot you. (When I told my dad about this, he laughed and told me he felt the same way in the 1950s during school drills to prepare for the Russians dropping the bomb. Being under a desk wasn't going to help.)

Anyway, all the classrooms had booklets on the wall saying what to do in case of a shooting. It made me feel a little paranoid because, I guess, it removed any sense that school was a completely safe place. It made me realize that anything can happen—there's only so much you can do to protect yourself.

Wilson Doun

Gen Yers React: We Need a Hug

Generation Y grew up in a conflicted time: a dangerous world that could hurt them combined with a safety net that has always protected them. The outcome is a risk-averse generation that sticks its tongue out at pessimism.

Gen Yers tend to be hopeful about their futures, even when confronted with such terrifying events as Columbine, the Virginia Tech shooting, and the attacks of September 11. If any event should diminish a young generation's enthusiasm, it would be 9/11. Yet a year after the attacks, a Harris Interactive poll showed that Generation Yers wanted to move on with their lives and were excited about their futures.[4] To us, this optimism may be a bit naïve but it is refreshing.

For their managers and coworkers, this can mean that Gen Yers are likely to be willing to trust you and that they expect openness, honesty, and fairness in return. They want you to be straight with them about what to expect on the job, like hours, pay, job conditions, and pitfalls. They expect you to keep them informed and to treat them fairly.

For this generation, you also need to consider that they are new to the workforce, so you may need to explain some things to them. For example, if you are hiring a Gen Yer part-time and the expected wait time to get a full-time position is 18 months, let her know. Show her the working conditions before you offer her the job. Will she have to work in a small, cramped cubicle? If so, don't just tell her: Show her. Remember, she has little or no experience in the real world to help her understand what you are describing. You'll probably have to explain more to her than you would to a Boomer or Gen Xer.

When interviewing Gen Yers, remember that they may not be interview savvy. They may not know what to ask. You can help them make informed decisions about the jobs being offered by answering the questions they should ask but don't think of. For example:

- Has he thought about how long the commute to work will take?
- Does she know her schedule may change?
- How does he feel about the dress code?
- Will she be expected to attend social events after work? Is that okay?
- How much time will he spend interacting with others?
- What's the policy on Web surfing, texting, Twittering, and other social networking while at work?
- What's the policy on exposing tattoos?

Answering such basic questions will lower the odds that a Gen Yer will leave you in six weeks because the job was "not what he expected." Coming from the structured environment he is probably used to, if you don't tell him, he'll consider it a breach of trust. Also, being proactive demonstrates that you are interested in his success at your organization and that it's not just a stopover.

Signpost: Technical Expertise

Twenty years ago, a lot of Baby Boomers went home after work and told their spouses, "We got to use a computer today! There's talk in the office that they're going to get everybody one. I'll believe that when I see it." Most Baby Boomers learned to use a computer at work. Gen Xers learned to use one at school. Most Gen Yers don't remember learning. Like the life laws we discussed in Chapter 1, using a computer has always been a part of their lives, so it's second nature to them.

According to *Connecting to the Net.Generation:*[5]

- 97% of Generation Y own a computer.
- 94% own a cell phone.
- 76% use instant messaging.
- 69% have a Facebook account.
- 44% read blogs.

> ➢ 34% use Web sites as their primary source of news.
> ➢ 28% author a blog.

The computer is as intimidating to Generation Y as the toaster is to older generations.

Gen Yers React: Technology Comes Naturally

Generation Y spends much more time than Baby Boomers surfing the Web, visiting blogs, and connecting on social networking sites. They are the experts, and this has given them respect and power in organizations that previous generations of young people did not have.

Gen Y has become our Internet tour guide. Former General Electric CEO Jack Welch once said that "e-business knowledge is usually inversely proportional to age and rank." To access this wealth of information, he established the practice of reversed mentoring at GE. The company paired 1,000 managers with 1,000 new Gen Y employees so the managers could be tutored by the Gen Yers in how best to use technology. The experiment proved to be a huge success.

Signpost: Online Social Networking

For those of you who think the term "social networking" means joining the Rotary Club so you can make business contacts, you're either a Baby Boomer who's out of touch or you've been living on Mars.

"Social networking" implies using Web-based services to connect people with similar interests. It's difficult to pinpoint the genesis of this phenomenon, but many experts agree that it started in the mid-1990s when service providers Compuserve and AOL made chat rooms and e-messaging services available to laypeople (as opposed to just scientists and geeks).

In 1995, Classmates.com allowed users to connect with old school chums. In 1997, Six Degrees of Separation launched. It was based on the idea that if you trace the connection from someone you know to someone that person knows and continue the thread, it will only take six leaps to find a connection to a person you want to know or to whom you are related. Then came Circle of Friends (1999), Friendster (2002), MySpace (2003), LinkedIn (2003), Facebook (2004), Twitter (a microblogging tool, 2006), and a host of others.

This phenomenon serves as a major signpost for Generation Y because it's how they socialize and connect with other members of their generation.

Gen Yers React: Constantly in Touch

According to a survey by Peanut Labs, 68 percent of Gen Y respondents said they visit social networks at least once a day.[6] That's 48 million people connecting every day with their friends through their computers, PDAs, cell phones, and smartphones. If you want to enhance your connections with Generation Y, embrace this technology and use it.

R. L. Polk & Co., a global company specializing in automotive information and marketing solutions, recruits Gen Y high-tech engineers through Facebook, LinkedIn, and Twitter. The company offers an internship program that allows potential hires to experience Polk from the inside out. Its philosophy is "hire slow, hire tough." As a result, employee turnover is well below the industry average, and 86 percent of employees surveyed recommended Polk as a good place to work.[7]

. . . .

A Gen Yer Comments

Through most of high school, I communicated with my friends every night via texting and Skype (a videomessaging service that uses Web cams so you can see the person you are talking to). We did homework, planned our weekends, and gossiped. My mother thought it was really cool because she grew up in a house with seven brothers and sisters and only one phone. Can you imagine how anyone could have survived that?

Madison Pikes

. . . .

Signpost: Economic Turmoil

In the 1990s, many Gen Yers watched their Baby Boomer parents make fortunes in the stock market only to see those fortunes evaporate in 2000 with the bursting of the tech bubble. Now, as they graduate from college,

Gen Yers see the economy in turmoil again. As a result, they're looking for jobs and financial security.

Gen Yers React: Wanting to Stay Put

A survey of 19,000 graduating college students by NACE (the National Association of Colleges and Employers) asked students to rank 15 job/employer attributes in order of their importance in choosing a job. The top three were:

1. Company provides the opportunity for advancement.
2. Company offers job security.
3. Company has a good insurance package.[8]

Unlike their Generation X predecessors, who saw job hopping as the road to success, Generation Y more often wants to do it within the confines of the company. They will, however, leave if they don't see potential for advancement. Concerned about turnover among its Generation Y recruits, consulting giant Deloitte created the position of National Director of Next-Generation Initiatives. This person's job is to create programs to help young people plan the next move in their professional growth—hopefully by staying at Deloitte. They figure this saves the company $150,000 for every employee retained.[9]

Signpost: Seeking Groups

If the Traditional Generation is motivated by company loyalty, and Baby Boomers are fueled by team development, and Gen Xers love to fly solo, Gen Yers get excited about the fellowship that takes place in the work environment. Not that they want to become blood brother or sister with all their coworkers, but much like the online community they have created outside of work, Generation Y is looking for a sense of belonging and kinship at work.

Perhaps because of an arrested sense of independence from their helicopter parents, or as a healthy result of being close to family and friends, Generation Y tends to relate to groups. They grew up engaging in structured activities in groups. They went to the mall in groups. They even dated in groups. We've had employers tell us that they've even had, on a few occasions, Generation Yers show up for the interviews in groups. One employer told us that he felt that if he hired one, he had to hire them all.

· ·

A Gen Yer Comments

In high school, I worked at Mimi's Café, a chain of restaurants. We had lots of high school kids show up in groups to interview or ask for applications. The managers would throw out any applications that came in as groups because they didn't want to feel pressure to hire all of them.

I think it is definitely a dependency issue. We've all grown up with a hand to hold all the time, and when it's finally time to answer to someone else, like a boss or manager, we sometimes shy away in fear. For this reason, people bring along a support group to apply for jobs, which obviously is even more of a detriment. Even if they do get hired together, it hinders their social skills. They are less likely to interact with new people they don't know.

Hannah Kuenn

· ·

Gen Yers React: Where Are My Friends?

In the NACE study[10] of 19,000 college students, the fourth most desirable company trait for Generation Y was: "There are friendly coworkers." After opportunities for advancement, job security, and good insurance, these young folks want to make friends and be part of a group.

That means making a special effort to welcome them. It doesn't mean you have to spend your days chatting with them on Facebook or applauding them when they pull into the parking lot, but you might want to consider what you're doing to welcome them aboard. Many companies put new hires on "probation." This seems like an odd term to apply to someone you are welcoming. Normally, it's criminals who get put on probation, and only after they've been convicted. We suggest you find a more creative term for the period of getting to know each other.

The Ritz-Carlton Hotel makes a special effort to welcome new employees that we think is commendable. It starts by making it clear it does not *hire* new employees, it *selects* them to try out for their varsity team. New persons are then immersed in a one-year orientation program that includes 120 hours of intensive training on the various aspects of their role in carrying out the gold standard of service for which Ritz-Carlton is so well known. They also spend 10 to 15 minutes before each shift reviewing these principles with their team and their supervisor. At the end of the year, they're tested and certified to be Ritz-Carlton's "ladies and gentlemen serving ladies and gentlemen."[11] Consequently, employee turnover is a low 18 percent compared to the luxury-hotel industry average of 158 percent.[12]

This fits with a study by PricewaterhouseCoopers that found that more than 30 percent of recent college graduates felt training and development were more important than salary and 98 percent believe that interacting with significant mentors is extremely important.[13]

Unfortunately, not every company is as farsighted in its efforts to connect with Gen Yers as the Ritz-Carlton. A Ramstad survey reported that 51 percent of Baby Boomers had almost no interaction with Generation Y and 71 percent of Generation Y had scarce contact with older employees.[14]

Signpost: Integrating Life and Work

Given their busy schedules when they were young, many Gen Yers are accustomed to meshing work with personal life. When they were kids, time spent in the classroom, at the soccer field, at drama lessons, and in karate class all flowed together with doing homework, spending time with family, and socializing with their friends. With the aid of a smartphone, the typical Gen Yer could manage it all on the fly.

Gen Yers React: Gimme Flexibility

Gen Yers tend to find an 8-to-5 structured job in cubical-land to be confining and tedious. They're happiest when they are held accountable for the results of their labor but have the freedom to come and go at work rather than logging hours on the clock. Technology has given them the ability to work and play at the same time.

Generation Y is the champion contortionist when it comes to working a flexible work schedule. One can text friends, write a proposal, check sales figures, send a tweet on Twitter, and pick up dry cleaning simultaneously. Of course, not every job is conducive to such an unstructured work routine. Someone has to mind the store. Service desks need to be manned, customers must be waited on, and meetings need to be attended.

Even so, smart companies understand that schedule flexibility is important to retaining Generation Y.

Upshot, a Chicago marketing firm that specializes in brand marketing and promotions, allows its employees an extra day off every month to reenergize themselves and keep their creativity fresh.[15] Upshot was listed as one of the top 10 places to work in Chicago and in the top 50 of *Ad Age*'s 2008 Agency Report.

Steve Swasey, vice president of Corporate Communications at Netflix tells us that the company's policy on vacations is "'Take some.' No one keeps track of how much time off anyone takes, as long as their manager knows and their work gets done."

The Peace Corps gives its volunteers 48 paid vacation days during a two-year hitch. This allows them to explore other countries or go back home to visit.

Signpost: Social Responsibility

Generation Y could easily be renamed "Generation Social Responsibility." These folks care about energy consumption, water and air pollution, carbon footprints, saving the whales, animal factory farming, and products made in sweatshops by child labor. Generation Y considers doing the right thing for the planet and for mankind important factors in choosing and staying with an employer.

Gen Yers React: Earn Our Respect

Two-thirds of Gen Yers want to work for an employer who acts responsibly toward the planet. According to a Cone Survey of Gen Y–age full-time employees, 69 percent are aware of their company's social/environmental commitments, 64 percent feel loyal to their companies as a result of their companies' social/environmental activities, 56 percent would refuse to work for an irresponsible corporation, and 79 percent want to work for a company that cares about how it impacts or contributes to society.[16]

Recruiters visiting college campuses in the past left giveaways like pens and stationary. Now recruiters come armed with tree seedlings and multiuse recycled bags. IBM recently launched the recruiting campaign slogan on college campuses titled "Work for the World. Start @ IBM."[17] Whole Foods is a favorite supermarket for Generation Y because it stocks items that weren't tested on animals and focuses on organic produce.

Another Gen Y favorite is Loomstate. The brainchild of Scott Hahn and Rogan Gregory in 2004, it's an eco-luxe label that uses 100 percent organic materials in its clothing and accessories, which are produced in factories that adhere to the highest standards of pollution control and fair labor practices.[18]

This Gen Y passion for being responsible residents of the planet can give you a way to connect with them. Don't have a recycling program? Assign the project to a Gen Yer. Need someone to research green alternatives for your office? Ask a Gen Yer. Make every effort to practice corporate responsibility to the degree you can. Gen Yers are watching you. If you want them to respect you, you must behave in ways they can respect. Practicing corporate social responsibility fills a big part of that bill.

A Gen Yer Comments

Right now, I'm a freshman at Northern Arizona University and living in the dorm. I've seen more Brita filters and aluminum water bottles than ever before. All incoming freshmen are required to read *Enrique's Journey*, a story about a young boy traveling from Honduras to the United States to find his mother. I suppose this is to inspire us to be even more "socially responsible" and "globally aware," and I think it's a good thing. NAU provides recycling bins in all of the dorms and encourages students to use them properly. Our newest dorm building, Aspen Crossing, as well as many other buildings on campus are considered "Green buildings."

Hannah Kuenn

Signpost: Volunteerism

Generation Y values volunteerism and puts a high priority on giving back—and their Baby Boomer parents deserve some of the credit for instilling this value. With a drive to raise their children "right," many Boomer parents have encouraged their Gen Y children to volunteer time to causes they feel are worthwhile. Doing so enhanced their children's real-world experiences, gave them an awareness of the needs of others, and beefed up college applications. Some schools even require volunteerism in order to graduate. More than 80 percent of high schools have some type of volunteer program.

Of course, cynics would say that 95 percent of the students participating do so to make their college application forms look good. That it's not a selfless activity—they do it to fulfill requirements of the school, honor society, or to get into college. Perhaps, but one way or another, Gen Yers are inclined to volunteer—to involve themselves in helping the world to be a better place.

Gen Yers React: We Want to Help

More than 60 percent of Generation Y want to work for a company that gives them the opportunity to volunteer. According to Stan Smith, Deloitte's national director of Next-Generation Initiatives, "Companies that facilitate meaningful community involvement opportunities for their people will be very attractive employers."[19]

Offering the chance to do volunteer work has several benefits for both Gen Yers and their organizations. Gen Yers get to see instant results from their work. It builds their confidence to try out new ideas in a less threatening environment than work. It builds the company's reputation for doing good things in the community. Most of all, it provides expanded training for Gen Y employees.

SalesForce.com is a software company offering online sales applications and customer service management tools. In January 2008, *Forbes* magazine called it the second-fastest growing technology company in the United States. Its Web site claims that its employees have a "change the world mentality." SalesForce.com places one percent of profits into a foundation that reimburses employees who volunteer one percent of their time. SalesForce.com employees have volunteered a whopping 50,000 hours a year under this program.[20]

A Harley-Davidson Dealer's Approach to Gen Y
Told by Author Larry Johnson

I spoke at an annual Harley-Davidson dealer meeting in San Antonio, Texas, where, at dinner one evening, I met Pablo Lee. I had been told that Pablo owns and operates HDK (Harley-Davidson Korea), one of the most successful Harley dealerships in the world.

In the gym the next morning, Pablo happened to be on the stationary bike next to me. How often do you get to chat with someone of this caliber? So between pants and puffs, I asked him what he considered to be the key to his success.

In a polite but firm manner, Pablo corrected me, saying that he does not consider himself or his business as "successful." He said that when you start thinking of yourself as "successful," you stop being successful.

"Huh?" I said.

He went on to explain that success, like happiness and enlightenment, is a journey one does not achieve, but something one must continually pursue.

Well, this was all sounding a little too mystical for my limited spiritual capabilities to grasp, so I rephrased the question, asking him what secrets he might share that would help others move through this journey as effectively as he has.

I expected him to refer to his business acumen, or his willingness to balance risk with caution in making strategic decisions, or perhaps something about hard work, sacrifice, and a bit of luck. But he simply replied that he makes it his business to make people happy. It sounded a little weird, but his dealership is financially successful by any measure and his employee turnover is almost zero, so I figured that he must be doing something right.

Pablo went on to explain that all people want to be happy, that we spend most of our time, energy, thoughts, and actions pursuing happiness. He said that HDK's vision is to be a leader in pursuing the happiness of his company's four major stakeholders:

1.   Customers
2.   Staff and investors
3.   Harley-Davidson Motor Company (suppliers)
4.   Korean society

I asked him how he does this, and he explained how he tries to make each of these four stakeholder groups happy:

Customers

"We provide our customers with nice motorcycles and an experience they will never forget," Pablo said. "Also, we always treat our customers with a 'family-minded' approach. In other words, the staff is taught that their relationship with their customers is like a brotherhood, that each employee should value each customer as if he or she was a sibling."

According to Pablo, given the strong emphasis on family relationships in Korean culture, doing business this way is essential.

Staff and Investors

Ninety percent of Pablo's employees are Generation Yers under the age of 25. He pointed out that treating his staff well is essential because they are the ones who contribute the most to making his customers happy. To do this, he generously offers them:

▷ **Higher pay**. Pablo pays his staff an average of 10 percent more than they could earn working in similar jobs for other motorcycle or car dealerships.

▷ **Company trips based on the company's annual performance**. This year he took all his staff to Bali for a seven-day stay at Club Med. Pablo says that almost all his employees are young, so this was a hugely popular reward. I noticed that he had a cadre of 10 or so staff attending the meeting with him in San Antonio.

▷ **Blueprints for their prosperous future**. Every staff member understands that HDK is the best place to learn his or her skill and that they can grow into competent professionals because HDK is simply the best place to work in the Korean motorcycle industry. I guess it's like playing for a championship sports team. When you work with the best, you can't help but become better.

▷ **Empowerment**. Every staff person is trained and empowered to decide and do his or her work independently. They are encouraged to see themselves not as "machines" but as valued souls who are important units that make the HDK organization perfect.

At this point, Pablo emphasized that of these four items, "blueprints for their prosperous future" and "empowerment" are far more important than "pay" and "award trips."

Pablo also believes that employees—especially these Gen Yers—want a sense of belonging, which fits with the family/brotherhood value. He makes this a reality by:

▷ **Asking employees for ideas on how to improve the company**. He implements the ideas that look worthwhile while publicly recognizing all who contribute.

▷ **Sponsoring many clubs such as a baseball club and a mountain bike club**. These clubs offer staff the opportunity to build special friendships with others, develop better communication, and create a more pleasant atmosphere in the workplace.

▷ **Spending time out on the floor interacting with and listening to his employees**. Pablo says that everyone wants to be heard and recognized for his or her contributions to the team. He makes sure he's around to do that.

▷ **Organizing community fund drives to benefit local orphanages and other charities**. Pablo says he's discovered that people have a powerful need to give to others and that when they do, it makes them happy. So he makes it easy and fun for them to do so.

Suppliers

Pablo emphasized that HDK not only focuses on selling motorcycles but also on trying to deliver the Harley-Davidson brand properly in Korea. "If we fail to keep the value of the Harley-Davidson brand and succeed in sales (which is impossible, I think), Harley-Davidson Motor Company would be 'glad' but not 'happy.' We believe Harley-Davidson is 'happy' now because HDK has succeeded in both sales and brand management."

Korean Society

"The idea of a 'motorcycle lifestyle' was completely foreign in the Korean market," Pablo said. "Korean riders used motorcycles just to get around, not to have fun experiences. HDK opened in 1999, and we immediately began working to translate the Harley-Davidson lifestyle in a way that was meaningful to the Korean culture. To do this, HDK and the Korean chapter of H.O.G. (Harley Owners Group) organized fund-raising events for local orphanages and other charities. Gradually, Korean society started considering motorcycling as a wonderful leisure activity and hostile eyes on motorcycles began to disappear."

Pablo pointed out that these community involvement activities also make staff and customers happy because they have opportunities to participate with the dealership and the H.O.G. chapter to contribute to Korean society.

△   △   △

The bottom line of all this is that Pablo makes the four major stakeholders of his business happy and that translates into more customers riding Harley-Davidsons. And that makes Pablo happy. (The views of Pablo Lee are his own personal views and are not representative of the views of the Harley-Davidson Motor Company.)

A Great Place for Gen Yers to Work

Google offers its employees on-site medical and dental care; unlimited sick leave; an educational program under which employees can take a leave of absence to attend school for up to five years with tuition reimbursement; and on-site educational programs in topics like Japanese, Spanish, and Mandarin. It also offers a philosophical approach to employment that would pluck the heartstrings of most Gen Yers. On its Web site, it lists the 10 top reasons you would want to work at Google[21]:

1. **Lend a helping hand.** With millions of visitors every month, Google has become an essential part of everyday life—like a good friend—connecting people with the information they need to live great lives.

2. **Life is beautiful.** Being a part of something that matters and working on products in which you can believe is remarkably fulfilling.

3. **Appreciation is the best motivation**, so we've created a fun and inspiring workspace you'll be glad to be a part of, including on-site doctor and dentist; massage and yoga; professional development opportunities; shoreline running trails; and plenty of snacks to get you through the day.

4. **Work and play are not mutually exclusive.** It is possible to code and pass the puck at the same time.

5. **We love our employees and we want them to know it.** Google offers a variety of benefits, including a choice of medical programs, company-matched 401(k), stock options, maternity and paternity leave, and much more.

6. **Innovation is our bloodline.** Even the best technology can be improved. We see endless opportunity to create even more relevant, more

useful, and faster products for our users. Google is the technology leader in organizing the world's information.

7. **Good company everywhere you look.** Googlers range from former neurosurgeons, CEOs, and U.S. puzzle champions to alligator wrestlers and Marines. No matter what their backgrounds, Googlers make for interesting cube mates.

8. **Uniting the world, one user at a time.** People in every country and every language use our products. As such we think, act, and work globally—just our little contribution to making the world a better place.

9. **Boldly go where no one has gone before.** There are hundreds of challenges yet to solve. Your creative ideas matter here and are worth exploring. You'll have the opportunity to develop innovative new products that millions of people will find useful.

10. **There is such a thing as a free lunch after all.** In fact we have them every day: healthy, yummy, and made with love.

The question to ask is: How Googley is your approach to hiring? Could you create a "Top 10 Reasons to Work Here" list for your company that would excite Gen Yers as much as Google's does?

The Bottom Line

Although Generation Y is accused of being spoiled by caring, but sometimes overprotective, parents, they are poised to contribute significant value to any organization. They are better skilled in technology and in traversing the Web. Because of their youth and the way they were raised, they may need instruction and coaching on taking responsibility beyond their specific job descriptions. More than anything, they will do best when they feel connected to the people who manage and work with them.

CHAPTER 7

Managing Generation Y

"If you want happiness for a lifetime—help the next generation."

—Chinese Proverb

Welcome to Generation Y

Generation Y accounts for more than 35 percent of the workforce. Like any group of people, you will find some difficult or impossible to manage, but with most, you'll do just fine as long as you're willing to work with their idiosyncrasies.

Kasey is a Gen Yer who has worked for a manufacturing company for six years. She was recently promoted to sales administration manager. Kasey says, "I never wake up dreading to go to work. As cliché as it sounds, we are like one crazy family. This is a fun place to work, everyone is relaxed, and customers love us. I am constantly being challenged with new things to do in addition to the items already on my to-do list. I have two bosses and I get feedback, mostly positive, from one of them at least once a day. If they say something critical, they do it in a nice way. And that's part of why I like this job. I trust and respect my bosses. Much like my parents, I know they have my back in tough situations. They're there for me when I need them and I can tell they care about me. If it weren't for them, I don't think I would like this job nearly as much as I do."

David, a Gen Yer, just got an MBA from a major university. At an interview with an international trading company, he told the interviewer he needed a flexible schedule. The interviewer told him the company allowed working from home a couple days a month. "No," David said, "I'm a marathon runner. I do four or five races a year. I need to be able to take time off throughout the year to compete across the country. Also, I normally do my training at four in the morning before I come to work, but in the winter it's too dark and cold, so I'll need to come in at 10 rather than 8."

Steve is a Gen Xer who manages an office supply store and supervises a group of 10 Gen Yers. The parents of one Gen Yer visited Steve to find out why he had fired their daughter. He explained to them that while their daughter was on the phone talking to a customer who had called to complain about a product, she told him to "f*** off" and hung up on him. Steve said the parents seemed shocked that he would fire her without hearing her side of the story and felt that he should give her another chance.

Generation Y has different work requirements and expectations than the Baby Boomers and Gen Xers who manage them. Understanding these differences will help managers to be effective and their Gen Yers to flourish.

The goals for managing Generation Y include:

1. Help them integrate into the work setting without scaring them off or turning them off.
2. Provide them with solid primary experiences that lay the groundwork for their careers.
3. Keep them from self-destructing.

Tips for Managing Generation Y

1. Create Opportunities to Bond

One complaint employers have about Generation Y is that they don't seem to care about their jobs. We agree: Many Gen Yers, especially the younger ones, don't care about their jobs in the same way many of us didn't care about jobs when were that young. But like any generation, they need jobs to earn money to pay the bills. Given their close family upbringing, jobs that offer Gen Yers a sense of belonging and a family-like atmosphere will have the most appeal to them.

Nick, a 22-year-old Gen Y college senior we interviewed, told us that the most lucrative job he's had during his schooling was parking cars for a restaurant. He said he didn't like it much, however, because he essentially worked alone. He finally quit to take a job at a local coffeehouse after a friend who worked there told him how much fun it was. He makes half the money but he gets to connect with people his age every day, both coworkers and customers. Nick went on to say, "With a job like this, who needs to go to a party?"

Gen Yers also like to feel bonded to their bosses. The perception that they are not loyal is a myth. According to Cam Marston, author of *Motivating the "What's in It for Me?" Workforce,* they have a tendency to seek tight bonds: They want a boss who is close, caring, and aware, so it makes sense to provide that kind of relationship. It's important to remember, however, not to cross the line from "boss as advocate" to "boss as friend."[1]

This puts you in the role of concerned coach. It's a step beyond "benevolent boss" but short of "loving parent." Your challenge is to show you care about Gen Yers but not to get lovesick. You still must insist they follow the rules, complete their tasks, meet their deadlines, and produce for the organization. If they do, you will applaud them. If they don't, you will help them, coach them, encourage them, and counsel them—just like their teachers did at school and their moms and dads did at home. If they continue not to meet expectations, however, unlike their parents, you will fire them.

Emma, a Gen Yer, works as concierge at a boutique hotel. She described to us how she connected with her supervisor:

> The interview process included meeting with a panel of hotel employees. I liked this approach because it gave me a snapshot of the variety of personalities at the property. There was one supervisor I really liked, right off the bat. She was pretty direct when she asked me questions, but she didn't seem like she was trying to uncover some awful truth about me. When the hotel offered me the job, I asked if I could speak to her privately before deciding. She called me the same day. I felt I could ask her questions about the company's culture and she would give me straight answers. She has since become my unofficial mentor. She's not my manager but it's reassuring that she is there to ask questions when I'm in a pinch. I also know she will not throw me under the bus if I make a mistake. I have been with the hotel for a year now and I don't have plans to leave anytime soon.

2. Tell It Like It Is

Unlike Traditionals and Baby Boomers, who had to compete for every award, Generation Y got trophies for just showing up. As a result, there is a perception that they can't handle bad news because they've had it too easy. This may be true for some, but they've also witnessed tremendous tragedies from Columbine High School to the Virginia Tech shootings. Generation Y wants to know the truth and sugarcoating bad news doesn't help them develop, nor does it enhance their trust in you. If the assignment you are giving them will be hard, tell them so, but follow up with why you think they can handle it. If they have done something incorrectly, let them know and tell them how they should change it in the future.

For example, Marianne is a Baby Boomer who works as a lead park ranger for the U.S. Forest Service. She has a group of Gen Yers who work for her. "Sometimes I feel like I'm their mother," says Marianne. "I have to remind them to put on sunblock, wear their name badges, and drink enough water to stay hydrated. I do, however, love the enthusiasm they bring to the job. I listen to their input and they've gotten me up to speed with some of the new weather technology. But I am very clear that, in the end, I am the one who makes the decisions. We will discuss new strategies when it comes to animal control or cleanup duties and I often ask for their opinions, but this is not a democracy. I explain to them that it's my butt on the line, so I make the final calls. It seems to work."

3. Avoid the "Good Old Days"

"When I was your age . . ." "Back in the day . . ." "The way we used to do it . . ." Blah, blah, blah. It's tempting to reminisce about the past. Really, Generation Y can't imagine being as old as you are, so stop rambling on about the way it used to be. Your responsibility is to coach them to succeed, not to relive the touchdown you scored back in high school.

4. Create Gen Y–Friendly Rules

Every environment requires rules to run efficiently, but some are as out of date as radio tubes and eight-track players. In Chapter 5, we suggested that you get rid of stupid rules when working with Gen Xers. This is even more important for Gen Yers.

If you spend a lot of time reinforcing certain rules with Generation Y, or you notice that they spend a lot of their time trying to figure out a way around certain rules, apply the "Why" test.

Ask yourself why the rule in question is important. If it doesn't impact customer service, sales, safety, quality, or cost, consider changing or getting rid of it. For example, why must your Gen Yers refrain from listening to their iPods while working? If they interact with customers, there is a good reason for the rule because you've found that customers, especially older ones, find it irritating. So you wouldn't want to change it. If, on the other hand, they don't interact with customers, and listening to their iPods doesn't present a safety hazard, why shouldn't they be able to work with white buds in their ears?

▷ PricewaterhouseCoopers answers the common Gen Y question, "When am I going to get promoted?" by pairing Gen Yers up with mentors who provide a prediction that if the employee develops the skill set required, he or she will be promoted within three years.[2] It's not a guarantee because there's always the big "if" included, but at least they give them a time frame.

▷ Capital One, a credit card company headquartered in McLean, Virginia, offers its employees the opportunity to purchase an additional week off if the three weeks it offers is not enough.[3]

▷ Stockamp & Associates, a health-care consulting firm located in Lake Oswego, Oregon, helps new Gen Yers to hit the ground running by having them meet with major clients under the watchful eye of veteran consultants who hold their hands through the process. Stockamp & Associates believes this gives its young members an immediate avenue to learn about their clients and what their clients want.[4]

Not every workplace can abolish the same rules. It depends on the type of job and industry you're in, so you'll need to decide what's right for your organization. The important thing is that to the degree you can, you create an environment to which Gen Yers will be attracted. Gen Y–friendly rules go a long way toward that end.

5. Be Open to Virtual Work Environments

Hank, a Gen Yer, is completing his last year at college, where he is studying to be a CPA. He takes all his courses online and never goes on campus. His professors have office hours that include live chat sessions on the Web. Hank has several team projects he must complete with other classmates. Some of the work can be done online, but for other portions, he must meet with his team, which they do at a bar or coffee shop.

Baby Boomers live to work. Generation Xers work to live. Generation Yers don't see work and life as any different; they blend into one. To most Baby Boomers and many Gen Xers, there is a clear distinction between working face-to-face and working remotely. A Gen Yer feels comfortable being home at 10:00 on a Sunday night listening to iTunes, editing his blog, checking his Facebook page, and sending a report to a client with a CC to his boss.

Cisco Systems surveyed its employees and found the company saved $277 million by allowing them to telecommute. Sixty-nine percent of those surveyed claimed their productivity improved.[5]

You need to make sure your technology is up-to-date. Generation Y comes to work assuming you are as high tech as their latest iPhone or Wii. If your organization's technology is old and making it current is out of the question, be clear about that before you hire them and point out any benefits that might offset your technological deficiencies. For example, many high-security areas of the government forbid employees from bringing cell phones and PDAs into the building. To compensate for amputating these devices from the bodies of techno-dependent Gen Yers, the government touts the other benefits of the job that would appeal to Gen Yers: highly challenging work, working with other bright Gen Yers, instant implementation of ideas, and participation on top-secret projects.

6. Offer Flextime

Firefighters and medical personnel have been working longer but fewer days a week for many years, and this kind of flexible schedule has become more common in a variety of occupations.

The ability to plan their own time and the freedom to work when they want to are major motivators for Generation Y. Not all work schedules can be a free-for-all, but examine the work schedule and determine if more flexibility can be offered. Establish what duties and assignments must be completed at the office and what can be done on the Gen Yer's own schedule. Does it have to be 8 to 5? Does the Gen Yer have to work set hours to produce products, collaborate with colleagues, solve problems, deal with customers, and get the work done? Or could it be done off hours or virtually? If the Gen Yer must be in the office for a certain number of hours a day, can he decide which hours?

The more options you can give to Gen Yers who show they are responsible enough to handle them, the more likely they will stay loyal and go the extra mile for you.

7. Interact Often

If you manage Gen Yers, you may have to function as a surrogate transitional parent for them. Surrogate in that they will look to you as the authority figure who will protect them, mentor them, and help them succeed. Transitional in that you may have to pull them from adolescence into adulthood by insisting they perform and holding them accountable for their mistakes, a parental role many of their Baby Boomer parents abdicated.

Part of this will include giving lots of encouragement and reassurance. The owner of an auto repair shop complained to us about the Gen Y mechanics she employs. "These young people expect a standing ovation if they just show up for work. I have better things to do than applaud the fact they remembered to set their alarms." As cranky as the owner sounds, she has a point: Generation Y does want recognition for actions the rest of us may not believe they deserve. On the other hand, given the way they've been raised, they probably need it, at least in the beginning.

A Generation Yer told us that she talks to her boss every day. She said she likes to have the daily interaction because it reassures her that she is on the right track. She said it also makes her feel good to have someone listen to her.

Generation Y has built a tremendous community online and at home. The workplace sometimes can be a lonely, intimidating place. Touching base with the Gen Yer reassures her that there is someone looking out for her.

If you work with Gen Yers, offer guidance and suggestions to help them with those parts of the job that weren't covered in new-employee orientation. If you manage them, provide a thorough orientation to the job that breaks down their duties and your expectations into bite-sized chunks. Go out of your way to give them regular feedback, both reinforcing and correcting, and give it often. This means cheering them when they do well and gently but firmly correcting them when they stray (just like their moms and dads did). Ask them often how they are doing and be willing to listen. Don't be afraid to correct them, even for behaviors you would assume they should know better, because often, they don't.

8. Stir Up a Little Fun

We recently spoke for a chain of convenience stores on the East Coast. The theme of its meeting was "We're First in Class," with a motif focused on school and sports.

The meeting started with a local high school band playing lively marching music while 45 managers divided into groups according to region marched into the ballroom dressed in football jerseys and chanting well-rehearsed cheers for their respective regions. The master of ceremonies then conducted a cheering contest to see which region could cheer the loudest. It was absolute pandemonium, outdone only by the final act: the CEO and top executives of the company—a bunch of Baby Boomer men with expanding paunches and spindly legs—coming onstage dressed in female cheerleader outfits including short skirts, bouncing busts, makeup, and wigs. These "execs in drag" proceeded to have their own cheerleading competition, complete with shoulder stands and wobbling pyramids. The crowd passed judgment by shouting, applauding, and cat-calling the executives' performances. To say everyone was having a ball would be an understatement.

It was the most energetic, creative, and *fun* way to start a meeting we've ever seen.

You don't need to wait for an annual meeting to have fun. One company we know has a monthly get-together where top management shares company financials and passes out awards. Each month, they include some fun along with the business. They've had karaoke contests, Tinker Toy tower-building contests, and spelling bees. The meeting lasts 90 minutes: 45 minutes for business and 45 minutes for fun.

We know another manager who has a five-foot by five-foot corkboard in the break room. Every month, she assigns the board to a different employee. The employee can put whatever he or she wants on the board as long as it represents his or her personality and as long as it is "family friendly." People post baby pictures, samples of their kids' artwork from kindergarten, pictures of their kids, and their favorite recipes.

The manager told us, "I am 20 years older than most of my employees. The board gives me a handle on things to discuss with them besides work. It also allows employees to learn about each other, even if they don't work together every day."

Someone once told us, "If work was supposed to be fun, we would call it fun, not work." We agree that the workplace is not an amusement park; however, we spend half our waking hours at work, so why not have a little fun? When we have fun at work, attendance increases and tardiness decreases. A survey of 100 directors found 84 percent believed employees with a sense of humor did a better job than people with little sense of humor.[6] Generation Y has blended fun into their lives, so it makes sense that they blend fun into work. This does not mean you create a playground with no expectations. It does mean that once the standards have been set, you allow some personality to come through.

9. Tell Them Why

Generation Y's signposts include an explanation for everything. They were told why they must wear a seat belt, look both ways before crossing the street, and not talk to strangers. They were made to understand why they needed to volunteer, join teams, and excel in school (to get into a good college). Most important, Generation Y was told they deserve to know why because their opinions matter.

When communicating your expectations to a Gen Yer, begin with the end in mind:

1. Explain the end result of the task. This can include the due date, the budget constraints, the physical description, the way something will behave or act, or the amount.
2. Tell Gen Yers "why": why this project is important for customers, them, or the organization.
3. Identify what assets or backing Generation Y will need to get to the end result.
4. Identify the roadblocks that could get in the Gen Yers' way and help them devise a plan to avoid or master the roadblocks.
5. Ask for questions.
6. Follow up to monitor progress.

Here's a small project we assigned to one of our Gen Y assistants as part of writing this book:

Katie, we want to put an interesting factoid at the beginning of each signpost chapter. For example, at the beginning of the Traditional signpost chapter, we're going to use: "*There is no cause to worry. The high tide of prosperity will continue.* Andrew W. Mellon, Secretary of the Treasury, September 1929." The idea is to catch the reader's attention and set the stage for what he or she will read in the chapter. We'd like you to put together a list of about ten factoids per decade so we can choose the ones we like best. We'll also need to know if permission to use each quote is required. Some require it and some don't. You may run into some roadblocks there because many of the authors of the older quotes are no longer living, which usually makes them fair game, but the rights to their words may be owned by some other entity, so you'll need to check that out. We'll send you a copy of our publisher's guidelines, which should be helpful. If you have any questions or you run into any snags, feel free to call either of us. In fact, after you've found a few, why don't you send them to us so we're sure you're on the right track? We'll need the whole list by Wednesday, July 8, at close of business.

Katie finished the list on time, with all the correct permissions in place.

10. Offer Close Coaching and Guidance

Kasey, the Gen Yer who was recently promoted to sales administration manager, has a yearly review but also receives feedback on a daily basis from one of her supervisors. She's responsible for all email newsletters and press announcements. Her supervisor tells her roughly what needs to be in the newsletter. Kasey puts it together and takes it to the supervisor for review.

"He tells me what he likes about it and what he would change," said Kasey. "He asks me why I included or failed to include some information and he makes suggestions to tweak it. I make the changes and have him go over it again. He allows me to shoulder the responsibility but I don't feel like I am going to fall on my face, because I trust his advice."

This approach may sound like coddling and micromanaging if you're used to giving employees free reign to perform. We think it's an effective approach to use with Generation Y until they get their sea legs and prove they can operate without it. In Chapter 12, we'll discuss how to apply Mode Management to determine when and how to move away from such close supervision, but for now, it's probably the best approach to meet Kasey's (and her Gen Y counterparts') needs.

11. Give Feedback Often

Generation Y is accustomed to getting instant feedback from parents, friends, and even video games. Waiting until a six-month review starves a Gen Yer of the information he needs to know if he's on track. We suggest weekly or even daily doses of feedback from you, the manager, to each of your Gen Yers. It doesn't have to be elaborate. A couple of comments describing what he's doing well or where he needs to improve can do wonders.

Some schools of thought encourage managers to "sandwich" any criticism of an employee between two compliments. This approach springs from a Baby Boomer/Dr. Spock mind-set that it's important to maintain the employee's self-esteem at all costs. Using the sandwich technique to give corrective feedback, the manager might say, "John, you are a very dependable employee. I'm concerned, however, that your mistake rate is way above standard. It's a shame because otherwise your work is nicely done."

We don't like this approach because employees see through it very quickly. The praise at the beginning and the end was just a sham to cushion the blow of the real message. Employees often refer to it cynically as the WOHICA (Watch Out, Here It Comes Again) approach.

We believe it's better to be generous with the praise and sparing with the criticism but never to mix the two. Give people lots of reinforcing feedback (praise) often and provide corrective feedback (criticism) when they need it, but do each at separate times so you don't send mixed messages.

12. Praise and Correct Them Correctly

Feedback comes in two varieties, reinforcing and corrective. Reinforcing feedback tells the receiver what she is doing is right and to continue to do it. Corrective feedback tells the receiver what she is doing wrong and how to correct it and prevent it from recurring.

Giving Reinforcing Feedback (Praise)

For praise to achieve maximum return, it should follow the Three *S* Rule:

> - **Specific:** When someone does something well, he appreciates knowing that you know specifically what it was and why it is important.
> - **Significant:** Reinforcing trivial actions weakens the credibility of the person giving the information. The praise should describe something that the recipient values. For example, praising an en-

gineer just because she keeps her desk neat may cause her to question your credibility, especially if you never praise her for the value of her work.

> **Sincere:** The difference between honest feedback and flattery is that the former comes from the sincere belief that the feedback was deserved.

Keep in mind these praising tips:

> **Deliver the information as soon as possible.** The longer a person has to wait for a compliment, the less effect it will have in reinforcing future positive behavior.

> **Praise in public.** Public reinforcement not only allows a person to gain prestige among his peers, but it also creates a standard for other team members. *Caution*: Be sure that public praise is indeed deserved. Using public praise to prop up a mediocre performer is a sure way to create disillusionment among those who perform well.

> **Put it in writing.** Make sure that a copy is put in the person's file and another copy is passed upstairs to your boss.

> **Do it often.** Although it is possible to praise too much, most people are starved for enough feedback that says, "Hey, you're doing the right thing." Gen Yers are used to getting lots of praise from their parents. What you may consider a normal amount (say, once every few weeks) may seem scant to the Gen Yer.

> **Describe the impact on the organization.** This tip applies to praising anyone, but is especially germane when giving feedback to Generation Yers. They may not understand the impact of small things, such as how smiling at a customer can increase loyalty, which can affect the bottom line of the organization for years to come.

Giving Corrective Feedback (Criticism)

There's an old rubric about advice: Most don't need it, and those who do won't heed it. Although this saying contains a great deal of truth, it is your job to provide advice that will help your team members correct problems and stay on track. This is known as *coaching*. A coach's challenge is to make sure corrective information is not only passed along but received and put to work.

Here are some tips:

1. **Pick the right time.** The purpose of giving corrective feedback is to facilitate learning. When someone makes a mistake, it is tempting to jump right in and "chew her out." This is probably the worst time to let the person know that you don't approve of what she just did. Emotions can hinder the learning process, especially if one or both of you are upset. Try holding your feedback until a teachable moment.

2. **Make sure the purpose of your feedback is to coach rather than punish.** Again, your emotional state can hinder the delivery of helpful information. Take time to cool off and examine your reasons for giving the feedback and the outcome you would like to achieve.

3. **Select a private place.** Nobody likes to receive criticism in public. The chances of defensive behavior soar when negative information is given in front of peers, regardless of your intentions.

4. **Be specific.** An example or a story where you made the same mistake or had the same problem can diminish the accusatory nature of the feedback. Demonstrating what you would like the person to do instead can maximize the teaching impact of the feedback. This is especially important for Gen Yers, who may not understand how to correct what they did.

For example, suppose you overheard a Gen Yer tell a customer that an item was out of stock, and you didn't like the way he did it. If you tell him, "John, you need to be nicer when you tell a customer something she doesn't want to hear," the Gen Yer won't get enough information to adjust his behavior appropriately. It's better to demonstrate the specific behavior you want: "John, when you have to tell a customer something she doesn't want to hear, I'd like you to say, 'Mrs. Jones, I'm so sorry, but we're out of that item. What I can do is special order it and have it here in two days. Would that work for you?'"

5. **Make the feedback descriptive and prescriptive.** Stay away from accusations, blame, and threats. It's better to tell the Gen Yer what you want her to *do* in place of what she just did, rather than telling her what you *don't* want her to do. Instead of saying, "Jan, don't file your court documents after the due date," it's better to say, "In the future, please make sure your documents are filed on time."

6. **Be sure that the feedback is targeted toward something the person can actually change.** Describe behavior that needs to be changed, standards that need to be met, events that need to occur differently, pro-

cedures that need to be changed, and your expectations that need to be met.

7. **Focus on the present and the future, but use the past for supporting data.** The past cannot be changed. Telling someone he made a mistake puts him in the powerless position of not being able to change what he did. Instead of saying, "You made a mistake," it's better to say, "In the future, I'd like you to make sure it's done flawlessly."

8. **Beware of derogatory labels.** Because they've been handled with kid gloves throughout their childhoods, Gen Yers can easily get their feelings hurt.

For example, Scott Cole and his wife, Linda (both Baby Boomers), manage a hairdressing school in Phoenix, Arizona. Scott told us about Jill, a 22-year-old Gen Yer whom he hired as a receptionist. She did such a good job that, after four months, he elevated her to the position of admissions leader. She seemed to handle the added responsibility well, so Scott and Linda decided to invest in Jill's development by sending her to a three-day seminar in Las Vegas.

A few days before she was to go, Jill did something that violated company policy and showed poor judgment. The envelope with all the employees' paychecks arrived from the corporate office. Before taking it to the payroll person, Jill opened the envelope and removed her own paycheck. When the payroll person saw it had been opened, she was upset and brought the incident to Scott's attention.

When Scott and Linda asked Jill about it, she replied defensively, "What's the big deal? It's my check. I was just trying to save the payroll person some time." Scott and Linda explained that what Jill did violated the privacy of the other employees whose checks were in the envelope and it put the payroll person in a bind because she's responsible for the security of the checks until they are handed to individual employees. During the conversation, Linda said, "Look, we understand that with your new workload things must seem a little overwhelming and it can make you feel kind of incompetent. But it's important that, if you have a question about what you should do, you please check with one of us." Jill said she would and the meeting ended.

After Jill left the office, Scott said to Linda, "I don't think that went so well. Did you notice the tears in her eyes? I won't be surprised if she quits." And sure enough, that night Scott received an email from Jill saying she was resigning, effective immediately. In her notice, she complained that she had never before been spoken to that way and that she couldn't work in a place where the management considered her to be "incompetent."

Jill's response may sound a little oversensitive. It seems that way to us, but we're not Gen Yers who've been raised by aging Baby Boomers trying to protect their children from any bruising of their self-esteem. When you give a Gen Yer corrective feedback, keep the conversation focused on what you want him to do or not do and stay away from words that could be interpreted as attacking his character, intentions, work ethic, or intelligence. It lowers the odds he'll get his feelings hurt and quit.

The Bottom Line

Generation Y grew up with parents who spent time communicating with them, who praised them for even the smallest victories, who asked for their opinions when they were children, and who devoted time to making life fun. They expect similar services from their Baby Boomer and Gen X bosses.

You don't have to coddle Gen Yers, but you do have to understand what they need from you to succeed. Get in the habit of checking in with them daily, offering praise when it is deserved and corrective feedback when it's needed. Be specific about jobs and expectations. Offer flexibility in when and how they work, as long as they perform.

And have some fun. Managers and employees of all generations can benefit from that.

CHAPTER 8

Old Dogs Have Lots to Offer: Signposts for the Traditional Generation

"There is no cause to worry. The high tide of prosperity will continue."
—Andrew W. Mellon, Secretary of the Treasury, September 1929

Critical Events in the Lives of Traditionals

1927 Lindbergh flies the Atlantic
1929 Stock market crash
1929 Great Depression
1932 FDR elected
1933 Roosevelt launches the New Deal
1935 Dust Bowl
1935 Social Security Act passes
1937 Hindenburg explodes
1939 Hitler invades Poland
1941 Pearl Harbor attacked
1944 D-day
1945 FDR dies
1945 Atom bomb dropped on Japan—Word War II ends
1950 Korean War begins
1952 Eisenhower elected
1953 Korean War ends

1954 McCarthy hearings begin
1955 Jonas Salk announces release of first polio vaccine

Mary, a 68-Year-Old Supplier Data Management Representative (Still Working)

Since 1970 Mary has worked for a large manufacturing company that she says she just *loves*. "They always keep their promises," says Mary. "They offered me the job when my previous company was moving to another state. They wanted me to start right away, and I told them I'd have to wait a month or I'd lose my severance package from my then-present employer. The new company needed me to start earlier and told me they'd make it right if I came immediately and lost the severance. I took them up on the offer, and true to their word, they compensated me fairly for the severance package I lost." Mary went on to say that most of all, the manufacturing company has always been there for her, far beyond what an employer should have to do. For example, when Mary's parents' house burned down, the company encouraged her to take time off to care for them until they could get settled. When her husband was stricken with cancer, the company insisted she take time off to care for him. When Mary decided to go back to school to get her bachelor's degree, the company paid her tuition and let her work a flexible schedule so she could attend classes.

Mary told us that she feels blessed to work for this organization and has no patience with the young people there who complain about it. "These kids don't know how lucky they are to have a job with such a great company. I've worked hard for the company, and the company has repaid me with a good living and its loyalty. What more can you ask for?"

A Traditional Comments

Cheryl is a retired nurse manager we know who is in her mid-70s. She worked in a hospital all her life. When she retired, she wanted to do something different, so she volunteered to work for her local chamber of commerce. "Volunteering with the chamber allows me to do something new: to work in a lower-stress environment, and still contribute to my community," Cheryl told us.

She works three days per week for four to six hours each day, coordinating the hospitality details for chamber functions. Cheryl is by far the oldest member of her work group, which consists of three Gen Xers and a Baby Boomer (all regular employees).

She told us that her biggest challenge was the team's initial lack of trust in her:

"Even though I had extensive management experience, all I was given to do were menial tasks like answering phones and getting coffee. I suspect the younger employees saw me as a 'grandmother' type of person and did not understand that I had spent my career making decisions in a high-stress environment that had severe consequences if I made a mistake. One day, a nurse friend of mine who's active in our local nursing association told me she was involved in planning next year's state nursing convention. I put her in touch with our chamber director and the association ended up booking the convention in our city. As a result, I was given my present job of coordinating hospitality details for the chamber. I feel like I'm contributing something of real value now and I love it."

△　　△　　△

Larry Remembers

Hearing Mary's and Cheryl's stories reminded me of an experience I had in college with a member of the Traditional Generation. I worked as a janitor on the evening shift in an aluminum extrusion plant. It was the perfect job for a college student. I had the freedom to walk around the huge factory, pushing a cart with cleaning supplies, mopping restrooms and office floors. The workload was easy: I had time to finish my route and then find a place to hide where I could study. To make it even better, it was a union shop, so it paid more than twice minimum wage. As a working college student, I was in tall cotton. (Tall cotton is a southeastern phrase that implies good times or financial success. Cotton growers would harvest their cotton after it reached a certain height—the taller the better—and take it to market to sell it and hopefully reap financial gain.)

On the crew was an older lady named Maude. As a young woman, she had worked in the plant during World War II making parts for B17s. When the war was over, she stayed on and was now in her late 70s. She was one of the hardest workers I have ever known. She never stopped moving and was always looking for something to do.

One evening I was studying in one of the women's restrooms. This was a perfect place to hide because my boss, who was a man, was required to knock and announce himself before entering. That gave me time to jump up and grab a mop. Maude came in and even though this restroom was my responsibility, she started scrubbing the toilets with her usual enthusiasm. I told her that wasn't necessary, that I'd clean the toilets when I finished my chapter. She replied, "That's okay. I'm done with my route, and I might as well help you. You just keep doing your studies."

I was somewhat embarrassed (as I should have been), so I got up to help her do my job. We chatted while we scrubbed. She said she had come to Arizona from Oklahoma in 1937 to escape the Great Dust Bowl. She and her husband had no work for the first three years they were here and were desperately poor. They lived in a tent on the banks of an irrigation canal where they drew their water and washed their clothes. They acquired most of their food from the garbage bins of local grocery stores. They had two small children at the time. One died of pneumonia during those years on the canal because they had no money for medical care.

Then the war broke out and Reynolds Aluminum started hiring. She said she was so thankful to them for taking her on, even though she was an uneducated "Okie," that she vowed she would give them her very best every minute she was there.

I never studied on that job again, and I've never again cheated an employer out of my time and effort.

Cheryl, Mary, and Maude are true testaments to the value the Traditional Generation has to offer all of us if we just give them the chance.

. . . .

The Greatest Generation

The Traditional Generation began with the end of World War I. Born between 1918 and 1945, many of them passed through childhood in the

Roaring Twenties, came of age in the Great Depression, and spent their 20s fighting and winning World War II. They were the parents of the Baby Boomer Generation and were responsible for the prosperity following World War II. In his book *The Greatest Generation*, Tom Brokaw wrote about these ordinary citizens who were called upon to do extraordinary things for the United States.

There are 52 million members of the Traditional Generation.[1] Because of their advancing age and retirement, they are the smallest segment of employees, representing only 8 percent of the workforce.[2] Their roles, however, go far beyond the 164,000 greeters employed at Wal-Mart. From professional ranks to security guards, they continue to contribute their talent and labor. Our bookkeeper is 74 years old. She works part-time to supplement her retirement income, and she does a terrific job. She's accurate, pleasant to have in the office, and the chances that she'll call in sick because she was at a kegger last night are virtually zero.

Many Traditionals work as nonpaid volunteers. For example, AARP (American Association of Retired Persons) enlists the services of retired accountants and businesspeople to help 2.5 million people file tax returns every year.[3] Hospitals depend on retired volunteers to do everything from manning the front desk to accompanying patients to clinics.

The result is that, although the number of paid employees from this generation is low, Traditionals remain a viable though declining presence in today's workplace.

• •

Larry Remembers

My mother taught first grade for 45 years. She always said that her real passion in life was making sure that by the end of each school year her students could read at the second-grade level. She knew that if they couldn't, their chance of doing well in later grades was near zero.

She was a terrific teacher. Most of her students met the criteria and passed, but if they didn't, she never hesitated to hold them back to repeat first grade. Over the years she fought many battles with parents who wanted their children to avoid the stigma of flunking the first grade. She never backed down and came close to being fired more than once over the issue.

When she retired in 1985, she immediately volunteered her services at the school. For the next 18 years, she spent her mornings tutoring individual children who were struggling with reading. The last three years she lived in an assisted-living facility. The staff would drive her to the school three days a week; she would hobble into the classroom with a walker. She finally "retired" from volunteering at the age of 84, six weeks before she died but not before the school district named her Volunteer of the Year and held a special banquet in her honor.

. . . .

Signposts for the Traditional Generation

Signpost: The Great Depression

During the Roaring Twenties, the stock market experienced spectacular growth and speculation drove stock prices to unprecedented highs. Thinking the growth would last forever, people borrowed money to buy stock. The bubble burst in 1929 and the United States plunged into the Great Depression. By 1932, the market had lost 80 percent of its value, one-fifth of the country's banks closed, and 9 million people lost their life savings. Unemployment climbed to 25 percent as 15 million people were put out of work.

As income levels declined, people spent less money so the government collected fewer taxes. Construction ground to a halt, and farmers struggled as commodity prices weakened. People sold off their possessions to survive. Children were often sent to live with relatives.

Men looking for work faced signs that read, "Jobless Men Keep Going." Many families pulled up roots and crossed the country in search of employment. The hard times changed Traditional family structures. While men had been the primary breadwinners, women now joined their husbands looking for work. Some could find domestic jobs easier than men and became the family breadwinners. Not all husbands responded positively to this new paradigm. More than a million men abandoned their wives and families.

President Herbert Hoover was often blamed for the crash. Hoovervilles, which were communities of cardboard shacks used by the homeless for shelter, began to dot the countryside. A Hoover Blanket was a blanket made of newspapers. A pocket turned inside out was a Hoover Flag, and a Hoover Wagon was a car pulled by horses.

Not everyone had it as tough as Maude, but everyone was affected.

Traditionals React: Stubbornly Independent

Many members of the Traditional Generation remember the embarrassment of asking relatives for help or being sent to Aunt Jane's to live because parents couldn't afford to keep them. Consequently, they tend to be extremely hesitant to ask for help or impose on others. Those who are still working tend to accept their roles in the organization and rarely complain. In 1951, *Time* magazine named this "the Silent Generation" because of its fatalistic attitude and nonconfrontational nature.[4]

Meagan Comments

My grandmother on my mother's side comes from the Traditional Generation. She is 81 years old and spends her time playing bridge, entertaining guests, and volunteering. I recently took her to the doctor. She had not been feeling well for weeks but kept insisting she was fine.

Being a Gen Xer, I believed her and thought we ought to leave her alone. My mother, a Baby Boomer, was smarter than I. She recognized that my grandmother needed to go to the doctor whether she wanted to or not. She asked me to take her and told me to go into the exam room with her.

When the doctor asked her what was wrong, I was shocked to hear her reply, "Nothing." She said she was only there to get her eyes checked! (Her eyesight was perfectly fine.)

After the doctor left the room, I asked my grandmother why she did not tell him about her symptoms. She said he was a busy man, and she didn't want to bother him. Besides, any remedy he was going to prescribe she could easily make at home. Fearing my mother's wrath if I brought my grandmother home without a diagnosis, I quickly returned her to the doctor's office and insisted she tell him what was wrong.

Signpost: Waste Not, Want Not

The deprivation of the Great Depression taught people the value of frugality. When you have very little, every little bit counts. Family meals often consisted of potatoes, pasta, and beans. Everything was used and nothing was wasted. Soap was made from lard. To save on fuel, the heat under cooking food was turned off; the covered food would continue to cook with its own heat, saving on energy costs.

The inclination to "waste not, want not" was further reinforced during World War II. The government rationed gas and food and promoted recycling. Consumers were encouraged to reuse tin cans and recover metal and rubber. All this reclaiming and reusing meant more ammunition and supplies for the soldiers.

Traditionals React: The Benefits of Frugality

A client told us that her fridge was full of little packets of aluminum foil after a weekend visit from her Traditional Generation mother. Any scrap of food her mother found, she wrapped up and saved for another meal. Larry remembers his mother patching his jeans, mending his socks, saving milk cartons to store food in the refrigerator, and collecting brown paper bags from the grocery store to wrap parcel post packages. Today many people only patch jeans for decoration. Very few people will take the time to mend their socks; it's easier to throw them away and buy new. Milk cartons join the plethora of other throwaway items in the recycling can, and brown paper used for posting comes in a roll from the local FedEx Kinko's store.

In truth, such frugality benefits everyone. If you have Traditionals working for you, ask them to help watch your costs. They can often be a great source of ideas on how to save money. They will also appreciate your recognition of what they consider to be a virtue.

Meagan Recalls

A friend of mine who wears prescription glasses showed up one evening with pieces of tinted plastic wrap taped over the lenses. It looked bizarre. She explained that she was visiting her great aunt (from the Traditional Generation) before meeting me and had mentioned that she wanted to buy prescription sunglasses. Her aunt got very agitated and told her niece she could not believe she would spend so much money for something she could make herself. Her aunt went about cutting pieces of saved Saran wrap and taping them to my friend's glasses. My

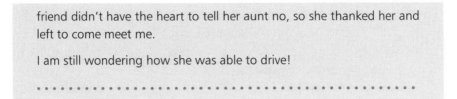

friend didn't have the heart to tell her aunt no, so she thanked her and left to come meet me.

I am still wondering how she was able to drive!

Signpost: World War II

America's declaration of war against Japan in 1941 eventually brought an end to the Great Depression. Unemployment disappeared as 16 million men and women joined the armed forces and millions more were hired to work in the factories that built the equipment the soldiers needed.

That didn't mean times were good. There were shortages of everything. Food, clothing, shoes, tires, nylons, and fuel were all strictly rationed. No one escaped having to make sacrifices, but the sacrifices were considered small compared to the soldiers risking their lives on the battlefields.

Through the combined efforts of those fighting abroad and those working at home, the nation defeated Japan, Italy, and Germany, making the world safe for democracy. It was the greatest team effort to which the United States had ever contributed.

Traditionals React: Trust in God, Country, and General Motors

After the war, the U.S. Government rewarded the Traditional Generation with the GI Bill, which enabled them to acquire homes and advance their educations. Big business rewarded them with jobs for life. Traditionals responded by developing a strong sense of faith in those institutions. If you work with or manage Traditionals today, that faith can be seen in their sense of loyalty to your company. Like Larry's stepfather, who worked for Procter & Gamble (mentioned in Chapter 1), Traditionals tend to stand by you, especially if you treat them with respect and fairness. They're unlikely to fudge facts or cheat on their time. According to Employer-Employee.com,[5] they have lower absenteeism rates, lower turnover rates, and fewer on-the-job injuries than younger employees. They also bring a wealth of experience to the job, have a strong work ethic, and usually find great satisfaction in their work.

Signpost: GI Bill

At the urging of the American Legion, Congress passed The Servicemen's Readjustment Act of 1944. It became known as the GI Bill of Rights, adapting the acronym *GI* (government issue), which was commonly used to describe anyone in the military. The bill gave military personnel returning home from the war immediate financial support in the form of unemployment insurance. More important, it included generous educational opportunities ranging from vocational and on-the-job training to higher education. It also included liberal access to loans for homes and businesses.

Traditionals React

For the first time, people for whom going to college, owning a home, or starting a business would have been impossible were able to do all three. This remarkable bill served as a major signpost, not only for the Traditional Generation that directly benefited from it, but also for Baby Boomers. It established a milieu of prosperity and high expectations in which Baby Boomers would be raised in the 1950s. GI Bill–educated parents expected their Baby Boomer children to follow in their footsteps and go to college.

Smart Companies Hire Traditionals

With the economy struggling, many members of the Traditional Generation are looking to remain in the workforce to help pay the bills. Several smart companies are using creative approaches to tap into this resource:

> Home Depot has partnered with AARP to recruit more retired people. Stating that "passion never retires," it actively seeks skilled elderly candidates with expertise in areas like plumbing, flooring, electrical, kitchen, and bath.[6]
> Borders bookstores attract retired teachers to sales jobs with discounts and the promise of reading and discussion groups.[7]
> PETCO advertises for senior citizens on seniors4hire.org, where it pitches the joys of spending every day with animals.[8]
> The Smithsonian offers what it calls "the perfect *career* choice for senior citizens in Washington, DC. A peaceful fulfilling job helping tourists and DC natives enjoy history."[9]

> ☞ PostcardMania of Clearwater, Florida, started hiring more senior citizens after CEO Joy Gendusa's mother passed away and she needed to find something for her father to do. The company was subsequently named one of the fastest-growing privately owned companies in the United States by *Inc.* magazine.[10]

The Bottom Line

Senior citizens who want to work have much to offer an organization compared to their much younger counterparts: lower absenteeism, lower turnover, higher commitment to quality, good communication skills, better work ethic, willingness to learn, good interpersonal skills, and dependability.

What's not to like?

CHAPTER 9

Managing the Traditional Generation

"We've put more effort into helping folks reach old age than into helping them enjoy it."

—Frank A. Clark

Larry's stepfather, Joe, whom we mentioned earlier, retired at the age of 65. During his first year away from the job, he became sick with a severe case of flu that lasted for three months. He developed a rash of cold sores that made it difficult for him to eat, suffered from chronic insomnia, and slipped into a depression that sapped all his energy. By the end of the year, he looked terrible and felt worse. His doctor referred him to a psychiatrist, who put him on various psychotropic medications, which only exacerbated his symptoms.

At the urging of a friend, he went to a second psychiatrist, who, after chatting with him for only 15 minutes, said, "Joe, here's my diagnosis: You're driving yourself crazy sitting around the house. I'll take you off all the meds and you go get a job!" Two weeks later he had three part-time positions: working mornings as a sales rep with a consumer products company, working afternoons for the Census Bureau, and working weekends in a liquor store located in the red-light district. He said the liquor store was his favorite because he got to chat with the prostitutes and the winos who frequented the place. He claimed they were much more interesting than anyone he ever met in the corporate world.

The Census Bureau job ended after six months. Joe continued with the other two for 19 years until he died at the age of 84. He never had another twinge of depression. At Joe's funeral, the owner of the liquor store told us that Joe would be sorely missed. He was dependable, honest, and hardworking and, most of all, his customers loved him as much as he loved them.

Joe proves that turning 65 doesn't mean you are no longer useful in the world of work. Our society has many Traditionals like Joe who continue to contribute well past this unofficial retirement age. One even ran for president in 2008.

The goals for managing someone like Joe should include:

1. **Give them something to do that contributes to the common good.** The Great Depression and World War II taught Traditionals the importance of contribution. Much of their self-esteem depends on feeling like their efforts are improving things for those around them.
2. **Capture and apply the wisdom from their wealth of experiences.** Being 60, 70, or 80 years gives people knowledge and insights that can be of great value to any organization.
3. **Help them adapt to and embrace new systems and methodologies.** Because they are old, it's tempting to think they can't learn something new. Not true.
4. **Provide them with a fulfilling experience.** They can probably use the extra income your job provides, but they're primarily there to do something interesting with their time.

Traditionals can be a valuable asset to any organization. According to a study of employers by SHRM (Society for Human Resource Management) and AARP:

- ▷ 77 percent agreed that older workers have a higher level of commitment to the organization than younger workers (only 5 percent disagreed)
- ▷ 68 percent concluded training older workers costs less or the same as training their younger counterparts (6 percent disagreed)
- ▷ 57 percent reported that age does not affect the amount of time required to train an employee (14 percent disagreed)

➤ 49 percent determined that older workers grasped new concepts as well as younger workers (18 percent disagreed)[1]

As many employers have discovered, recruiting and retaining Traditionals can help them achieve their goals.

Tips for Managing Traditionals

1. Recruit Traditionals

Not all Traditionals will offer the kind of loyalty and good work that Joe did. Like any generation, some will be more productive than others, some will be brilliant, and some will be duds. The more you have to select from, the better your chances of finding good ones. We suggest you actively recruit them so you can have a large group from which to choose.

Ironically, less than 20 percent of American companies have a game plan for recruiting older employees, and less than one-third have plans for how to keep them.[2] If you wish to lure these potentially valuable employees into your workforce, take a hint from the rapidly expanding retirement and assisted-living industries. Notice how the ads for a retirement community always include full-color pictures of attractive senior citizens playing golf, swimming with grandchildren, and having cocktails by the pool while watching beautiful sunsets. A 36-year-old acquaintance told us that they make those places look so good she's tempted to see if they'll waive the age requirements so she can move in now. There's something to be said for thoughtful marketing.

The same applies to attracting employees. If you want to lure older workers, design your Web site and job descriptions so you look like a place where older people would want to work. Use phrases like "Welcome Home, Retirees" and "We Value Workers of All Ages." Include lots of pictures of people of all ages, including Traditionals, engaged in doing interesting work, socializing with coworkers, and contributing in meaningful ways. Barbara McIntosh, PhD, author of *An Employer's Guide to Older Workers: How to Win Them Back and Convince Them to Stay*, suggests that you avoid using language that seniors might find offensive like "elderly" and "senior citizen." "Experienced," "mature," and "reliable" are more appealing.[3]

It's important to remember that you can't discriminate on the basis of age, nor should you. *You must be an equal opportunity employer.* However, nothing prevents you from designing your Web site and recruiting materials to attract certain segments of the age spectrum.

Domestic & General Group PLC, an insurance group in Nottingham, UK, takes recruiting of the senior population a step further by sending its senior-age employees to job fairs to talk directly with Traditionals who are looking to reenter the workforce.[4] The U.S. Postal Service recruits retirees to serve as substitute carriers and replacement postmasters by advertising on senior-oriented Web sites, such as seniorjournal.com. Southern Metal Roofing in Atlanta, Georgia, advertises on its Web site for people who are fit enough to handle walking door to door and passing out brochures. A big selling point is that their dogs are welcome to accompany them. Seniors who hire on get exercise, their dogs get walked every day, and they get paid for it.[5]

SICK AG, an industrial equipment and commercial machinery company in Waldkirch, Germany, continually invites retirees to join current employees at company events and social functions.[6] The University of California at Berkeley actively recruits office professional retirees for part-time positions to write grants, do budget work, conduct strategic planning, and facilitate organizational development by simple postings on its Web site.[7]

Other ways to attract talented seniors include:

- Partnering with senior associations like AARP who provide job-finding assistance to Traditionals
- Asking your current employees for referrals, such as parents or relatives interested in working part-time
- Posting jobs at local adult community centers, retirement communities, and churches
- Contacting your own retirees who may be bored and looking for part-time employment
- Using Traditional job-posting sites like Monster.com, Jobsearch.com, and CareerBuilder.com

2. Make Them Mentors

While visiting a client who uses retirees for part-time office work, we observed a familiar situation. One lady who must have been about 75 was having difficulty with her computer. She called IT, and a young man in his early 20s appeared. The difference in their dress and demeanor was stunning. She wore a pantsuit and patent leather pumps and had a permed helmet of tiny silver curls on her head. He wore a pair of low-slung cargo pants, boxer shorts showing, and had tattoos that crept up the side of his neck like kudzu vines on the side of a Georgia road.

He walked up to her and said, "What's up with your computer?" She looked a little taken aback but told him about her problem. After he fixed it, he showed her what she needed to do the next time it happened. She demonstrated that she could do it and he said, "Cool," and got up to leave.

She called to him. "Young man," she said, "my name is Betty. What's yours?"

"Tim," he replied.

She said, "Nice to meet you, Tim. Thank you for your help. You did a great job. Next time, you might want to introduce yourself first. We old folks like stuff like that." Then she winked at him. He looked a bit astonished and then laughed and said, "Okay, Betty."

In one brief moment, an invaluable lesson in courtesy and etiquette was passed from one generation to another. Several organizations have formalized approaches that help them take advantage of the wisdom of our oldest generation:

> Centers for New Horizons (CNH), a Chicago-based social service agency, is one of Chicago's "101 Best & Brightest Companies to Work For." CNH uses the Traditional Generation as trainers and mentors for younger staff members. CNH also has members of the Traditional Generation on advisory committees and relies on their knowledge to help make informed decisions.

> "The Good Working Life" is a program at Horsens Kommune in Horsens, Denmark, that encourages retiring teachers not to retire.[8] By pairing up the retiring teacher with a teacher new to the job, the younger teacher gains experience and the class benefits from a multigenerational teaching approach.

3. Teach Old Dogs New Tricks

Conventional wisdom tells us the Traditional Generation can't keep up with changes in technology. Untrue! They may be resistant, but once they buy in, they can learn quickly. In fact, they are the fastest-growing age group joining the Internet today. In one year, their presence on the Web increased 25 percent.[9] While it may be true that some Traditionals take longer to absorb the material than their younger peers, they tend to have better study habits, especially when motivated.

Jan is an aerospace technical writer/project manager we know who retired and now travels the world. She graduated from high school in 1951 and landed a job with Hughes Aircraft Company as a clerk (which Jan calls the lowest life form in the Hughes aquarium). Like a lot of other women her age, she hadn't gone to college but should have. She'd been a straight-A student in high school. She was intelligent, perceptive, well organized, and could type at lightning speed. She married shortly after starting work. Unlike a lot of other women in her situation, however, she was able to escape the role of clerk, and work her way up the ladder to technical writer because of her superb English skills and her willingness to work hard. Her career path was limited, however, because she lacked an engineering degree. Over the years, by attending night school, she earned a BA in philosophy because she found it interesting, but in the aerospace industry, engineers rule. And of course, there was the glass ceiling to break through.

Jan learned quickly that moving ahead in this 1950s, male-dominated environment meant distancing herself from being perceived as a clerk, which translated into "secretary" or "typist." As soon as she got her first promotion and could have someone else do her typing, she swore to *never touch a keyboard again.* For 40-plus years she kept that vow. It served her well until the late 1980s, when organizations started replacing clerks, secretaries, and typing pools with computers on every desk. At that point, Jan was able to take early retirement, so she managed to avoid having to learn how to use a computer.

For the next several years, she continued to avoid keyboards, resisting all attempts her friends and family made to convince her to get computerized. This year, however, she finally gave in and bought one because sending email was the only way she could stay in touch on a world cruise. Now, six months later, she surfs the Web daily, uploads photos to her Facebook page, stays in touch with friends and family by email, buys and sells on eBay, and is planning to start a Web-based editing service for technical writers.

Old dogs *can* learn new tricks.

Many organizations are helping their Traditionals get up to speed by setting up reverse mentoring partnerships with young people. Gen Yers and Linksters are teaching Traditionals to use the Internet, program their

DVRs, use their Blackberries, and embrace technology. In turn, Traditionals are teaching young people etiquette, organizational politics, and the subtleties of good interpersonal communication skills. In the process, the groups are bonding in ways we have not seen before:

   ▷ At Ballard High School in Seattle, Washington, AARP teamed up with Earthlink to pair teenagers and Traditionals for technology tutoring.[10] As a result, the Traditionals significantly increased their ability to use technology to communicate with their family and friends. Additionally, homebound senior citizens were better able to remain up-to-date on current events. The program is now available in a number of schools across the country.

   ▷ The AARP Foundation sponsored an event called "Ready, Set, Internet!"[11] Hundreds of participants took four 45-minute classes on how to surf the Web, shop online, and buy computers wisely.

   ▷ *Generations on Line*, a Philadelphia, Pennsylvania–based not-for-profit that specializes in Internet literacy, offers Hispanic seniors courses on how to use the Internet. The program includes tutorials in Spanish and large type on the screen. There are enough large "help" buttons and email links so the learner can get her "Web" feet wet with a minimum of pain. More than 1,300 libraries, senior centers, and retirement homes are using this learning tool.[12]

   ▷ TriHealth Inc. in Cincinnati, Ohio, actively recruits and trains retired nurses using Gen Y and Gen X nurses who are working directly with patients. Their reentry training programs have been designed to bring returning nurses up to speed with current working systems and technology. Upon completing the training, returning nurses go to work either full- or part-time.

   ▷ Lee Memorial in Fort Myers, Florida, provides $1,000 tuition reimbursement to returning retired nurses who choose to take refresher courses at accredited academic institutions.

Have you returned to visit your hometown and been struck by how much it has changed? That's nothing compared to the pace of change in the workplace. Your work environment may not seem different to you than it was a year ago, but even a few small changes can seem daunting to someone who has been out of the loop for a while. Offering refresher courses to members of the Traditional Generation can help get them up to speed and integrate them into the workplace.

4. Accommodate Their Needs

Alfred Baucam and Robert J. Grosch point out in their book *Hospitality Design for the Graying Generation*,[13] that after our teen years, our drive to socialize with our peers tends to wane as we focus on career and family but then returns as we approach retirement. As we get older, we tend to want to interact with others in our age group.

This year, we were speaking at a convention of convenience store/ truck stop managers. One told us about a fellow who cleaned the locker rooms, showers, and bunk rooms at her truck stop. It was a family-run operation and the old guy had started working for her father 40 years ago. She said he was getting to the point where his arthritis was preventing him from doing the kind of physical work the job required. He told her he would have to retire.

She hated to see him go because he was dependable and the drivers liked him, so she offered him a job in the convenience store manning the cash register. It required some training and close supervision until he got the hang of it, but she said it was well worth the investment. He worked there another six years, never missing a day of work, and he did a terrific job.

One morning he didn't show up. His daughter called later in the day to say that he had had a stroke and died. She said the last thing he asked her to do was to call the truck stop and apologize for not coming to work that day. He was 86 years old.

5. Recognize and Applaud Their Contributions

Mary Kay Cosmetics in Dallas, Texas, thanks its long-term employees with stock contributions. After five years, an employee receives 20 shares of stock and continues to receive increasing amounts of stock every five years.

If pay raises are economically out of the question, use tangible rewards that represent how much upper management respects and values Traditionals' contributions. Take pictures of productive Traditionals receiving a certificate of achievement from the company president. Frame the pictures and hang them in the front lobby or reception area. Putting an article in the company newsletter about an employee's years with the company and his contributions can have a powerful motivational effect.

Plaques with the Traditional's name and number of years of service are also effective because they celebrate the Traditional's contributions.

First Chicago Bank awards high-achieving mature employees with the Service Products Group Performance Award.[14] Presented monthly, it includes a memento and a meal. At the end of the year, all the winners attend a reception where they can bring their spouses and guests and more awards are presented.

6. Give One-on-One Support

Although motivated to learn, Traditionals may need some extra support to help them grasp new skills, especially around technology. A few years ago, we hired Charlie, a retired insurance salesman, to join the sales force of our training company. Our sales manager, Jane, who had been instrumental in hiring him, set up a time to train him on our systems. As the principals of the firm, we thought it would be a good update for us to sit in on the training.

Jane began by quickly showing him the features of our client management software, the way we access our call lists, and the various approaches we use with customers. Jane tends to talk fast, and she covered a lot of ground in a short time. From time to time, she would ask Charlie if he had any questions, and he would shake is head. His face, however, told us he was somewhere between confusion and panic.

When Jane was finished, Charlie said he couldn't wait to get started. The next morning he resigned, citing family conflicts. We suspected, however, that the training experience was the real cause. Charlie felt overwhelmed and didn't want to suffer the embarrassment of admitting he felt that way. Rather than losing face by admitting he needed help, he exited the situation.

It was a good lesson for us. When training older employees on new systems or technology, it's wise to go slow, step by step, assuming they don't know much and won't tell you if they don't get it. Ask lots of questions to make sure they understand. You may have to prime the pump to engage them by saying something like, "When I first learned to run this equipment, I found it confusing that there was more than one setting for the calibrators. How about you?"

When you can, conduct this kind of training one-on-one instead of in a group. More than Boomers, Gen Xers, Gen Yers, and Linksters, Traditionals tend to be very sensitive to public embarrassment.

Managing Volunteers

Most Traditionals in the workplace today are volunteers. (In 2008 the Peace Corps had its oldest volunteer, an 85-year-old who taught science to children in Ghana.) In addition to all the tips for managing Traditionals listed, here are some suggestions for managing them when they are volunteers:[15]

1. Avoid the "Warm Body Syndrome"

The number one complaint from Traditional Generation volunteers is that employers do not tap into the skill set they can offer. Filling a volunteer position should be more than a "mirror under the nose" test. Find out what they are capable of doing and balance it with what they would like to do. You want to take advantage of their skill sets without putting them back in jobs they did all their lives and might not want to do again. An in-depth conversation with them about their experiences and their goals for volunteering will raise the odds that you will place them in jobs that they will enjoy doing and that will maximize their contributions.

2. Give Them Titles Commensurate with Their Experience and Responsibilities

The volunteer should have a title other than "volunteer." It can include the word, but should also describe the volunteer's responsibilities and contain elements of cachet and prestige. A title gives the position a sense of worth in the eyes of the volunteer and the people with whom the volunteer interacts. Cheryl (whom we mentioned at the beginning of the previous chapter) has the title of "Volunteer Director of Event Logistics."

3. Explain the Job's Contribution and Importance

Since most people volunteer because they want to contribute to a cause greater than themselves, explaining how their role in the organization contributes to the welfare of the organization, its clients, and the community as a whole is critical to keeping volunteers motivated.

4. Make a Task List or Clear Job Description

Create a list of all the tasks, duties, and responsibilities the volunteer position requires. The list should be straightforward and clear. Many volunteers want to work without having to engage in the intricacies of office politics in which regular employees who are vying to get ahead often engage. Having a straightforward list of responsibilities for which the volunteer can come to work, accomplish, and then go home helps make this a reality for them.

Cheryl's chamber listed the top three characteristics it was seeking in a volunteer as:

> A clear speaking and phone voice
> Comfortable with multiple details
> A sense of satisfaction when getting answers to people's questions

5. Identify Reporting Responsibilities Clearly

Define to whom the volunteer reports and to whom the volunteer is accountable.

Cheryl reports directly to Steve, a Baby Boomer who is the manager of customer service. Cheryl also takes direction from other staff members but whenever there is a conflict of priorities, Steve makes the decision.

6. Clarify WIFV (What's in It for the Volunteer)

What are the benefits to be gained by the volunteer for committing her time and talents to your organization or cause?

Cheryl's chamber told her she would be assisting the pillars of her community by providing a service to their business members and visitors. Cheryl wanted a chance to give back to the town she had called home most of her adult life and it helped that Steve was able to clearly define how she could do that in her volunteer position.

7. Lavishly Express Appreciation

Volunteers have their own reasons for volunteering for you. They may or may not want to be thanked and appreciated constantly, but it's a sure bet they will resent it if they don't get an occasional word of acknowledgment. So play it safe and pat them on the back often by describing how their work contributes to the betterment of the organization, the clients, and the community—and be sure to thank them for the effort.

The Bottom Line

It's easy to write off the Traditional Generation as over the hill, but such snap judgments can do your company a disservice. Research shows that Traditionals can learn what they need to do the job, even if it involves a computer. They tend to be more social the older they get. They're reliable and hardworking. And they have a lifetime of experience upon which to draw.

You can tap into this precious resource by understanding what will draw older employees to your company. You can hold on to them by offering personal support such as mentoring a younger employee—or being mentored by one—and one-on-one training. Modify their jobs to accommodate their capabilities. Recognize their achievements.

Your workplace will be enriched by their contribution.

CHAPTER 10

Cell Phones and Hanna Montana: Signposts for the Linkster Generation

"It is all that the young can do for the old, to shock them and keep them up to date."[1]

—*George Bernard Shaw*

Critical Events in the Lives of Linksters

1998 TiVo first launched at CES
2000 *Survivor* reality show debuted
2001 New York becomes first state to ban handheld cell phone use while driving
2001 The Netherlands becomes first nation to grant same-sex marriages
2004 Janet Jackson "accidently" exposes her breast at the Super Bowl
2007 Washington becomes the first state to make texting while driving illegal
2008 Financial meltdown
2009 President Barack Obama takes office
2009 U.S. Airways Flight 1549 crashes into Hudson River
2009 Swine flu outbreak
2009 Death of Michael Jackson
2009 Jay Leno moves to prime time
2009 First AIDS vaccine shows promise

. . . .

Larry's Story

When I was a teenager, I spent many after-school hours at my best friend Frank's house playing Vibration Football. This is a board game consisting of one-inch-high plastic football players, a felt "ball" the size of a BB, and a three-foot-long electric playing board painted to look like a football field. The board was made of metal, with a vibrator hidden in the frame. The game was played by lining your players up against the opposing team, placing the ball in a slot on one of the players, and turning on the vibrator. This would cause the players to scurry all over the board. If your ball carrier happened to run into an opposing player, he was considered "tackled." If he ran across the goal line, you scored a touchdown. All the while, we would cheer our own players and razz the opposition, just as if we were at a real game. It was great fun and, at the time, considered very "high tech."

I recently witnessed a similar scene at the home of a friend who has two teenage boys. They were playing an interactive video game projected onto a large screen by an LCD projector. As they were cheering and razzing each other, I noticed they were wearing telephone headsets. My friend said that was because the people they were playing against were in France, Australia, Japan, and Canada.

. . . .

Generation Linkster

Welcome to Generation Linkster, so called because no other generation has ever been so linked to each other and to the world through technology. Born after 1995, they are currently in their teens and preteens. There are approximately 20 million Generation Linksters in the United States,[2] and they represent 18 percent of the world's population.[3] As of this writing, they are entering the workforce as part-time employees, working after school and during the summers.

Most Linksters don't remember the O. J. Simpson trial, the disputed 2000 presidential election, the dot-com collapse, or the 9/11 attacks. Their vocabulary lessons included words like "terrorism" and "Google." The nice lady who gives you directions from your GPS is an icon for them and as trustworthy as a police officer. In fact, the people they trust most are their parents, who are, for the most part, Generation X.

Signposts for Generation Linkster
Signpost: Parental Involvement

Baby Boomer parents wanted their Gen Y children to grow up with a strong sense of self-esteem and an advantage in getting into the best schools. Generation X parents, although caring about self-esteem, are rejecting some of the overscheduling and overparenting tactics of their Baby Boomer parents. Remember from Chapter 3 that these are the folks who waited until their mid-30s to marry and then embraced familyhood with relish. They're involved, caring, and willing to devote the time to be good parents. Generation X includes more stay-at-home dads than the Boomer parents of Generation Y. And more Generation X moms than Boomers are staying home or working part-time to be with their kids.[4]

On the other hand, they have often been criticized for overindulging their children. In her article on child-centered parenting, Kathi Alexander complains that many parents today are so "child-centered" that they're afraid to deny their children anything.[5] She uses the example of, "Okay, but honey, that's your last package of Twizzlers before breakfast," to brilliantly paint a picture to which many of us can relate. She goes on to say:

> It's not just that many American parents are under-parenting by not setting reasonable limits. Paradoxically, we are also over-parenting by making every effort to ensure that our children are not given the opportunity to fail. At the same time our pediatricians are urging us to cut back on the excessive use of hand sanitizers and antibiotics (kids need exposure to some germs if their immune systems are going to successfully fight the really bad ones), our child development experts are telling us to stop excessively slathering our children with the word "Yes." Our kids' emotional "immune systems" need exposure to life lessons that involve at least the risk of disappointment, failure, or emotional turmoil if they are going to be able to withstand the bigger setbacks and losses they will inevitably face in adulthood.

Dr. Michael Brody, a child psychiatrist and chair of the Television and Media Committee of the American Academy of Child and Adolescent *Psychiatry*, explains that Gen X parents "are trying to heal the wounds from their own childhoods through their children."[6] Remember, Gen Xers were the latchkey kids who often watched their families dissolve in divorce.

The parents of Generation Linkster seem concerned with creating a more rational, traditional family atmosphere than did their Baby Boomer predecessors. By traditional, we mean having dinner together and spending more connecting time in activities that bring everyone closer. By rational, we mean that it's okay to let their children be themselves. The result is a generation that remains close to their parents. According to Youth-Trends.com, a marketing and research company in Ramsey, New Jersey, 70 percent of this generation call their parents their best friends.

Linksters and their primarily Gen X parents participate in similar activities from skateboarding to snowboarding. Nickelodeon is a U.S.-based television channel with programming aimed at children between the ages of 6 and 15. The number one song on Nickelodeon's 2009 Kid's Choice Awards was "Single Ladies" by Beyoncé, which was also listed on the *Rolling Stone* list of 100 Best Songs.[7] Linksters and their parents are turned on by the same music.

Linksters React: Keep Things Flexible

As of this writing, the majority of working Linksters are doing so part-time while going to school. Since they are essentially still kids, if they work for you, expect their parents to be heavily involved. They may be relying on their parents for transportation to and from work. They may have other obligations at school. They may be involved with volunteer groups or they may need to study for a test. So keep their stage of life in perspective when dealing with them.

We were in a hotel recently and had to catch an early morning flight. The young man who loaded our luggage said he's a high school student who works part-time. We asked him what he likes best about the job, and he replied that he really appreciates the free reign the hotel gives him to arrange his schedule around his classes. If he needs to study for a test, he can move his hours around or even work fewer hours. We couldn't help noticing that he did a terrific job: courteous, friendly, helpful, and efficient. Just the kind of customer-oriented employee every hotel wants.

If you want to hold on to Linksters, providing a schedule that reasonably accommodates their needs and the needs of their parents will improve your chances.

Signpost: Connecting Through Technology

As grade school children, Generation Y embraced technology and brought online social media into the mainstream. Linksters have been online since they were toddlers. Today, 62 percent of American homes have access to the Internet and 82 percent of those homes have a high-speed connection.[8] If there is a Linkster in the home, you can be sure he or she is using that high-speed line to connect with friends and cruise the Web. According to a study by Pew Internet, 50 percent of American Linksters go online every day.[9] We think it's likely that most of them pity anyone who only has dial-up!

These kids have been accessing email, putting pictures on their own Web sites, and making calls on cell phones since they were three or four years old. In an informal survey of several hundred teenagers, 100 percent told us they had access to the family computer or owned their own laptop. When asked at what age they started using a computer, several said, "I don't remember. We've always had one."

For this generation, the computer is just another appliance. They use it to do homework, visit social networking sites, surf the Web, and chat with friends. In fact, sending traditional email has become passé for Linksters. They much prefer to text friends using a cell phone or PDA.

Linksters React: Cell Phone Addiction

In the United States, 63 percent of teens have a cell phone.[10] Jason, a 14-year-old Linkster, told us he takes his cell phone with him wherever he goes—not to make calls but because he wants to stay "connected." (His record is 8,569 text messages in one month.) When he got his first cell phone at 12 years old, his agreement with his parents was to stay at or below 1,500 texts per month. If he went over, he had to pay the difference. Consequently, every month he knew exactly how many texts he had and how close he was to going over the limit. He told us that part of his criteria for texting his buddies or pursuing a potential girlfriend was (1) Were they part of his network? and (2) How many texts did he have left before going over his limit? He explained this was somewhat limiting when he would receive a text but couldn't respond, hoping the person on the other end didn't think he was ignoring him or her. Thank goodness now for unlimited texting, which is what many Linksters have. Jason tells us, "Now we don't talk on the phone. We just text."

According to a Nielsen study, 83 percent of U.S. mobile teens use text-messaging and 56 percent use MMS/picture messaging. The average U.S. mobile teen now sends or receives an average of 2,899 text messages per month compared to 191 calls.[11]

Currently, one 13-year-old girl holds the record for number of texts in one month at 14,528. That means she sent 484 texts per day, or an average of three per minute. Her father's cell phone bill was over 440 pages long.[12]

A study by Jan Van den Bulck, PhD, on mobile phone addiction found that only 38 percent of Generation Linksters never used their cell phone after going to bed.[13] As many as one in five are awakened in the middle of the night because of an incoming text message or the anticipation of one.[14] Another study found that teenagers who have high cell phone usage are more aggravated, have a harder time falling asleep, and are more prone to other addictive behaviors such as drinking or smoking. According to the study's author, Gaby Badre, MD, PhD, "Addiction to the cell phone is becoming common. Youngsters feel a group pressure to remain interconnected and reachable round the clock."[15]

Many Linksters describe their cell phones as extensions of their hands, their lifeline, and the only thing they cannot live without. The jolt of energy someone gets from a friendly text has been compared to the buzz a gambler gets from winning. According to a UK news article, two Linksters were taken to a treatment center for their cell phone addiction after their parents discovered they were swindling money from their relatives to pay their cell phone bills.[16]

Not every member of Generation Linkster is so far gone, but there is no denying that Linksters have incorporated technology into the way they communicate with each other and the world.

A downside to all this virtual interaction has been a deterioration of face-to-face communication and social skills. As children, we were told not to chew food with our mouths open. Linksters are told not to text during dinner. A survey by Computerworld identified poor interpersonal communication as a common problem among this age group.[17] One of our clients who runs an amusement park said he has to remind his Linkster employees to look patrons in the eye, smile, welcome them on the ride, and even to not spit in front of them. Otherwise, they often don't know any better.

Another told us about Madison, who works as a cashier in a grocery store. She was upset because her manager told her it was impolite to wait on customers while she listened to her iPod. She said, "I don't know what the big deal is. I had one bud in my ear and the other bud out. Anyone could see that by having only one bud in, I was accessible. I mean, it's not like I can't listen to the customer talk and listen to music at the same time."

Signpost: Dearth of Face-to-Face Contact

All this reliance on technology and lack of face-to-face contact has resulted in diminishing opportunities for Linksters to learn how to deal with life's difficult encounters. It's so much easier for a teen to break up with a love interest by texting him rather than facing him, but by avoiding the encounter, the teen never learns how to have those kinds of tough conversations. Texting your parents to ask them if you can stay out beyond your curfew may be less intimidating than calling them, but it robs you of the chance to practice your powers of persuasion. Writing negative thoughts about someone on MySpace may be easier than confronting her directly, but it cheats you out of learning to temper your criticism with compassion.

In all of these cases, you never get to see the other person's face and sense his or her response. You only see the words. Texting and email may be convenient tools for sending messages, but they lack the richness and subtlety of face-to-face communication.

The good news from the key signpost "connecting through technology" is that kids are communicating more than ever. The bad news is that their communication skills may be suffering as a result. The implication for managers is this: If you place these people in any situation where they must interact with others, provide them with the training to overcome their inadequacies. If you work or live with them, try to engage with them in face-to-face conversation as much as possible, even if it means asking them to put down the PDA and give you their full attention.

Signpost: Environmental Awareness

Baby Boomers remember when the government drained the Florida Everglades to create more farmland. Gen Xers remember the *Exxon Valdez* spill in 1989—and many are still boycotting Exxon. Generation Y made

Green the new Black (i.e., fashionable) and is playing a part in bringing natural water flow back to the Everglades.

Generation Linkster is growing up knowing *An Inconvenient Truth*. (*An Inconvenient Truth* is a book and movie featuring 45th Vice President Al Gore. The movie demonstrates the damage humans are causing to the planet with pollution, and the imperative need to stop global warming.[18]) They are keenly aware of problems facing our world like global warming, melting ice caps, thinning ozone layers, and depleting oil reserves. They often know their own carbon footprint before they know their own shoe size.

According to a survey by American Camp Association (ACA), over 80 percent of resident camps offer at least one type of environmental program or activity for teens.[19] PEAK (Promoting Environmental Awareness in Kids) is a program developed by the partnership of REI (Recreational Equipment, Inc.) and the Leave No Trace Center for Outdoor Ethics. PEAK coaches both urban and suburban kids in how to enjoy the outdoors more responsibly and respectfully. Since 2002, PEAK has taught over 550,000 children how to treat and take care of the wilderness and hiking trails. In 2009, PEAK received the Special Recognition Award from ACA for its outstanding efforts in educating the next generation about the great outdoors.[20]

Examples of Linksters acting on their environmental awareness regularly appear in the news.

A group of kids in Maryland Heights, Missouri, completed a project at their local school to turn garbage into methane gas that now heats all the classrooms and two gymnasiums.[21]

Two third-graders in Gloucester, Massachusetts, were so moved by the decimation of the rain forests for commercial purposes that they wrote a play about it and, with 11 of their friends, performed the play in front of classmates and teachers.[22]

Green Children's House is a Green Montessori School located in Pompano Beach, Florida. Its curriculum focuses on being green and teaching children how to reuse and recycle. Children's reports can be printed on recycled paper at the parents' request, but the goal of the school is to be totally paperless. All the food that is provided to the students is organic and comes from Whole Foods Market or is grown on a sustainable farm. According to the school's Web site, its mission is to develop student EQ (Environmental Quotients) along with IQ (Intelligence Quotients).[23]

Green Children's House is not alone; the number of ecofriendly preschools is on the rise. According to the U.S. Green Building Council there are 127 preschools that have been certified as Green.[24]

Linksters React: Environmental Passion

Linksters tend to care deeply about the state of the world. They assume greenness should be a priority for all companies. Being so connected to the Internet, they are aware of events and conditions all over the world. It turns global issues into backyard issues for them and gives them a sense of urgency to do something to make the world better. In preschool, Baby Boomers were told to finish their lunch because there were starving children in Africa. Linksters held food drives in preschool to help solve world hunger.

As teenagers, Linksters are moving to make the world a better place. According to the Corporation for National and Community Service, in 2004, 55 percent of American teenagers volunteered, which is almost twice the rate of adults.[25]

They are directing a great deal of that energy toward the Green Movement. The movie *The Graduate* made a lasting impression on Boomers because it defined their alienation from their parents' values. *The Breakfast Club* had an impact on Generation X because it celebrated their independence from adults. Generation Y will long remember *Napoleon Dynamite* because it reflected their desire to be unique. Linksters will likely remember *Hoot, Happy Feet,* and Al Gore's *An Inconvenient Truth* because these and other "green" movies helped define their mission for the future.

Smart companies are capitalizing on this eco-inclination. Whole Foods Grocery Market, the world's largest retailer of natural and organic foods, recently created a line of body care products targeted at teens called Teens Turning Green. The products are unique because each is chosen by a committee of teens that evaluates and compares how different skin products affect the changing conditions of teenage skin.

A portion of all sales is donated to Teens for Safe Cosmetics, a coalition of young women dedicated to educating peers and the public at large about using cosmetics free of pollutants and toxic chemicals. Sponsored by Whole Foods and other ecofriendly corporations, their projects include campaigning for the adoption of green laws. They played a major role in the passage of California's Safe Cosmetics Act in October 2005 and the California Toxic Toys Bill in 2007.[26]

On a smaller scale, Linksters are organizing to make a difference at the local level. Green Teens is an environmental group in northeastern Connecticut founded by three high school freshmen. Their mission is to spread environmental awareness through education and simple, positive lifestyle changes. Accomplishments include operating cloth bag booths, running lightbulb swaps, and attending community events to spread their message.[27]

The good news is that Linksters care about causes outside themselves and are willing to work hard to make a difference, especially around environmental issues. The bad news, which isn't really bad, is that as they enter the workforce, their expectations of similar sentiments from their employers will be very important to them. If you haven't started recycling your scrap, reducing your energy consumption, and cleaning up your carbon footprint, you'd best start. The Linksters are coming and their reactions to eco-unfriendly companies will likely be harsh.

A Great Workplace for Linksters

Hot Topic is a retail store that sells music and popular, culture-themed clothing. The majority of Hot Topic shoppers and employees are under the age of 20. Staff is encouraged to turn the music up. Employees are outfitted in Hot Topic ultracool wear. The store wants its employees to look hip but not be too cool to wait on customers.

To remain current, Hot Topic encourages employees to go to as many concerts as possible. The cost of the ticket is reimbursed as long as the employee fills out a fashion report after the show.[28] Retail staff are encouraged to call or text store buyers with their opinions about fashion, a highly unusual practice in an industry where buyers and retail staff are traditionally kept separate. Linksters love this because it's just how they're treated at home: as equals. The company benefits because no one knows and cares more about Linkster fashion than Linksters.

The Bottom Line

As Generation Linkster enters the workforce, managers and coworkers face new challenges to integrate young people who have been shaped by the attitudes of their Generation X parents, by technology, and by a growing environmental awareness.

Linksters are close to their parents, whom many in this generation consider their best friends. Managers need to be aware of the influence parents have and the Linksters' need to affirm their decisions with their parents. As much as possible, schedules need to be flexible to allow Linksters to fit work into their busy schedules.

A generation defined by white cords hanging from their ears while their thumbs fly across keypads inches from their noses understand technology. They're comfortable with computers. They love video games. They can't live without their cell phones. Most Linksters can easily handle job requirements that involve technology, but they will have a tougher time with face-to-face communication with customers and coworkers. Managers will need to help them develop these skills.

Generation Linkster recognizes the impact we all make, individually and collectively, on our environment. They want to contribute to creating a better world, and they expect their employers to want the same thing. Corporate social responsibility is fast becoming a new emphasis for companies that wish to compete for talent—and business—in the future.

CHAPTER 11

Managing the Linkster Generation

"Young people are in a condition like permanent intox-
ication, because youth is sweet and they are growing."
—Aristotle[1]

Every new generation brings a different mind-set to the job. Linksters, the generation just entering the workforce now, are no different.

Linkster #1 Comments

Jordan is 16 years old and works part-time at a retail clothing store. "The pay's not great, but I like the employee discount and the opportunity to see some of the new fashions before everyone else has them," said Jordan. "What sucks about my job is that being reliable is punished rather than rewarded. If you show up early, or on time, management tags you as dependable. When you are dependable, you are given all the less than desirable shifts like the day after Thanksgiving, New Year's Eve, and Saturday night. My supervisor knows I won't be a 'no-show,' even on Christmas Eve. Sometimes I think I should be one of the jerks who calls in sick when he doesn't want to come in."

Linkster #2 Comments

Kylie, a 13-year-old Linkster, is on a competitive swim team. One of Kylie's teammates, an extremely good swimmer, complained that he was not winning enough individual races and thought if he swam in the second heat instead of the first, he might win more blue ribbons. Kylie told him, "Yeah, but what about the team? We can only score team points if you swim in the first heat. You might win more blue ribbons for your trophy scrapbook, but our team will suffer." For Kylie, doing the right thing for the team (her group of friends) is as important as looking out for yourself.

Linksters primarily work part-time while attending school. Similar to previous generations, many of their struggles spring from their youth and inexperience. Do not think, however, that they are younger versions of yourself. As we said in the previous chapter, Linksters have a different set of generational signposts that sets them apart. You'll need to think strategically if you want to have a successful working relationship with this new breed of workers.

Goals for Managing Linksters

1. Settle them down and help them feel comfortable.
2. Get them into a routine to which they can adapt and master.
3. Provide them with fun and engagement to hold their attention.
4. Reward them often and correct them immediately when they need it.

Tips for Managing Linksters

1. Ride Herd on Them

Linksters are currently at an age where they may seem like rambunctious calves on a cross-country cattle drive. (For all you nostalgic Baby Boomers, think Rowdy Yates and Mr. Favor.) They may have short attention spans and will lose interest, especially if they find the work boring.

Paul is a high school sophomore. He is an avid reader and video game player. He wanted to make money to buy additional video games and magazines; we needed packets stuffed for a large mailing scheduled to go out July 1. This was the ideal summer job for a teenager: He could do the work at home while he watched TV if he wanted.

It was the first of June. It should have taken him about a week to finish the job if he worked on it just two hours a day. We figured it was a safe bet the packets would be ready to go out on time. We told Paul we would pay him when the job was completed.

Initially, he was enthusiastic about the work and expressed great interest in being given additional assignments. By the end of June, however, he had completed only half the work. He returned the remaining supplies to us and said he was sorry, but the job did not have enough "intellectual stimulation" for him.

He was right. Like any repetitive task, putting packets together lacks intellectual stimulation. People do them because there's another reward at stake. It's usually money, but it could also be because they want to contribute to a group effort, they find it socially stimulating, or they don't want to disappoint their parents. But usually it's money.

In Paul's case, the money was not enough motivation. He stood to make $100. If it had been enough to buy a new Xbox, and he had a burning passion to have one, he might have been motivated to endure the dreaded "lack of intellectual stimulation" and done it. Or, if he was starving and living on the street instead of with his parents, he would have finished in record time just to get something to eat. But neither was the case.

In retrospect, we made several mistakes. We should have paid him for every 50 packets he completed. Having to wait a month for a reward is a long time for a Linkster. We also should *not* have let him work at home. The hands-off policy was a disaster. There were just too many distractions. Again, teenagers tend to have short attention spans and distractions like the video game player, television, and friends dropping by are simply too tempting. Finally, we should have hired two Linksters to come into our office so they could work together as a team and where we could watch them. They could have socialized while they worked and their pay would have depended on the numbers they achieved together. They would have been under close supervision so we could have done a Rowdy Yates–like herding job on them every time they wandered off task.

If we had done these three things, we wouldn't have been scrambling around at the end of June trying to get our mailing out the door.

2. Provide Them with Job Descriptions

Like any new employees, Linksters need clear direction about what you expect from them. Know the job you want them to perform. Write a job description to clarify your expectations and give the job a greater sense of importance. Part-time jobs are sometimes treated provisionally and have a disposable feel to the worker. A job description helps elevate the job's importance to the manager and the Linkster.

In the interview process, be clear about the times they are to work, the duties of the job, and the number of hours you want them to be available. Setting clear expectations in the job description and the interview process helps keep the Linkster on track.

3. Treat Them Like Valued Coworkers

Being part-time means Linksters have less time to connect and feel part of the group than full-timers. This can lead to a second-class syndrome. Linksters can often feel like outsiders, especially when full-time employees view them as disposable.

Linksters have had a steady diet of feedback and connections through their friends and family. Remember, it was Linksters who said their parents were their best friends. A work atmosphere that is less than inviting will seem hostile to a Linkster. Since most of them don't really need a job, feeling that way raises the odds that they will leave.

Communicate with your full-time employees the importance of including part-time employees in office chitchat, meetings, and social events. Remind everyone that part-time employees add value by completing the tasks that full-time employees don't have time to complete. Whatever Linksters contribute should be seen as important spokes in the wheel of work.

To that end, keep your Linksters in mind when scheduling meetings or corporate events. Encourage Linksters to attend company functions and after-work celebrations (except those who, because of their young age, are not legally allowed to attend). The more you include Linksters, the tighter the connection they will feel with you and the place where they work.

Meagan Reminisces

Recently, after a speech I gave where I told the "$1.69 story" that I told at the beginning of this book, a Gen X audience member approached me and said, "I was standing in the checkout line at the grocery store with my 10-year-old son when I saw a $100 bill on the floor! I casually picked it up and shoved it into my pocket. Out of the corner of my eye, I could see my son watching me. I was torn about what to do. I thought, 'If I give this money to the cashier, how likely is it that she will look for the bill's owner?' Then I thought, 'What would I want my son to do and how will I explain to him the reasons I kept $100 that didn't belong to me?'"

The man gave the bill to the cashier, who told him she knew to whom it belonged and would make sure it was returned. The man told me he didn't know if the money made it back to its owner, but in the long run, it didn't matter. "My son couldn't believe I had turned in the money," he said. "It allowed me to explain the importance of giving back what does not belong to us. It also made me realize that we frequently expect our children to do what we don't have the courage to do ourselves. The awe and amazement my son had for me were worth much more than $100."

This reminded me that parents and managers fill a leadership role for their children as well as their employees.

Larry Responds

You got that right, Meagan. Now I don't mean to go on a rant, but an event in the news in 2009 caused me to pause and think about how personal behavior is what leadership is all about.

Mark Sanford, the Republican governor of South Carolina, disappeared from his post for five days with no word of where he was. Upon returning, he said he was hiking the Appalachian Trail before admitting he had been in Argentina having an extramarital affair.

We often hear "to err is human" and let's face it, we have all erred a time or two. I can understand Sanford's falling from the "holier than thou" pedestal on which he placed himself in 1998 when he criticized Bill Clinton for doing something similar. It simply made him a hypocrite in addition to a philanderer. From my perspective as a student of corporate culture, however, the more egregious sin Sanford committed was his blatant disregard for those who had placed their faith and trust in him.

Besides his family and the citizens of South Carolina, Sanford arrogantly displayed an incredible disrespect for the employees of the state of South Carolina. He blatantly broke a state policy that would get any regular employee fired on the spot. The South Carolina Budget and Control Board Disciplinary Policy, which, according to Mike Spanhour, director of public affairs, serves as the personnel policy guide for South Carolina state employees, reads:

> SECTION VI, ABANDONMENT OF POSITION An employee who voluntarily fails to report to work for three consecutive workdays and fails to contact the appropriate supervisory authority during this time will be considered to have voluntarily resigned from the Budget and Control Board. The resignation is automatically accepted. A voluntary resignation is not a grievable issue.

Will Sanford be fired? Of course not. Spanhour went on to say, "It's not clear that the governor has to abide by the rules that employees must follow."

There's probably no legal standard for canning him. That's little comfort to the supervisor in the field who decides to discipline an employee for the same infraction and is confronted with, "If the governor can do it, why can't I?"

Everything a leader does demonstrates what is or is not acceptable. Sanford's behavior told the state of South Carolina employees that it's okay to abandon your position and lie about what you do on state time. Of course, everyone knows that's not true. The governor gets to behave according to a different standard than the rest of us. Is it any wonder government employees are sometimes perceived as having an "attitude"?

The bottom line is that people follow leaders because they trust them. When leaders are dishonest, when they lie, when they act without integrity, when they adopt special rules for themselves, they betray that trust. Think about the last time someone you cared about betrayed you. Did your level of cynicism about the world not go up a notch or two? Keep that in mind the next time you are treated rudely by the clerk at the DMV.

> Of course, few of us are state governors. Most of us are supervisors and managers doing our best to lead and manage our folks—and that includes me. None of us would ever act in a way we wouldn't want our employees to act, would we?
>
> **Meagan Responds**
>
> Gosh, Dad, I'm sure glad you didn't want to go on a rant.
>
> •

4. Lead by Example

Linksters are hatchlings in the workplace. They are still trying to figure out how to act and behave. They look to us for examples, and it behooves us to provide those examples. If you want your Linksters to come in on time, get there on time yourself. If you want Linksters to go the extra mile with customers, make sure they see you do the same. If you want Linksters to be honest and not steal from you, be scrupulously honest with them on their hours and paychecks. Remember, they are watching your lead.

One of Starbucks' core values is equal participation. Everyone does what needs to be done to get the job done. Nobody has a title, everyone is called a partner, and when addressing another employee, you use the person's first name. In South Korea, men do not traditionally perform domestic duties like cleaning or washing dishes. Rather than abandon their value of equal participation to fit with South Korea's culture, Starbucks demonstrated to its South Korean employees that everyone from the front counter staff to corporate management would scrub and clean by hanging a picture on the wall in every store of the international director cleaning a toilet.[2]

5. Orient Them to the Obvious

Be specific about expectations that may seem obvious to you but may not be to them. For example, tell the new Linkster employee, "If you are sick and unable to come in for your shift, give us as much notice as possible." Linksters are usually still in school, and their mom or dad calls the attendance office when they are ill to tell the school they will be absent. It might not occur to the Linkster to give you as much notice as possible.

Be clear about the consequences of not showing up on time, missing their shift, or breaking core company values. Just as important—and this goes back to leading by example—be willing to enforce the rules.

McKenna, a Linkster we know, works as a barista in a trendy coffee shop. She told us, "It is infuriating to watch people show up late or not at all and our manager just shrug his shoulders. I asked him why someone that is a no-show is not fired like it was explained in orientation and he said, 'Yeah, you're right, but I'm busy and it's too hard to find replacements. An unreliable employee is better than none at all.'"

McKenna went on to say, "With people showing or not showing, it's hard to give good customer service, and besides, it's just not fair." We don't expect McKenna to remain a barista at that shop much longer.

David, a Baby Boomer research manager, often hires Linksters as lab assistants. "I understand they are students and are still learning about the ways of work, but there are areas where I draw the line," said David. "I hired a teenager who did a great job in the interview. Then he rescheduled his appointment with HR twice to fill out his paperwork and he showed up 45 minutes late on his first day. When he arrived, I explained to him that it didn't look like we were going to be a good match so he should go home. Other employers may have been more lenient, but I know my staff. If I had let this person stay on, it would have been a rub with my other employees."

6. Welcome Them with Open Arms

Let your people know when Linksters are joining your team and ask everyone to welcome them. Pair Linksters with buddies. (Pick good role models. Choose the kind of person who models the values, work ethics, and job performance you want Linksters to emulate.) Buddies can make the workplace seem a little less intimidating, like having someone to eat lunch with on the first day of school. Buddies should introduce the Linksters to everyone and show them where the fire exits and bathrooms are, where they can get something to eat or drink, and the layout of the building. Assigning Linksters to buddies also gives them someone they can ask the questions they may have forgotten to ask during training, like, "What holidays are you closed?"

Call Linksters the night before their first day. This sends the message that you are interested in them. On the calls, remind Linksters of:

> ▷ Dress code. This avoids the embarrassment of having to send a Linkster home if he or she is inappropriately dressed.
> ▷ Time they should arrive. Be clear about criteria for tardiness.
> ▷ Items they should bring, such as driver's license and Social Security card.
> ▷ Traffic. Remind them if they will be driving in rush hour. Let them know that heavy traffic is *not* considered a valid reason to be late.
> ▷ Snacks and water. Will the Linkster be working several hours before his first break? Remind him to bring a snack or a bottle of water, if appropriate.
> ▷ Where to park.
> ▷ Whom to contact once they arrive.
> ▷ Quitting time.

7. Know What Songs Are on Their iPods

The greater the number of personal connections you have with the Linkster, the greater her loyalty will be to you and the team. Take time to listen to the Linkster. Young people have a language that is distinctively their own and it may be easy to dismiss what they have to say because of their youth. Do not assume Linksters do not want to learn. Their interest level increases the more they feel in touch with you.

8. Create Microcareer Paths

"Young people want to work the register. It's the most prestigious job," says Michelle, co-owner of Lox Stock and Bagel, a busy bagel shop in Scottsdale, Arizona. "Before they can do that, they need to understand our line of offerings and how the flow of customer orders works. The only way they can learn that is working the line, taking orders, preparing the food, and delivering it to the tables. Learning all that doesn't happen in a day; it usually takes a year before they're ready. Then, I have them run the register under my close supervision until I feel they can do it on their own. At that point, they get a special badge that says Certified Cashier, and a bump in their wages. We make a big deal about it so it becomes a goal they can strive to achieve. I know they won't be with us for long, but why not give them something to work toward while they're here? The practice has served us well for 20 years. In fact, we've had people who worked for us as teenagers return years later to thank us for the training we gave them."

A Gen Y manager of a clothing retail store created the V.I.P. Salesperson honorary position. The manager took all the small tasks that were required of her Linkster salespeople, like colorizing a rack, cleaning a dressing room, and unloading shipments, and listed them on a chart in the back room. On one side was the list of tasks and on the other were all the employees' names. Once an employee masters a new task, meaning he can complete the task without being told how to do it, the manager places a star next to the Linkster's name at the weekly meeting. After the employee has stars by all the duties, she promotes him to V.I.P. Salesperson. It doesn't pay more, but he gets a special name badge, a place on the recognition board, and the right to accumulate seniority points to be eligible for premium days off like the day after Thanksgiving, the prom, and New Year's Eve.

The manager told us, "The V.I.P. status gives my part-time employees something to work toward. Since they are part-time, they won't be promoted into management, but as their manager, I want to help them focus their energy. The best part is, as I hire new people, the V.I.P.s assist me in training them. Also, several V.I.P.s have chosen to go full-time and have progressed into management positions inside the store, as well as with our corporate office."

9. Reexamine Your Uniform Policy

Part of being young is having a heightened interest in how you look and a preoccupation with your physical appearance. Examine the uniforms you are asking Linksters to wear. Are they embarrassing? Do your current Linkster employees complain about them? When was the last time the uniforms were updated? Are the uniforms comfortable to wear?

Gwen Stefani, lead singer for the band No Doubt, was recently hired by the trendy W Hotel chain to redesign its uniforms for female employees. Stefani wanted to create a dress for the employees that she imagines being in her own closet.[3]

If you hire young people and/or want to appeal to young customers, you may want to reexamine what you ask them to wear. The more fashionable (does not mean trendy) and comfortable the uniforms are, the fewer objections you will receive from Linksters and Gen Yers alike. Bruce Oldfield, better known for designing celebrity clothing, helped redesign the uniforms at McDonald's in London. The new uniforms are more contemporary looking and more comfortable to wear. McDonald's wanted the staff to feel more confident with the new uniforms and gain greater respect from the customer.[4]

Linksters want their personalities to shine through: The more you allow that to occur, the more enthusiasm Linksters will bring to the job. Be prepared to explain why certain dress codes exist. Any grooming, uniform, or clothing expectations should be relevant to the industry in which you operate.

Home Depot, for example, branded itself with its famous orange aprons. All employees are required to wear an apron to distinguish themselves from customers and to prevent damage to their own clothes. Employees are permitted, however, to choose what they want to wear under the apron.

For its uniform, a paint store provided all its employees with a golf shirt embroidered with the company logo. A group of employees at a West Coast location decided to tie-dye their golf shirts. Management decided to let the employees wear the shirts because the dye job better represented paint than the conservative, original brown color.

10. Thank Their Parents

Linksters are young and many still live at home with their parents. Mom or Dad may be getting up early to drive the kids to work and waiting in a dark parking lot to take them home. Taking a few minutes to meet the Linkster's parents and thank them for their efforts provides a tremendous amount of goodwill.

Tell Linksters to invite their parents for a visit or hold an open house and encourage the Linksters to bring their parents and family members. (No, you don't need to display their work on the walls and give them a report card, but it doesn't hurt to talk about what value Johnny brings to the organization.)

Also, it's highly likely that Linksters will voice any complaints about their job to their parents. Having the parents onboard increases the chance that they will help their child overcome her work challenges.

Linksters will probably be short-term employees. Consequently, they usually receive the lowest pay and get the least amount of training. Ironically, they often have the most interaction with your customers. The more you invest in creating a strong Linkster workforce, the better your brand image will be and the happier your customers will be.

Remember, Linksters will eventually become adults and their buying power will only go up. Giving them positive work experiences with your company plants the seeds for future business.

The Bottom Line

People entering the workforce need special attention during their first jobs. They don't know what to expect. They have little or no work experiences upon which to draw. They are anxious and tentative until they get a few shifts under their belt and discover that they can, indeed, do the job.

A new generation entering the workforce faces these issues from a new perspective shaped by new signposts. For Linksters, those generational signposts include close ties to their parents, technology as a regular part of their daily lives, and a heightened concern for their community and their planet. Keep these signposts in mind as you design work and jobs that Linksters will want to do, and do well.

Different Strokes for Different Folks: A Model for Managing Across Generational Boundaries

"All Fords are exactly alike, but no two men are just alike. Every new life is a new thing under the sun; there has never been anything just like it before, never will be again."

—Henry Ford, 1863–1947

. . . .

Larry Remembers

In the mid-1970s I managed a 60-bed inpatient unit at a government psychiatric hospital. A staff of 42 people reported to me, and I managed a budget of about a half-million dollars (big bucks for the time). From the beginning, the goal was to discharge all the patients to more appropriate placements and shut the unit down. The goal was accomplished in two years, and I moved into the hospital training department temporarily until another managerial position opened up.

I tell you this to let you know that, at that point in my life, I'd earned some managerial chops.

My new boss in the training department, Mike, was a Baby Boomer like me and had recently taken over that position. We didn't know each other except by reputation. We were as different as dirt and water. I had long hair and a beard; he was clean shaven and sported a crew cut. My politics were liberal; he was a Nixon Republican. I attended protests against the Vietnam War; he had completed two tours of duty there and was a decorated Marine Corps officer. I liked to wear Navajo shaman shirts and moccasins; he was never caught without a sport coat and tie.

You get the picture.

Shortly after I started, the director of purchasing called and asked me to go over some invoices with him. I told him I'd be right over. I signed out on the whiteboard we had in the front office of our building and told the receptionist I'd be back in a couple of hours.

When I returned, she pulled me aside and said that Mike had been looking for me. She said that when he saw I had signed out for two hours to go to purchasing, he said, "Why is he taking so long? It shouldn't take more than 30 minutes."

I was furious. Who was this "soldier boy" to question how I spent my time getting my job done? I have a *master's degree*, for gosh sakes. Of course, the logical thing to do would have been for me to ask Mike what he wanted and clarify why I needed to take two hours. It also would have been a good time to discuss our mutual expectations about how I manage my time.

But did I do that? Nooooooo. I sulked and stewed about it for weeks without saying a word to him. I was civil, but not friendly. I avoided him when I could and avoided eye contact when I couldn't. I did my job, kept to myself, and counted the days until I could get out of there.

A few weeks later he walked into my office, closed the door, and asked to talk. He said that he had heard I was really easy to work with, but that this had not been his experience. "I get the feeling you're ticked off at me. Is that true?" he asked. I did my best to look puzzled and denied there was anything wrong. He looked me in the eye and said, "B- - -s- - -. I can tell when something's wrong. I want you to level with me."

Through clenched teeth I told him what I'd heard he said about me taking two hours to go to purchasing and how it felt like he was questioning my integrity. I told him I didn't appreciate him treating me like some kid; I was a professional with extensive managerial experience.

I could tell he was dumbfounded. He replied, "Gosh, Larry, I don't even remember saying that. I guess I must have, but I can assure you, I feel no need to look over your shoulder to monitor how you use your time. If you produce and make this department look good, I don't care where you go, what you do, or how much time you take doing it."

From that day forward, Mike and I got along just fine. In fact, he proved to be one of the best bosses I've ever had. He knew when to leave me alone (which was most of the time) and when to intervene (which I occasionally needed). We've long since gone our separate ways, but we stay in touch, and I consider him a friend.

Looking back, I realize there were several factors that led me to behave so childishly. First, I was accustomed to running my own operation. Second, my ego was a bit bruised because I had lost the prestige of having people report to me. And third, I was feeling a little paranoid because Mike was my total opposite. I had created such a negative image of him in my head before I ever met him that I was ready to jump on anything he did. At the first hint that he perceived me as anything less than an equal, I responded irrationally. It doesn't excuse my behavior; it's just what happened.

If Mike had met with me on the first day, acknowledged my experience, and established a more collegial relationship, I probably wouldn't have overreacted the way I did. It would have rolled off my back or I would have asked him what he meant. Of course, I could have initiated the same discussion.

. . . .

Management Principles

In this chapter we discuss some basic management principles and introduce a tool for choosing a management mode that is appropriate for the person and situation you are managing. You should find the tool especially helpful for managing across generations. The management principles apply to all people and every situation.

Management Principle #1: Everyone's Different

Larry's experience with Mike reminds us that every individual is different and requires an approach tailored to his or her needs. This chapter explores a model for customizing how you manage and coach people to address their specific needs based on their experiences, abilities, individual desires, and generational signposts.

Management Principle #2: There Is No "Truth"

People are complicated. With every event in their lives, their memories, emotions, and thoughts filter their perceptions. What may be taken as an innocent comment by one person may be seen as an insult by another. (Mike and Larry proved that.) What may be interpreted as helpful advice by one person can be seen as micromanaging by another. Anyone who has more than one child will tell you that siblings tend to be quite different: What works with one is not likely to work with the other—but it might. What works with one child once might not work with the same child again—but it might. And what works with both children today might only work with one tomorrow—or it might not. In other words, there is no "truth." There is no "one way" to handle people.

For example, imagine you have two people working for you who are very good at their jobs, but you notice signs that they are falling in love. They hang out together. They come to work together, go to lunch together, and go home together. You say to yourself, "That's okay. As long as they maintain a professional demeanor and it doesn't affect their work, it's none of my business."

Unfortunately, you notice that it *is* affecting their work. They seem distracted. They flirt inappropriately at meetings. They take long, long lunch breaks together. And customers are beginning to notice.

Being a person of action, you take them aside, tell them their relationship is beginning to cause a problem, and ask them to cool it at work. They look you in the eye and say they will. How long do you think that commitment will last? They may be able to do it if they are responsible adults, but wait until they have their first fight. They won't want to speak to each other. Tension in the office will spiral. One of them will probably start looking for another job. It won't be pretty.

There is no one way to deal with this. You want to be sensitive to their dilemma, but you've also got to keep the organization productive and not have disruptions. In one situation, it might be best to separate them. In another, you might want to remind them of their promise to cool it. In another, you might decide to let one or the other go. All the while, you've got to be careful not to sexually discriminate against either person.

It's not easy.

Or let's suppose you're trying to choose a project manager for an upcoming project. On the one hand, you have a Baby Boomer you trust. He's a capable engineer who's overseen many projects, always bringing them in on time and under budget. On the other hand, you've got an up-and-coming Gen Xer who has fewer accomplishments to her credit and sometimes goes over deadline and budget, but has an incredible ability to think outside the box. One of her projects gained the attention of your industry's professional journal, which did a cover story on it. Who do you pick: Mr. Tried-and-True Baby Boomer or Ms. Up-and-Coming Gen X Superstar? And how do you deal with the one you don't pick?

There is no one way to do it. There is no "truth."

Management Principle #3: The One with the Most Tools Wins

All things being equal, the person with the most options will excel in any situation. For example, if you have two mechanics with exactly equal skills, abilities, intelligence, common sense, and motivation (yes, this is a fantasy), the mechanic who has one more tool in his toolbox will eventually surpass the other.

It's the same when you are dealing with people. All things being equal, the person with more options for handling a given situation will, in the long run, be more effective than someone with fewer choices.

For example, after reading this book, you may be more inclined to provide more structure and continuous feedback to the Gen Yers and Linksters working for you, as we suggest in Chapters 7 and 11. There's no guarantee that such an approach will work with all of them. You may have a precocious Gen Yer who has a Gen Xer's preference to work on his own. He will find your continual "attending" to him smothering. If you're not comfortable backing off, you must figure out a way to balance the two approaches or risk losing him. The manager who can flex her style to provide what the employee needs will, in the long run, be more effective than the manager who approaches every situation the same way.

In the past 25 years, participative management has gained a great deal of popularity. Savvy managers have learned that soliciting employee input into the decision-making process raises the odds that they will make better decisions and that the decisions will have greater support. Does that approach always work? Of course not. Sometimes it's a terrible approach that only frustrates the employee.

We are fervent proponents of participative management, both giving it and receiving it. If we're working for someone, we want that person to ask for our input before making a decision. Usually.

Our family went on a whitewater river rafting trip a few years ago. There were seven people in the raft, three on each side plus the hired guide who sat in the back. We all had paddles and were expected to row in sync forward or backward to steer the boat. The guide sat in the back and shouted the orders: "Right side forward, left side back . . . left side forward, right side back," and so on. As we raced through the rapids, the orders came quickly as we dodged boulders and tree trunks at breakneck speed.

This was not a time when we wanted the guide to ask for our input on which direction we should paddle. We just wanted, and needed, to be told what to do. Luckily, he was good at that. Later, around the campfire, as we discussed the next day's journey, the guide asked us for input on more comfortable seating arrangements in the raft, how we'd like to time the breaks, and what we'd like to have for lunch. He stepped out of the telling mode and into the asking mode—and we appreciated his ability to do both.

Management Principle #4: Mutual Reciprocity

To the degree you can give people what they need, they tend to give you what you need. Put another way: "What goes around, comes around." Think of someone who's made a positive change in your life. Perhaps it was a manager or a special teacher. Maybe it was a mentor who went out of his way to help you grow or a friend who was there for you when you needed emotional support.

Imagine you haven't seen this person in many years and he calls you in the middle of the night. He's been arrested and he asks you to come down and bail him out of jail for a minor infraction. Would you do it? Given no extenuating circumstances, of course you would. It's the principle of mutual reciprocity at work. The person invested in you and now you feel obligated to repay the debt. If there had been no previous investment—say, the person was a casual acquaintance—you may still bail him out because doing so enhances your perception that you're a good person, but you're just as likely to tell him no.

On the other hand, if he's wronged you in the past, like not repaying a loan, wrecking your car, or running off with your spouse, you're likely to hang up on him. That's negative mutual reciprocity. Either way, what goes around, comes around.

Work relationships tend to be particularly susceptible to mutual reciprocity. Unlike people you meet at a party and never see again, you see and interact with the people at work every day. There's a lot of give-and-take. We do things for our employees, and they do things for us. Consequently, the opportunity for mutual reciprocity, both positive and negative, is great.

For any relationship to be healthy, there needs to be a balance between the positive and the negative. Things work better when both parties feel like it's a fair deal. As a manager, you should do what you can to meet the needs of your employees. It simply raises the odds that they will go the extra mile to meet your needs when the time comes.

You may be saying, "Yeah, but we pay them. Isn't that enough?" Not necessarily. Think about all the special needs each generation has that we've discussed in this book. Baby Boomers need respect for their experiences and opportunities to contribute to the team. Gen Xers need independence and recognition for individual achievement. Gen Yers need structure and watchful interest. Not once have we discussed pay and benefits. We're simply saying that when people get their needs met at work they're more likely to be there for you when you need them.

This doesn't mean you must give them everything they want. There is a difference between wants and needs. *Wants* come from the surface; *needs* run deeper. Children want everything they ask for and will throw a tantrum if they don't get it. Children need love combined with discipline, even if they don't always like the discipline part. Most adults want to make more money but need to feel they are paid a fair amount for the contributions they make. Most of us want things to be easy but need to successfully overcome challenges. Some employees want constant approval but need genuine, honest feedback. The principle of mutual reciprocity applies when you give people what they need, which is not necessarily what they want.

Tailoring Your Mode of Management

Since each person brings with her a set of unique needs and the principle of mutual reciprocity dictates that we do what we can to meet those needs, it makes sense that we tailor our management approach to create the best working relationship.

In the following model, we offer five different modes of management: directing, teaching, persuading, collaborating, and coordinating. We'll introduce each and then look at how you can apply them in the right circumstances.

Directing Mode

As the name implies, when you are in this mode, you call the shots and give the orders. You tell people what to do, when to do it, and where to do it. This doesn't mean you are rude or overly authoritative or we would have named it the dictating mode instead of the directing mode.

The guide on our whitewater rafting trip is a perfect example of someone using the directing mode. He told us what to do, and we did it. There was little interaction among us except to clarify what he meant. The line of communication was mostly one way, from him to us. Occasionally, someone would ask him to clarify what he meant or whether that person should do something about the tree branch up ahead, but otherwise, he directed, and we followed.

We normally think of the directing mode when dealing with Gen Yers and Linksters. They're young and new and often need to be told what to do. Of course, that's not always the case (there is no "truth"), but the rule of thumb is to turn first to directing mode when working with younger people. They will appreciate it because it removes any fuzziness from their tasks. Essentially, first timers are not ready for anything more advanced or subtle.

Teaching Mode

Jack Welch, the legendary CEO of General Electric, once said of his stint at GE, "My main job was developing talent. I was a gardener providing water and other nourishment to our top 750 people. Of course, I had to pull out some weeds, too." He often said that the main job of a manager is to be a teacher. He practiced what he preached. Over 17 years, he presented more than 250 lecture sessions to over 15,000 managers at GE's training center.[1]

In the teaching mode, the manager seizes opportunities to encourage the growth of those she manages. She shows people how to do what she wants done. It can be as simple as demonstrating how to perform a task on the computer or as complex as conducting a lecture about the intricacies of a new microprocessor.

The question is: What makes a good teacher? We've been conducting seminars all over the world for 30 years, and we've discovered some basics of teaching that seem to raise the odds a seminar will be successful. They also happen to be the same steps, modified to fit the situation, that good managers use to teach subordinates and colleagues effectively, whether it's a group lecture or a one-on-one discussion.

1. **Start with a story or facts that capture the listener immediately.** Stating that the reject rate in a manufacturing setting is outside acceptable parameters is not nearly as compelling as saying, "This month, 92,000 wafers had to be scrapped. That cost the company $4,324,000. That's $51,888,000 per year. If we can reduce that waste by one percent, we'll save the company more than half a million dollars per year."

When Larry teaches seminars on management techniques, instead of starting out with a long-winded introduction of himself (boring), followed by a lecture on Theory X versus Theory Y (even more boring), he tells a story about a fellow he met at Southwest Airlines who went out of his way to help him. He wraps up the story by saying that when he asked the fellow what made him so enthusiastic about his job the fellow replied that he had a great boss. Larry uses that story to start a discussion of what constitutes a great boss.

2. **Engage the learner.** Larry then asks the audience members to write a list of words describing the best and worst managers they've ever had. He engages them in a back-and-forth discussion of these characteristics. As the discussion proceeds, he lists the characteristics on a flipchart under one of two headings: good or bad. Once the audience members are engaged and have a framework in their minds of what good managers and bad ones look like, they are ready to hear about Theory X and Theory Y and how they can apply those theories to their own management practices.

3. **Show rather than tell.** You can tell someone that a poor manager is indecisive or you can show it by having the person think of a poor manager he's known who couldn't make a decision. Because there's a personal connection, the latter approach is always more powerful.

Making it personal makes it real. You can tell someone that a one percent reduction in the interest rate on a home loan will result in significant savings, or you can show him by working out the numbers on his own mortgage so he can see for himself what the savings will be. You can tell someone how to drive a car, but it's better to show her so she can see how you do it. You can tell someone that if you never say no to a child, you will likely create a monster, or you can show that person by telling a story about someone you know who created a little monster.

Stories are powerful ways to show concepts, which is why books and movies are so popular.

4. **Have them try while you watch.** In many cases, showing is not enough. You can tell someone how to drive a car and demonstrate it until the cows come home, but until he gets behind the wheel and experiences it for himself, he will never be able to do it. No amount of discussion prepares him for the feeling he will have when he presses on the gas and the car jumps ahead. That's why driving schools always include time on the road with a driving instructor.

Until you watch the student perform, you don't know if he truly understands how to correct his mistakes. Two years ago, we hired a part-time Gen Yer to help with office duties. His first assignment was to do a direct mailing. It required folding 18,000 brochures, sealing each with a sticker, and stamping them. Larry demonstrated how it was to be done for the young man and then left for the airport without watching him do it.

When Larry returned at the end of the week, all 18,000 brochures were sealed, stamped, and ready to go—except that the address had been folded to the inside so there was no way to deliver them. They say that life is a series of learning experiences, and that day Larry learned the importance of Step 4 in the teaching process.

Like Jack Welch, good managers apply the teaching mode across the generational spectrum. It is likely, however, that you will use this mode most when interacting with Gen Yers and Linksters because they usually have the most to learn about everything from policies and procedures to the subtleties of organizational politics.

Persuading Mode

When in persuading mode, the manager tries to convince people by help-ing them understand why something must be done. If the directing mode means the manager tells the person what to do and the teaching mode means she shows him how to do it, the persuading mode means giving him the reason to do it. This is where inspiration, eloquence, and the power of personality combine to show the bigger picture, demonstrate why it's important, and influence the follower to get on board.

When Kim Jordan, CEO of New Belgium Brewing, stands before em-ployees every month and shares the financials of the company, she's in the persuading mode. She's persuading them to go the extra mile by helping them see what's in it for them.

In the movie *Saving Private Ryan,* the platoon led by Captain Miller (played by Tom Hanks) comes upon the bodies of several GIs. After tak-ing cover in the bushes, they realize the men were ambushed by a German machine gun nest located up the hill. When Miller starts making prepara-tions to attack the nest, the men try to talk him out of it. One says, "Captain, we could still skip it and accomplish our mission." Miller im-mediately shifts into persuading mode and replies, "Is that what you want to do, Mellish? You just want to leave it here so they can ambush the next company that comes along?" The soldier replies, "No sir, that's not what I'm saying. It just seems like an unnecessary risk, given our objective." With that, Miller retorts, "Our objective is to win the war." Then he picks up his rifle and heads up the hill. The men follow him with no further argument.[2] With two brief sentences, Miller persuades his platoon to act by making it clear there was a higher purpose at work.

You may be saying, "Hey, it was the military. No officer needs to do any persuading. You just give orders and they follow." And that was Miller's ace in the hole—"Get up that hill. That's an order." But people do things a lot more enthusiastically when they understand the reason for doing so, especially when it's something they don't want to do. So, in this case, Miller's *persuading mode* paid off. He could always resort to the *directing mode* if he needed to.

Whether it's explaining to a Linkster serving food in an assisted-living facility why chewing gum is inappropriate or convincing your team of Gen X engineers of the value of coordinating their efforts on a project, the persuading mode is an effective approach to getting people on board and motivating them to get the job done.

Collaborating Mode

In the collaborating mode, the manager relates to her colleagues in a more collegial fashion than in the directing mode, teaching mode, and persuading mode. She may reserve the right to make the final decision, but will consult with colleagues and subordinates before doing so. If there is a problem, she asks for input and discusses possible solutions rather than tells people what to do to solve it.

Whereas the collaborating mode would have been highly inappropriate for our guide to use while we were shooting rapids, it was perfect when discussing plans for the next day around the campfire.

Collaboration assumes a certain amount of trust in the abilities of those with whom you collaborate. For example, you would apply the collaborating mode if you were discussing with your son which graduate school he should attend. You'd ask him about his interests and what his concerns are. You'd want to know why he was considering one school over another and you'd offer your thoughts on what factors he should consider when choosing. In the end, however, the decision would be his. The relationship during the discussion is collegial.

You would use the persuading mode to convince him to go to one particular school. In the directing mode, you would tell him what school he must go to if he wants your support. Assuming the young man is an adult and is competent, the collaborating mode is by far the superior approach.

On the other hand, the collaborating mode would be highly inappropriate when discussing with your six-year-old daughter what school she should go to. In that case, you are the adult, you know far more than she, and giving her a real choice in the matter would be ludicrous.

As we noted, the collaborating mode requires a certain level of trust among those who are collaborating. If the manager hopes to get honest answers when he solicits input, it helps if those being solicited feel comfortable giving him input. If they don't trust him, they're likely to withhold vital information. Likewise, the manager must trust those with whom he is collaborating enough to know there can be a give-and-take of ideas. If the follower hasn't proven she can contribute, the conversation becomes lopsided.

Larry Tells a Story

Last year my wife, CJ, had a cornea transplant. As you can imagine, any transplant is a serious operation. Once the ophthalmologist determined she needed it, we searched for the best cornea transplant specialist we could find. We settled on the one everyone said was the best. He had a habit, however, that almost convinced us to find another surgeon: Every time there was a decision to be made, he would ask us what we would like to do.

For example, CJ needed a lens implant in the other eye to repair an injury that had occurred when she was a teenager. We asked him whether it would be advisable to do both eyes at the same time. Rather than telling us, he said it was up to us. We asked about the risks associated with doing one eye at a time versus doing both. He went over them but repeated that it was really up to us. It was very frustrating. He didn't seem to understand that we were the laypeople in this situation and he the professional. We wanted him to assume the directing mode and *tell us what was the best thing to do*. He persisted in using the collaborating mode, and we were ready to strangle him.

We finally decided to do both eyes at the same time. The operations were successful, and he proved to deserve his reputation as a brilliant surgeon, but he almost lost a customer because he wouldn't use the right management mode for the situation. You don't collaborate with those who are not qualified to collaborate with you. If you do, you'll get lousy input from them, and they'll get frustrated with you.

Because of their experience, you would apply the collaborating mode of management most often when interacting with Baby Boomers and Gen Xers. Again, however, there is no "truth." You may have some Gen Yers who have established enough credibility to hold their own in a collaborative discussion.

For example, you may go into directing mode when you explain roles and responsibilities to a new Gen Yer. You will probably have to shift into teaching mode to show him the best way to get things done. You may have to use the persuading mode to convince him that it's necessary to cover up his tattoos when dealing with customers. You probably wouldn't use the collaborating mode unless you ventured into an area where he has the chops to engage with you as an equal. For example, if he's a technical guru, you would probably collaborate when you discuss technology with him. If he has more knowledge than you on the subject, he may, at times, move into directing, teaching, and persuading you.

Coordinating Mode

This is the mode most managers want to use and most followers want to receive. You use the coordinating mode when you trust that your followers know what they are doing and you want to stay out of their way so they can do it.

Used appropriately, it is the mark of good management. You clarify what you want your followers to accomplish and then you hold them accountable for results. They decide how to accomplish the task. There is very little discussion about methodology, incremental progress, organizational problems, or anything else pertaining to the job.

When this mode is used inappropriately, it's called management by abdication. We saw a classic example of this during Wall Street's 2008 financial meltdown. The SEC and other regulating bodies managed the financial industry with the coordinating mode exclusively, and they even did a lousy job of that because they didn't hold the industry accountable for results.

On a local level, a good example of the coordinating mode would be the project manager of a building project. She hires subcontractors to complete various tasks according to a schedule. Once the direction is set, she leaves them alone but is available if they need help. She would probably slip into collaborating mode to discuss a problem with them and arrive at a solution. She may resort to persuading mode, teaching mode, or directing mode to communicate what needs to be done, why it needs to be done, how to get it done, and the consequences of not getting it done. But primarily, she simply coordinates the work and holds the subcontractors accountable for results.

In general, Baby Boomers have reached a point in their careers where they expect their bosses to deal with them in the coordinating mode. They feel they've earned it and they probably have. Gen Xers, by virtue of their latchkey signposts and their independent nature, expect to be treated with the coordinating mode on the day they start, whether they deserve it or not. By now, most have the experience to legitimately demand it. Because of their relative inexperience, most Gen Yers are not candidates for the coordinating mode of management, especially early in a new job, but that will change as they get more experience.

Working the Mode Management Model

The question facing managers who use the Mode Management Model (Figure 12.1) is when, how, and with whom to use each mode.

The table in Figure 12.1 is designed to give you general guidelines for applying the five management modes. We remind you that these are only general guidelines and not hard-and-fast rules. *There is no "truth."*

For example, the model indicates that you would normally operate in the directing mode with a Linkster. That doesn't mean all Linksters can't work on their own and should be directed. When Meagan was 16, she worked in a hobby shop. The woman who owned it came to trust her enough that she gave her a key and empowered her to open the store and run it on weekends with no supervision. At that point, she was managing Meagan in the coordinating mode.

Likewise, you may have a Baby Boomer you need to bring up to speed on some new software. If he has no familiarity with the product, you'll probably apply the teaching mode and even the directing mode to tell him what to do and how to do it, even though you normally deal with him in the coordinating mode. The point is, the model is flexible. You should adopt the management mode that fits each individual according to his or her needs at the time and in the situation.

Tasks and Procedures (Clear vs. Unclear)

From completing a claims form to carrying out a surgical step, tasks and procedures define how to do a job. When the tasks and procedures are clear, you either use the directing mode if people don't know what to do or the coordinating mode if they do.

For example, if you are working in a fast-food restaurant, the procedures for making a crunchy bacon jalapeno burrito are prescribed and clear. If you're working with a Linkster employee who doesn't know how to do it, use the directing and teaching modes. If the Linkster knows how to do this task and she's proven to be trustworthy, you would probably apply the coordinating mode.

Figure 12.1. Mode Management Model®

Situation/Mode	Directing Mode	Teaching Mode	Persuading Mode	Collaborating Mode	Coordinating Mode
Tasks and Procedures	clear	unclear	unclear	unclear	clear
Need for Speed	high	low	low	low	high
Need for Coordination	low	high or low	high or low	high	low
Generation	Linkster & Gen Y	all generations	all generations	Gen X, Boomers, Traditionals	Gen X, Boomers, Traditionals
Proven Competence	low	low	low and high	high	high

On the other hand, if the task or procedure is not clear, then teaching mode, persuading mode, or collaborating mode would be called for.

For example, a Gen X account executive who reports to you has a client who's threatening to take his business elsewhere because product shipments are chronically delayed. You can teach her about the system to help her fix the problem. You might say, "Jane, you might want to check with Smith in shipping. He can work wonders getting product out the door." You might have to use the persuading mode to get her to take an action she is resisting: "Jane, my experience with this client is that if you call him up and do some serious groveling, he usually calms down." Most likely, you would go into collaborating mode and brainstorm possible ways to approach the customer and then let her pick the best action. One, two, or all three responses would be appropriate.

Need for Speed

When the need for speed is high, the directing mode or coordinating mode are usually the best ways to go, depending on the proven competence of the person being managed. For example, imagine you are a fire captain. You arrive at the fire with your engine company. Decisions about how to attack the fire must be made quickly. There is no time to discuss the pros and cons of one approach or another.

You quickly go into directing mode and start making decisions and barking orders. It's the appropriate mode for the situation. Once you've told people where you want them to go, because they are professionals who know what they are doing, you slip into coordinating mode and let them do their jobs.

When the need for speed is low, you can take the time to teach, persuade, and collaborate. In the case of the fire captain, those modes would be appropriate back at the firehouse as you conduct a "lessons learned" discussion about the fire.

Need for Coordination

When you need consensus on details, there are differences of opinion as to the best path to follow, or the need for discussion and interaction is high, the teaching, persuading, and collaborating modes are preferable.

For example, June is a nurse manager in a nursing home. One of the residents has recently developed a contagious condition that will require quarantining him to protect the other residents and the staff. Although there are procedures in place to handle this sort of thing, this is the first time it's been necessary to apply them. It will require the coordination of everyone's efforts to make sure the quarantine stays intact. June will very likely apply the teaching mode to bring everyone up to speed on the quarantine procedures, the persuading mode to make sure people understand the seriousness of the situation, and the collaborating mode to work out the details of who's going to do what and to get everyone on board with the effort.

When there is little or no need for this kind of discussion, directing mode or coordinating mode will usually suffice. For example, one of our clients emailed Larry with a question about an item on an invoice. Since Heather (our Gen Y assistant) does the billing, she was in a better position to explain the charge to the client. Larry forwarded the email to Heather with a coordinating mode note: "Heather, please handle." She called the client, explained the item to him, and solved the problem. No need for a lot of discussion between Larry and Heather. He gave her a task. He trusted she knew how to do it and could handle it on her own. Coordinating mode was the appropriate approach in this instance.

On the other hand, if this had been a tricky situation with the client and Larry wanted to make sure it was handled properly, he would have noted on the email, "See me about this one." They would have discussed the situation and agreed on how she was going to handle it: classic collaborating mode. Or, if Heather had never handled a problem like this and Larry wanted to develop her skills, he would have applied teaching mode followed by directing mode and micromanaged her through the process.

Generations

The management mode you adopt is highly dependent on the situation at hand. Are the tasks and procedures clear or vague? Is there a need for speed? Is complicated coordination necessary? In general, you can assume that for Linksters and many Gen Yers you would adopt the directing, teaching, and persuading modes early on. As they develop and are able to operate more independently, you would transition your management mode from left to right across the model, with the ultimate goal of being able to adopt a coordinating mode as much as possible.

For Gen Xers, Baby Boomers, and Traditionals, the collaborating and coordinating modes will most often be the appropriate approaches.

Again, it depends on the situation and the needs of the individual. For example, a Traditional who's learning to use technology will appreciate the directing mode. Tell her exactly what to do and in what order. On the other hand, being so directive in how she deals with a customer she has dealt with successfully in the past might cause her to resent your intrusion.

Proven Competence

Of all the factors in the Mode Management Model, this one should have the greatest influence in determining which mode to use. The questions to always ask are:

> - Has the person proven her competence in handling the task at hand?
> - Does she know what to do?
> - Have I seen her do it?
> - If I were not there to monitor the situation, would she know what to do without my input?
> - Would I be pleased with her performance if she acted independently?

Being able to answer "yes" to these questions means the individual has proven competence regarding the issue at hand.

For example, Bob, a Baby Boomer, has been a top-producing account executive for a software company for eight years. His numbers exceed expectations, and he manages his territory superbly. Bob adjusts easily to change. For example, his company recently expanded its focus to include solution selling in addition to simple "product in a box" sales. Bob adjusted to this shift quite easily and his average solution/consultation revenues are among the highest in the company. To accomplish this, Bob effectively uses resources inside and outside the home office.

Bob has proven that he's competent in running his territory. Using any modes other than coordinating and collaborating risks making him feel like he's being micromanaged. To manage Bob, you leave him alone and let him do his job. You may collaborate with him on strategy, policies, or special problems, but the decisions on what to do and how to do it are up to him.

Compare Bob with Julie, a Gen Yer who has been an inside sales representative for the same company for the past three years. She was moved to outside sales two weeks ago. She now has face-to-face contact with customers and is responsible for coordinating efforts with inside sales. She is bright, motivated, and educated (MBA from Stanford), and has a wealth of sales talent (she was a top producer with the inside organization). At first, Julie seemed excited about the new position, but lately she seems overwhelmed by all there is to learn.

What management mode would you use with Julie?

It's tempting to say that you would use the coordinating mode because Julie sounds so smart, accomplished, and competent, but that doesn't make up for the fact that she has never done outside sales. For the time being, we have to assume her competency in this area is low. Until she proves otherwise, adopting the directing, teaching, and persuading modes will better fit her needs and is less likely to allow her to get into trouble.

For example, weeks ago, Julie made a cold call to a company that seemed to have great potential. The contact person seemed interested but said he would get back to her. Twenty minutes ago, the same person called and said his boss is interested. The catch is that the boss is only in town for the afternoon and wants to see what Julie has to offer before she leaves. If Julie gets this order, it would mean several million dollars in revenue for the company. Assuming you're not going to take this away from Julie to do yourself, in what mode would you manage her through the process?

The answer, of course, is that you would adopt a highly directing mode, hovering over her to help her get the sale. At this point, she would appreciate your mother hen approach. After she's been selling for a while, however, and has learned the ropes, she would resent being so closely *managed*. It would start to feel more like hen pecking to her. That's when you start moving toward collaborating and finally coordinating with her.

Here's another example. Dave is a Gen Xer. He started working in the warehouse of your plumbing supply company four years ago. Dave has an associate's degree in communications from the local junior college and is working on his bachelor's degree in business at the local university. Because of his outstanding performance, you promoted him to operations manager 18 months ago.

Dave is enthusiastic about his new position. He comes in early and stays late. He often works on weekends. Dave seems to believe in his employees and makes certain that they receive their share of resources.

He also seems eager to prove that his unit is the top performer in the company. Although you are pleased with the general performance of Dave's unit, you are concerned that he is burning himself out. You suspect that he is not delegating enough to his people, which is typical of independent Gen Xers. When you discussed this with him, he admitted that he sometimes does work that people on his team should be doing, but excused it by saying that they have plenty to do and that his job is to take the "tough assignments."

You fill in for Dave while he's on vacation. You notice that employees come to you to handle problems that, given the employees' time and job tenure, they should be able to handle easily themselves. When Dave returns from vacation, you watch him interact with employees. If there is anything unusual or problematic about what they are discussing, Dave usually says, "Let me handle that."

How would you proceed?

With Dave's experience and his gung-ho attitude, it's tempting to continue in the coordinating mode by leaving him alone, but that would constitute management by abdication on your part. He has proven himself competent in some parts of his job, but when it comes to delegating, he's only proven his incompetence. Obviously, applying the teaching and persuading modes will be necessary. If those don't work, your next step is moving to a directing mode by ordering him to delegate.

Or consider Jennifer. A Gen Yer, Jennifer is a contract monitor for outside vendors. She has been in the position for 12 months. She has a degree in business administration and previously worked for 18 months as a purchasing agent for a large electronics company.

Jennifer is very organized and meticulous about details. She makes a "to do" list every day and uses a daily planner. She follows up in writing when dealing with vendors, especially when there is a problem to be resolved. She usually avoids face-to-face discussions with problem vendors, however, and seems to lack confidence in her ability to deal with confrontation. You have observed her, on rare occasions, use confrontational skills with vendors effectively, but only when she could not avoid it. Up to now, you've been applying the coordinating mode of management with her.

Lately, you've received complaints that the building is not adequately cleaned at night by the contracted janitor crew. Jennifer took immediate action on these complaints by speaking to the janitors. The complaints, however, have persisted. As Jennifer's manager, you ask her about this problem using the collaborating mode. Her desired course of action is to speak to the janitors again because, she says, the owner of the janitorial service is mean, obnoxious, and sometimes tries to flirt with her.

It's tempting to let her handle it that way except that it doesn't get the problem solved. You may need to use the persuading mode to convince her that she needs to deal with the owner so that the problem gets resolved and so that she learns how to handle these kinds of situations in the future.

Dealing with Jealousy Generated by Mode Management

In our Mode Management seminars, we are often asked how one should deal with any jealousy that might arise among employees. A Gen Yer might think it unfair that you micromanage her while you let her Gen X coworker operate independently. Or a Baby Boomer might resent the fact that you spend so much time with the younger employees and seem to ignore him. A Gen Xer might feel like you're playing favorites with a fellow Gen Xer because she seems to get more direct coaching from you than he does.

The answer lies in complete transparency. If employees don't understand that there is a logical rationale behind your behavior, it is easy for them to think the worst and assume you are showing favoritism or arbitrarily picking on them. We tell managers using the Mode Management approach to be completely candid about what they are doing—that they share the model with their employees and explain that it is simply a formalized approach to doing what all good managers do anyway, which is to give people as much attention, guidance, and direction as they need, based on the needs of the organization, the circumstances in which the activities in question occur, and the capabilities of the person in question. In our management training seminars, we provide the students with a poster-size copy of the Mode Management Matrix to hang on the wall of their offices so they can refer to it as they apply or discuss the model. For example, when giving an assignment, say, "Jerry, I know that I normally take a *coordinator* role with you on your projects, but since this one has some sensitive political implications, I'd like to be more of a *collaborator* here, so I'd like you to keep me up-to-date on the project's progress so we can discuss strategy as we go along." Or, "Brenda, if it seems unfair that I'm giving Jan freer reign on her assignments than I do with you, it's that Jan's assignments are pretty straightforward, so she doesn't really require my input. Consequently, I can adopt the *coordinator* role with her. Your assignments, on the other hand, are a lot more complicated than hers, so I think it's appropriate for us to *collaborate* a bit as we go." Or, "Bob, you know that I practice Mode Management, and in this situation, I'm going to adopt the *director* role because we need to make a decision *now.*"

The Bottom Line

Managing people effectively means making sure they get what they need so they feel a balance between the efforts they put forth and the benefits they derive. In their heads, it needs to look like a fair deal.

Meeting people's individual needs requires adjusting how you deal with each person. One size does not fit all. It's useful to be able to flex your management mode to fit the needs of each person you manage in the different situations each faces.

One factor to take into account is the person's generational status, but you also need to consider the clarity of the tasks and procedures, the need for speed, and the need for coordination. Most importantly, you must account for the level of the person's proven competence with the task at hand.

Resolving Intergenerational Conflict

Conflict is a normal part of all work environments. People disagree about everything from how work should be done to who gets a better parking space. Often, these conflicts can be traced to differences in generational orientation. A Baby Boomer's need to have buy-in from the entire team before making a decision may clash with a Gen Xer's desire to make a unilateral decision and move on. A Gen Yer may need direction that her Gen X boss doesn't think he should have to take the time to give. A Traditional may find a Gen Yer's lack of formality and manners offensive.

As a manager in these situations, it would behoove you to consider the generational factors that can influence the situation. Here are some questions to ask and some steps to take as you deal with the situation:

What generations are involved?
Is this conflict generational or is something else going on?
What values are at stake for each generation involved?
What are the perceptions each participant has of the situation?
How would each participant describe the positions of those with whom they are conflicting?
How can I communicate to each of them that their values are important?
What Mode Management style normally works best with each of the people involved?
Is that management style appropriate for this conflict?
What do I need to change to improve the situation?

What would be the ideal outcome?
What solution would I find acceptable?
What will I do if the situation remains unresolved?

Steps for Resolving Conflict

Since conflicts often arise in a multigenerational environment, it's helpful to have a forethought strategy. Here are some suggestions, based on the concept of Constructive Confrontation® as covered in *Absolute Honesty: Building a Corporate Culture That Values Straight Talk and Rewards Integrity*, by Larry Johnson and Bob Phillips.[1]

1. Do Your Homework

If possible, take time to think about the disagreement. Prepare your thoughts, get your data together, think about what you want to accomplish, and prepare a plan for the discussion. We always do better in any kind of discussion or presentation when we are prepared. This step helps you prepare for the confrontation.

The steps for doing your homework are:

1. **Identify the issue.** If you don't know exactly what you want, how can you clarify it for the person you are confronting?

2. **Decide if it is an issue.** Not all issues need to be confronted. Balance the wisdom of picking your battles with the need to teach people how to treat you.

3. **Identify the desired outcome.** If you don't know what you want as a result of the confrontation, you'll probably end up with something else. Defining what you want ahead of time can help you avoid confronting the person just to make a point, prove yourself right, or punish the person.

4. **Determine your interests and theirs.** Behind every "position" taken in a negotiation or an argument, there is an interest. If you can identify your interest and theirs ahead of time, you will raise the odds you will find an agreement that meets your mutual interests.

5. **Identify alternatives.** It is rare that the outcome of a confrontation is exactly as you planned. In fact, this is appropriate since a confrontation always involves the input of one or more other people. If you have

thought about the alternatives prior to the confrontation, you are more likely to arrive at an outcome that will be satisfactory to you and the others involved.

6. **Create a plan to get there.** Even if your plan doesn't end up being the one followed, it provides a starting point.

2. Open the Debate

Ask the other person to describe the issue as she sees it. Then ask her to help you define the best outcome for the discussion: for example, increased profit, reduced risk, improved quality.

➢ **Describe the problem or issue specifically.** In clear, concise, nonaccusatory terms, describe the problem in detail.

➢ **Use "I" language.** The word "you" in a potentially negative situation will almost always be interpreted as accusatory. The thrust of Constructive Confrontation® is to focus on, and solve, problems and disagreements. It is not to focus on the faults and foibles of people.

➢ **Focus on the "present" and "future."** It is impossible to change the past. When the discussion dwells on events that have already occurred, there is a tendency for all involved to defend their positions and not move to solve the problem.

3. Open Your Ears

Listen to the other person's point of view without prejudice or thinking about the arguments you can marshal against her point of view. Ask questions to clarify her position and to validate the data. Good listening includes:

➢ **Attending.** This includes eye contact, body language, and the nonverbal clues that let the other person know that you are listening.

➢ **Paraphrasing.** This does not mean repeating exactly what the other person said. It is simply summarizing the content that the other person conveyed so you know that you interpreted it as it was meant.

➢ **Clarifying.** This usually takes the form of asking questions that ensure that the content you received was the content intended. It also can clarify if your interests will be met, and if not, where you can focus to meet those interests.

▷ **Empathizing.** Until the other person understands that you understand how he feels about the issue, he will not be willing to listen to what you have to say about the issue.

▷ **Contributing to their reality.** This is simply a way of showing respect for the other person's side by taking his perspective and adding to it.

4. Open Your Mouth

Offer your point of view in a clear and firm manner supporting your view with data. (Having done your homework really helps here.)

▷ **Use "I" language.** Remember, the word "you" can be accusatorial. Instead of, "Joe, you're wrong on this," try, "Joe, here's the way I see it."

▷ **Focus on the present and the future; beware of the past.**

▷ **Claim your reality as your own.** Phrase your case in terms of the way you see it, not as if it were the "truth."

▷ **Be clear and firm about what you need.** To paraphrase Mick Jagger: "You can't always get what you want, but if you try . . . you can get what you need."

▷ **Remember the difference between "position" and "interest."** What you need is your "interest"; what you want is your "position."

5. Open Your Mind

Direct the discussion toward a goal that works for both of you and, more importantly, is the best solution for the company.

▷ **Agree on the outcome.** Ask the other person to help you define the best outcome for the discussion: for example, increased profit, reduced risk, improved quality. The point is to mutually agree on a goal for the discussion that rises above turf or ego issues and goes directly to the heart of what is best for the company, the community, or even the world. Then direct the discussion to that end.

▷ **Review the data.** It is tempting to try to reach a solution before all the facts are in. Doing so will often result in a poor decision.

▷ **Integrate their concerns and wants if possible.** Remember, their trust comes from knowing that you have their interests in mind as well as your own.

➢ **Ask for possible solutions.** There is usually more than one way to solve a problem. By asking the other person for ideas, you increase the chances you will get a solution she can live with.

6. Close the Deal

Restate the agreed-upon solution. Assign responsibilities and follow-up dates. Agree to disagree and commit if necessary.

➢ **Clarify who will do what.** In a heated conversation, often the final assignments associated with a resolution of the confrontation can be vague. It is important to make sure each person in the discussion is aware of what he or she is going to do differently as a result of the confrontation. You might even want to write out the agreement to minimize misunderstanding.

➢ **Agree to disagree and commit.** No matter what your feelings are at the end of the confrontation, whatever decision made must now be supported. Bad mouthing a decision or the outcome of a confrontation is not acceptable.

➢ **Follow up and measure.** Set a date to rediscuss the issue to ensure that the solutions you agreed upon are working.

A Quick-Reference Guide to the Book

This appendix is a quick reference of key points in the book.

Signposts: Harbingers of Things to Come

Personal Signposts

From the day we are born, our lives are filled with experiences, some of which make a lasting impression on us and affect the way we live from that point on. We call these experiences *personal signposts.* In contrast, we acquire *group signposts* through associations with a particular group. Our feelings about race and gender differences are often associated with these *group signposts.*

Generational Signposts

A *generational signpost* is an event or cultural phenomenon that is specific to one generation. Generational signposts shape, influence, and drive expectations, actions, and mind-sets about the products we buy, the companies for whom we work, and our expectations about life in general.

Life Laws

Events that occur before you are born or when you are too young to remember them are called *life laws.* They've always been there. For example, the airport security procedures that we endure today are *life laws* for those too young to remember the way they were before September 11, 2001.

Generations Defined

There are a variety of methods for defining a generation: When the members were born, when they came of age, and the president who was in power when they were born are just a few. The definition we use for this book is:

> A group of individuals born and living contemporaneously who have common knowledge and experiences that affect their thoughts, attitudes, values, beliefs, and behaviors.

Five Generations at Work

History is in the making. Never before have five generations occupied the workplace as they do now. The three main groups are:

- Baby Boomers, aka the Woodstock Generation, born between 1946 and 1964
- Generation X, aka Latchkey Kids, born between 1965 and 1980
- Generation Y, aka the Entitled Ones, born between 1981 and 1995

There are also a few members of the Traditional Generation still working (aka Depression Babies, born before 1945), and we're beginning to see the first of the Linkster Generation appearing on the job site (aka the Facebook Crowd, born after 1995). As of this writing, there are five generations working.

A couple of thoughts about signposts:

- Generational signposts bond us.
- Signposts affect everyone—just not in the same way.

Cuspers

People born close to the dividing line between generations are known as cuspers. They have the advantage of having one foot in two generational worlds. According to Lynne C. Lancaster and David Stillman in their book *When Generations Collide: Who They Are. Why They Clash. How to Solve the Generational Puzzle at Work,*[1] cuspers have a natural ability to identify with multiple generations' beliefs and interests. They also have special access to both generations.

Generational Myopia

In our work as organizational consultants, we often hear managers complain that young people today have little or no work ethic. There may be some truth to this, but to tar an entire generation with one descriptor misses the tremendous value young people can contribute. Like them or not, young workers are the future of our companies, our communities, and our world. We call this tarring of one generation by another *generational myopia.*

New Generations of Leaders

According to a survey of 578 companies by the Boston College Center on Aging and Work, only 33 percent say they have analyzed workplace demographics and made projections about the retirement rates of their workers.[2] This is scary, because according to David Delong, author of *Lost Knowledge: Confronting the Threat of an Aging Workforce* (Oxford University Press, 2004), the vacuum in leadership that will be created by the exiting of Baby Boomers from the workplace will threaten the survival of every organization on the planet. Up-and-coming Generation X and Generation Y are looking for something far different from their careers than what the Baby Boomers wanted. Companies will be wise to take heed.

The Postwar Baby Boom

When the soldiers came home in 1945, the birthrate began to soar. By 1965, the largest generation in history, Baby Boomers, had been created.

Signposts for the Baby Boomer Generation

> ➤ The GI Bill
> ➤ *Dr. Spock's Baby and Child Care*

> The Soviet Union Goes Atomic
> Overcrowded Schools
> *Brown v. Board of Education*
> Television Reflects Our Angst
> *The Feminine Mystique*
> Watergate and Vietnam
> Civil Rights Movement
> The Decadent 1980s

Tips for Managing Boomers

As they prepare to retire, many Baby Boomers are looking forward to an encore, either by starting a new career or by engaging in an active retirement. Unfortunately, because their stock investments and 401ks took such a drastic hit during the economic meltdown of 2008, many Baby Boomers will have to wait to do either. In an AARP survey published in May 2008, 27 percent of workers ages 45 and up said the economic slowdown had prompted them to postpone plans to retire.[3] The good news for employers is that Baby Boomers will continue to be in the workforce for some time to come. The bad news for Gen X and Gen Y is that Baby Boomers will continue to be in the workforce for some time to come.

1. Don't Ignore Them

Boomers need love too. And they may be around a lot longer than some of your Gen Xers and Gen Yers.

2. Make Them Mentors

Assigning a *sempai* (mentor) to a *kohai* (mentee) is a common practice among Japanese companies. A promising young manager, the *kohai,* is assigned to an older, more experienced manager, the *sempai*. The *sempai* is usually outside the *kohai*'s chain of command and functions much like a "godfather" to him or her. In addition to his normal managerial duties, the *sempai*'s job involves helping the *kohai* succeed in all areas of work from technical questions to operational issues to organizational politics.

3. Ask for Continuing Contributions

Asking Baby Boomers to recommit themselves to their jobs in new and creative ways will often recapture their hearts and stimulate them to contribute until the day they leave.

4. Don't Give Up on Them

Neglecting the growth needs of Baby Boomers is understandable. After all, they'll be leaving soon, so why waste money training them when it can be better spent on someone younger?

That can be a mistake. With many Boomers planning to extend their careers because they can't afford to retire or because they simply like working, they may be around longer than you think. Since most Gen Xers and Gen Yers view their jobs as temporary assignments, paying to train older employees may be the safer bet. Even if Boomers retire before you get a return on your investment, you may be able to recover that investment with some creative planning like hiring them as consultants after they leave.

5. Deal with Resistance

Soon-retiring Boomers may resist adapting to changes your organization is implementing. If you simply let them resist, figuring they will retire soon, you risk eroding your credibility with the Gen Xers and Gen Yers who are watching. Down the road, you may want them to make a change they don't want and they'll remember how you handled change with your Boomers. Your failure to insist that the Boomers "get with the program" may come back to bite you.

6. Confront Negative Behavior

Occasionally, a Baby Boomer may adopt a less-than-positive attitude as she approaches retirement. It may be based on unhappiness with the company or her circumstances or on mixed feelings about leaving. Or, it may simply be a product of "Short-Timer Syndrome," where her mind and spirit have moved on to the next step in the road. Whatever the cause, if it's creating a problem that is affecting the quality or quantity of output, profitability, customer satisfaction, or team morale, the manager must deal with it. Here are five steps for having a problem-solving conversation with the wayward Boomer.

1. Describe the problem.
2. Explain your concern.
3. Listen to and acknowledge his or her issues.
4. Ask for an agreement to change.
5. Clarify what's been agreed upon.
6. Express confidence and confidently expect change.

7. Offer Opportunities to Volunteer

Many Baby Boomers have reached a point in their lives where they want to give back to society, perhaps to fulfill unrealized desires to change the world that have been dormant since the 1960s or because they feel it's time to balance the scales of karma. In 2005, nearly one-third of all Baby Boomers volunteered with formal organizations, which the Corporation for National and Community Service called the highest volunteer rate of any American group. According to the U.S. Committee on Education and Labor Web site, the recently passed Edward M. Kennedy Serve America Act will triple the number of volunteers nationwide to 250,000.[4]

Tips for Younger Managers Working with Boomers

- ➢ Respect their experience.
- ➢ Give them room without abandoning them.
- ➢ Prove yourself through performance.
- ➢ Practice "Radar O'Reilly Management."
- ➢ Capture the wisdom Boomers offer—before it's too late.
- ➢ Motivate them on their terms.
- ➢ Leverage strength in new ways.
- ➢ Arrange for recognition and credit.
- ➢ Find and ally with your veteran sergeants.

The Bottom Line

Every generation has value to an organization. Baby Boomers may be nearing retirement, but that doesn't mean they should be shunted to the side and ignored until they leave. They have the wisdom of experience that can provide historical perspective for the decisions you face. They have overcome many obstacles in their careers and that tenacity can help your organization meet new challenges. They are team players who can enhance any group in which they participate.

But they need to be engaged. They need to feel like they are still valuable to the organization. They need the freedom to act on their accumulated knowledge and skills without being micromanaged—but they don't want to be left totally adrift.

Successfully managing Baby Boomers means keeping them motivated and excited about their jobs, communicating—and listening—to ensure that they are aligned with the goals of your group and organization, and giving them the support they need to continue to perform at the highest levels.

And don't forget to capture their knowledge so all is not lost when retirement calls.

Generation X

In 1991, Douglas Coupland coined the term "Generation X" to describe people born between 1966 and 1980. His book, *Generation X: Tales for an Accelerated Culture,*[5] was a fictional story about a group of Americans and Canadians who reached adulthood in the late 1980s.

Signposts for Generation X

- ➤ 1965: Children Become Unfashionable
- ➤ The Disillusioning 1970s
- ➤ *Sesame Street* Rules
- ➤ The Decadent 1980s
- ➤ Latchkey Kids
- ➤ The 1990–1991 Recession: Parents Laid Off

Tips for Managing Xers

Gen Xers have become adults, but they haven't been completely tamed.

1. Give Them Individual Recognition

In addition to team recognition, make sure that Gen Xers are spotlighted individually for jobs well done. To the degree you can, put them in working situations where they can shine, even if it's in a team environment.

2. Create Collegial Teams

Although Gen Xers tend to seek individual recognition, it doesn't mean they can't or won't work well in teams. They tend to look for small groups within their teams or coworkers for support. The relationships tend to be based more on professional, mutual respect than on the fact they're all on the same team.

3. Establish a Meritocracy

Merriam-Webster's online dictionary defines "meritocracy" as "a system in which the talented are chosen and moved ahead on the basis of their achievement."[6] Notice that there's no mention of whom they know, how they schmooze, or how long they've been with the company.

4. Support Their Lifestyle

After watching their parents work 14-hour days at jobs they often didn't like only to be laid off, Gen Xers have realized that there is more to life than a paycheck. For Gen Xers, doing what they enjoy tends to trump bringing home more money.

5. Provide Schedule Flexibility

Gen Xers put high priority on being able to spend time with family. Being able to establish life/work balance is a major motivating factor for Gen Xers.

6. Help Them Prepare for Their Next Job

From their perspective, job security for Gen Xers has always rested in their ability to find another job. They have little faith in your being there for them 20 years from now. Too many saw that same faith their Baby Boomer parents had in their employers betrayed by the reengineering and downsizing in the early '90s. In their minds, every job is a temporary assignment—they are more like independent contractors than employees.

7. Vary Their Experiences

Since Gen Xers' long-range career goals are always lurking in the back of their minds, the more experiences they can acquire during their tenure with you, the more attractive the job will be for them. Consequently, opportunities to manage multiple projects, work on cross-functional teams, participate in job sharing, and be involved with volunteer projects are major motivators for Gen Xers. With each new assignment, they expand their growth portfolios for future opportunities.

8. Apply Donald Trump Training (aka White Knuckle Terror)

Gen Xers learn fast. After giving them the training to do the job, put them on the spot to perform and hold them accountable. They respond well to that kind of "White Knuckle Terror Training."

9. Get Rid of Stupid Rules

Since Gen Xers spent lots of time alone as children, they were forced to make up their own rules as they went along. Consequently, they have little tolerance for rules that make no sense to them.

10. Coach Office Politics

Gen Xers tend to lack the intuitiveness Baby Boomers possess when it comes to office politics.

11. Challenge Them

Gen Xers are happy working MTV style, meaning they like activities that require intense bursts of energy and challenge them to think quickly. According to J. Leslie McKeown, author of *Retaining Top Employees*,[7] Gen Xers work well with ambiguous assignments as long as the objectives and the deadlines are clear.

12. Keep Things Moving

Ready. Lights. Action. Gen Xers tend to be fast paced and will become frustrated when they feel things are lagging. They often turn their noses up at team meetings because they consider them bottlenecks that delay, rather than accelerate, decision making. One of our clients put a big red action button (think of the Staples Easy Button) on the conference table. If it looks like a meeting is starting to drag and go off course, anyone can hit the action button, which rings a loud bell, getting everyone back on task.

To make meetings more productive and more inviting to fast-paced Gen Xers, we suggest the following eight-step meeting strategy:

1. Determine the purpose.
2. Consider alternatives to meetings.
3. Create an agenda.
4. Start on time.
5. End on time.
6. Stick to the agenda.
7. Assign responsibilities.
8. Take notes and distribute minutes.

13. Reward Winners with Your Time

When we conduct leadership seminars, we ask the audience to divide their employees into three categories:

1. Eagles
2. Sparrows
3. Turkeys

Make it a point to spend 70 percent of your time with your Eagles, 25 percent of your time with your Sparrows, and 5 percent of your time with your Turkeys. You'll get a better return on your investment of time, and your Gen Xers will respect you for it.

14. Reward Action

Given their latchkey/independence-based signposts, Gen Xers are used to taking charge of situations and getting done what needs to be done. They also respect that in others.

15. Offer Sabbaticals

Progressive companies interested in catering to their Gen Xers often offer sabbaticals, some with the company paying full salaries while the employees are gone, and some who expect the employees to support themselves.

Either way, sabbaticals support the drive toward work/life balance that is so important to Gen Xers.

16. Beware of Hovering

No one likes to feel like they're being micromanaged, but given their signpost of latchkey independence, Gen Xers are especially sensitive to it.

17. Provide Feedback

In Chapter 4, we described the Gen X attitude toward supervision as, "Tell me what you want done, give me the tools I need to do it, train me to use them, and then leave me alone!" We omitted the final step in that process, however, which is, "When I'm done, tell me what you think." Here are some tips for giving Gen Xers feedback:

1. Do it often.
2. Keep it matter-of-fact.
3. Make it immediate or slightly delayed.
4. Make it constructive.
5. Convey high expectations.

18. Allow Them to Be Themselves

Give the Xer as much personal freedom as the industry or organization will tolerate. Xers value their individual style and the more they can bring that style into the workforce, the less resentful they will feel when you ask them to give up personal time.

19. Have Fun

The more fun Xers have with their work, the more they are willing to compromise on other issues.

The Bottom Line

Generation X has a slightly different take on work than the Baby Boomers and Traditionals who preceded them. They are not loyal for loyalty's sake—but they can be very loyal if the company meets their needs. They will not work long hours just because the company wants them to—but they will work long hours if they understand the need and can expect a balance of time off for their efforts. They prefer working on their own to working in a team—but they are team players if the other members of the team do their part to meet a goal. They won't schmooze their way to a better job—but they will seek better jobs on the basis of their abilities. They get bored easily—but they will be engaged if you challenge them, remain flexible, keep things moving, and recognize their achievements.

Attracting and retaining Gen Xers helps make your company better by making you more aware of employee needs, more open to different ways of doing things, and more agile and adaptable.

And it sets you up for an influx of Gen X managers who value independence, balance, variety, challenging work, and merit-based promotions—all qualities any organization would love to have.

Generation Y: Extending Their Families

By the 1980s, Baby Boomers who had postponed having children in the 1960s and 1970s were reaching their mid-30s and realizing that if they were going to start families, they needed to do it quickly. Their biological clocks were ticking. In addition, with divorce rates hovering around 50 percent, many Boomers who already had children were remarrying and starting second families. Together, they spawned Generation Y.

Signposts for Generation Y

> Helicopter Parents
> Columbine High School
> Technical Expertise
> Online Social Networking
> Economic Turmoil
> Seeking Groups
> Integrating Life and Work
> Social Responsibility
> Volunteerism

Tips for Managing Generation Y

Generation Y has different work requirements and expectations than the Baby Boomers and Gen Xers who manage them. Understanding these differences will help managers to be effective and their Gen Yers to flourish.

The goals for managing Generation Y include:

1. Help them integrate into the work setting without scaring them off or turning them off.
2. Provide them with solid primary experiences that lay the groundwork for their careers.
3. Keep them from self-destructing.

To get them to reach those goals:

1. Create opportunities to bond.
2. Tell it like it is.
3. Avoid droning on about the "good old days."
4. Create Gen Y–friendly rules.
5. Be open to virtual work environments.
6. Offer flextime.
7. Interact often.
8. Stir up a little fun.
9. Tell them why.
10. Offer close coaching and guidance.
11. Give feedback often.

Giving Reinforcing Feedback (Praise)

For praise to achieve maximum return, it should follow the Three *S* Rule:

- Specific
- Significant
- Sincere

Keep in mind these praising tips:

- Deliver the information as soon as possible.
- Praise in public.
- Put it in writing.
- Do it often.
- Describe the impact on the organization.

Giving Corrective Feedback (Criticism)

> Pick the right time.

> Make sure the purpose of your feedback is to coach rather than punish.

> Select a private place.

> Be specific.

> Make the feedback descriptive and prescriptive.

> Be sure that the feedback is targeted toward something the person can actually change.

> Focus on the present and the future, but use the past for supporting data.

> Beware of derogatory labels.

The Bottom Line

Generation Y grew up with parents who spent time communicating with them, who praised them for even the smallest victories, who asked for their opinions when they were children, and who devoted time to making life fun. They expect similar services from their Baby Boomer and Gen X bosses.

You don't have to coddle Gen Yers but you do have to understand what they need from you to succeed. Get in the habit of checking in with them daily, offering praise when it is deserved and corrective feedback when it's needed. Be specific about jobs and expectations. Offer flexibility in when and how they work, as long as they perform.

And have some fun. Managers and employees of all generations can benefit from that.

The Traditional Generation

The Traditional Generation began with the end of World War I. Born between 1918 and 1945, many of them passed through childhood in the Roaring Twenties, came of age in the Great Depression, and spent their 20s fighting and winning World War II. They were the parents of the Baby Boomer Generation and were responsible for the prosperity following World War II.

There are 52 million members of the Traditional Generation.[8] Because of their advancing age and retirement, they are the smallest segment of employees, representing only 8 percent of the workforce.[9] Their roles, however, go far beyond the 164,000 greeters employed at Wal-Mart. From professional ranks to security guards, they continue to contribute their talent and labor.

Many Traditionals work as nonpaid volunteers. For example, AARP enlists the services of retired accountants and businesspeople to help 2.5 million people file tax returns every year.[10] Hospitals depend on retired volunteers to do everything from manning the front desk to accompanying patients to clinics.

The result is that, although the number of paid employees from this generation is low, Traditionals remain a viable presence in today's workplace.

Signposts for the Traditional Generation

▷   The Great Depression
▷   Waste Not, Want Not
▷   World War II
▷   GI Bill

Smart Companies Hire Traditionals

With the economy struggling, many members of the Traditional Generation are looking to remain in the workforce to help pay the bills. Several smart companies like Home Depot, Borders Books, and PETCO are using creative approaches to tap into this resource.

Got Traditionals? Here's What to Do

Goals for managing traditionals:

1.   Give them something to do that contributes to the common good.
2.   Capture and apply the wisdom they have gained from their wealth of experiences.
3.   Help them adapt to and embrace new systems and methodologies.
4.   Provide them with a fulfilling experience.

Recruit Traditionals

Just like you cannot legally discriminate against older employees in your hiring practices, you cannot and should not discriminate against younger employees. You can, however, design your recruitment efforts to appeal to older citizens. You can tailor the careers section of your Web site to attract and appeal to seniors, you can place recruitment ads in locations that older potential employees frequent such as senior centers and churches, and you can partner with senior organizations like AARP that help older citizens find jobs.

Tips for Managing Traditionals

- Make them mentors for other employees.
- Give them training—old dogs can learn new tricks.
- Accommodate their needs.
- Recognize and applaud their contributions.
- Give one-on-one support.

The Bottom Line

You can tap into this precious resource by understanding what will draw older employees to your company. Your workplace will be enriched by their contribution.

The Linkster Generation

Born after 1995, they are currently in their teens and preteens. There are approximately 20 million Generation Linksters in the United States,[11] and they represent 18 percent of the world's population.[12] As of this writing, they are entering the workforce as part-time employees, working after school and during the summers.

Most Linksters don't remember the O. J. Simpson trial, the disputed 2000 presidential election, the dot-com collapse, or the 9/11 attacks. Their vocabulary lessons included words like "terrorism" and "Google." The nice lady who gives you directions from your GPS is an icon for them and as trustworthy as a police officer. In fact, the people they trust most are their parents, who are, for the most part, Generation X.

Signposts for the Linkster Generation

 ▷ Parental Involvement
 ▷ Connecting Through Technology
 ▷ Dearth of Face-to-Face Contact
 ▷ Environmental Awareness

Goals for Managing Linksters

1. Settle them down and help them feel comfortable.
2. Get them into a routine to which they can adapt and master.
3. Provide them with some fun and engagement to hold their attention.
4. Reward them often and correct them immediately when they need it.

Tips for Managing the Linkster Generation

 ▷ Ride herd on them.
 ▷ Provide them with job descriptions.
 ▷ Treat them like valued coworkers.
 ▷ Lead by example.
 ▷ Orient them to the obvious.
 ▷ Welcome them with open arms.
 ▷ Know what songs are on their iPods.
 ▷ Create microcareer paths.
 ▷ Reexamine your uniform policy.
 ▷ Thank their parents.

Mode Management for Every Generation

Here is a tool for choosing a management mode that is appropriate for the person and situation you are managing. You should find the tool especially helpful for managing across generations. The management principles apply to all people and every situation.

Four Management Principles

Management Principle #1: Everyone's Different

To successfully manage people across generational lines, it is helpful to vary your management approach to fit the unique needs of each individual.

Management Principle #2: There Is No "Truth"

Because people are complicated, no one single approach works for everyone.

Management Principle #3: The One with the Most Tools Wins

The most effective manager is the manager who has the most tools for dealing with different individuals.

Management Principle #4: Mutual Reciprocity

To the degree you can give people what they need, they tend to give you what you need.

Tailoring Your Mode of Management

Since each person brings with her a set of individual needs and the principle of mutual reciprocity dictates that we do what we can to meet those needs, it makes sense that we tailor our management approach to create the best working relationship.

Here we offer five basic management modes to draw from: Directing, Teaching, Persuading, Collaborating, and Coordinating.

Directing mode—you tell people what to do.
Teaching mode—you teach people how to do it.
Persuading mode—you help people understand why they should do it.
Collaborating mode—you confer with people to help them do it.
Coordinating mode—you clarify expectations and get out of their way.

Working the Mode Management Model

The question facing managers who use the Mode Management Model (see Figure 12.1 on page 203) is when, how, and with whom to use each mode.

The table in Figure 12.1 is designed to give you general guidelines for applying the five management modes. We remind you that these are only general guidelines and not hard-and-fast rules. *There is no "truth."*

The Bottom Line

Managing people effectively means making sure they get what they need so they feel a balance between the efforts they put forth and the benefits they derive. In their heads, it needs to look like a fair deal.

Meeting people's individual needs requires adjusting how you deal with each person. One size does not fit all. It's useful to be able to flex your management mode to fit the needs of each person you manage in the different situations each faces.

Notes

Chapter 1   Signposts: Harbingers of Things to Come

1. Salt, B. *Beyond the Baby Boomers: The Rise of Generation Y.* KPMG Publications. KPMG International is a Swiss cooperative. http://www.kpmg.com.sg/publications/fs_BeyondTheBabyBoomers.pdf (site last accessed on November 15, 2009).

2. "Live Births and Birth Rates by Year." *Infoplease,* http://www.infoplease.com/ipa/A0005067.html (site last accessed November 20, 2009) (data originally from the U.S. Census Bureau).

3. Lancaster, L. C., and D. Stillman. *When Generations Collide: Who They Are. Why They Clash. How to Solve the Generational Puzzle at Work.* New York: Collins Business, 2003.

4. http://www.jonathanpontell.com/aboutgenjones.htm (site last accessed on November 20, 2009).

5. Cullen, D. "*Newsweek* Rave and 'Columbine' Book Trailer." *Dave Cullen's Blog.* Salon.com, March 28, 2009, 7:54 P.M., http://open.salon.com/blog/dave_cullen/2009/03/28/newsweek_rave_columbine_book_trailer (site last accessed on November 9, 2009).

6. Brokaw, T. *Boom—Talking About the Sixties.* New York: Random House, 2007, pp. 117–119.

7. Weiss, A. *Million Dollar Consulting.* Quoted, with permission, from an email interview, March 26, 2009.

8. Schweitzer, T. "Report: Retiring Baby Boomers Expected to Hurt U.S. Companies." *Inc: Daily Resources for Entrepreneurs,* March 23, 2007, http://www.inc.com/news/articles/200703/boomers.html (site last accessed on November 9, 2009).

9. Aon Consulting's Benefits and Talent Survey, 2008, http://www.aon.com/

about-aon/intellectual-capital/attachments/human-capital-consulting/Aon
_Consulting_Benefits_Talent_Survey_2008.pdf (site last accessed on November 9, 2009).

10. "Engaging Millennials." *The Herman Trend Alert,* January 7, 2009, http://
www.hermangroup.com/alert/archive_1-07-2009.html (site last accessed on
November 9, 2009).

Chapter 2 Baby Boomers: The Elephant in the Python

1. Dr. Jean-Paul Rodrigue, Dept. of Global Studies and Geography. Hemp-
stead, NY: Hofstra University, 1998–2009.

2. Chafe, W. H. *The Unfinished Journey: America Since World War II.* New York:
Oxford University Press, 2003, p. 311.

3. Whitbourne, S. K., and S. L. Willis, eds. *The Baby Boomers Grow Up.* Mah-
wah, NJ: Lawrence Erlbaum, 2006, p. 12.

4. Spock, B. *Dr. Spock's Baby and Child Care.* New York: Simon & Schuster,
2004.

5. "Dr. Benjamin Spock, 1903–1998." *drspock.com.* http://www.drspock.com/
about/drbenjaminspock/0,1781,,00.html (site last accessed on November 9,
2009).

6. Waring, N.-P. "Dr. Spock: An American Life." *JAMA* 280 (November 25,
1998): 1796.

7. Twenge, J. M. *Generation Me.* New York: Simon & Schuster, 2007, p. 46.
http://books.google.com/books?id=tV4M1hpG-3wC (site last accessed on
November 9, 2009).

8. *Ibid.*

9. "Fallout Shelters: Cold War." *U.S.History.com.* http://www.u-s-history
.com/pages/h3706.html (site last accessed on November 9, 2009).

10. Deiro, J. A., and B. Benard. *Teachers Do Make a Difference: The Teacher's
Guide to Connecting with Students.* Thousand Oaks, CA: Corwin Press, 2004,
p. 4.

11. Feldman, R. T. *Don't Whistle in School: The History of America's Public
Schools.* Breckenridge, CO: Twenty-First Century Books, 2001, p. 57.

12. Levi, D. *Group Dynamics for Teams.* Thousand Oaks, CA: Sage, 2007, p. 274.

13. Taylor, S. J. L. *Desegregation in Boston and Buffalo: The Influence of Local
Leaders.* Albany, NY: SUNY Press, 1998, p. 87.

14. Pohlmann, M. "Black Mayors in Large Cities: A 35-Year Perspective."
All Academic Research. http://www.allacademic.com/meta/p_mla_apa_
research_citation/0/6/2/2/2/pages62229/p62229-1.php (site last accessed on
November 9, 2009).

15. Gerbner, G., L. Gross, M. Morgan, N. Signorielli, and J. Shanahan. "Growing Up with Television: Cultivation Process." In *Media Effects: Advances in Theory and Research,* edited by J. Bryant and D. Zillmann. Philadelphia: Lawrence Erlbaum Associates, 2002, pp. 29–30.

16. "HerStory: 1971–Present." *Ms.* magazine Web site, http://www.msmagazine.com/about.asp (site last accessed on November 9, 2009).

17. Telephone interview with a customer service agent at *Ms.,* May 26, 2009.

18. Wolbrecht, C. *The Politics of Women's Rights.* Princeton, NJ: Princeton University Press, 2000, p. 30.

19. Limbaugh, R. *The Way Things Ought to Be.* New York: Pocket Books, 1992, p. 192.

20. "The Baby Boomer Generation Is a Source for Trends, Research, Comment and Discussion of and by People Born from 1946–1964." *AgingHipsters.com,* July 18, 2003, http://www.aginghipsters.com/blog/archives/000135.php (site last accessed on November 9, 2009).

21. Uslaner, E. M. *The Moral Foundations of Trust.* New York: Cambridge University Press, 2002, pp. 66–67.

22. "Civil Rights Timeline: Milestones in the Modern Civil Rights Movement." *Infoplease.com,* http://www.infoplease.com/spot/civilrightstimeline1.html (site last accessed on November 9, 2009).

23. *Ibid.*

24. *Encyclopedia Britannica Online,* s.v. "Rubin, Jerry," http://www.britannica.com/EBchecked/topic/511997/Jerry-Rubin (site last accessed on November 9, 2009).

25. Schulman, B. *The Seventies: The Great Shift in American Culture, Society and Politics.* New York: *New York Times* Notable Book, 2002, p. 219.

26. Uzelac, E. "What a Long, Strange Trip It'll Be." *Research,* May 1, 2005, http://www.highbeam.com/doc/1G1-132561444.html (site last accessed on November 9, 2009).

27. "Survey Shows Baby Boomers Expect to Live Long and Well Using Variety of Alternative Health Care (Statistical Notes)." *Health Care Strategic Management,* January 1, 2004, http://www.highbeam.com (site last accessed on November 9, 2009).

Chapter 3 Managing Boomers

1. Cooke, C. "12 Reasons to Hire a Boomer." October 22, 2009, http://dentalrecruiterblog.blogspot.com (site last accessed on November 14, 2009).

2. *The Economic Slowdown's Impact on Middle-Aged and Older Americans.* AARP, http://assets.aarp.org/rgcenter/econ/economy_survey.pdf (site last accessed on November 9, 2009).

3. "Think Age Is Enough to Predict Worker Needs? Think Again. National Study of Multi-generation Workers Bends Prism of Age." Sloan Center on Aging and Work at Boston College, April 9, 2009, http://www.bc.edu/research/agingandwork/all_feeds/2009-04-09.html (site last accessed on November 9, 2009).

4. "How 'Ya Gonna Keep 'Em Down on the Farm? (After They've Seen Paree)." Words by Sam M. Lewis, 1885–1959, and Joe Young, 1889–1939, Music by Walter Donaldson, 1891–1947. New York: Waterson, Berlin & Snyder, Co., 1919.

5. *Volunteer Growth in America: A Review of Trends Since 1974.* December 2006, p. 2, http://www.serveminnesota.org/PDFFiles/VolunteerGrowthReport.pdf.

6. Kittredge, B. M. "National Service Bill Will Expand Service Opportunities for Seniors." *U.S. Committee on Education and Labor,* March 8, 2009, http://edlabor.house.gov/blog/2009/03/give-act-will-expand-service-o-1.shtml (site last accessed on November 9, 2009).

7. Delong, D. "Five Keys to Decisions Vis-à-vis an Ageing Workforce." Permission to use granted from David Delong, http://www.lostknowledge.com (site last accessed on November 9, 2009).

8. Printed, with permission, from an interview with Kathy Deel, June 6, 2009.

Chapter 4   Big Bird, *Wayne's World*, and *Home Alone*

1. http://www.brainyquote.com/quotes/quotes/h/haimginott106966.html (site last accessed on November 14, 2009).

2. Coupland, D. *Generation X: Tales for an Accelerated Culture.* New York: St. Martin's Press, 1991.

3. "50 Most Powerful Women in Business: FORTUNE's Annual Ranking of America's Leading Businesswomen." *Fortune* magazine, 2008, http://money.cnn.com/magazines/fortune/mostpowerfulwomen/2008/ (site last accessed on November 10, 2009).

4. http://www.edgetechcorp.com/company/press-release/ (site last accessed on November 10, 2009).

5. Munk, N. "The New Organization Man." *Fortune* magazine, March 16, 1998, http://money.cnn.com/magazines/fortune/fortune_archive/1998/03/16/239268/index.htm (site last accessed on November 10, 2009).

6. *The Future of Children* (a collaboration of the Woodrow Wilson School of Public and International Affairs at Princeton University and the Brookings Institution), http://www.futureofchildren.org/information2827/information_show.htm?doc_id=75526 (page no longer available).

7. "Generation X Redefining Family, Financial Needs." New York Life Insurance, http://www.newyorklife.com/cda/0,3254,13769,00.html (site last accessed November 20, 2009).

8. Farley, R., and J. Haaga. *The American People: Census 2000.* New York: Russell Sage Foundation, 2005, p. 89.

9. "Generation X Redefining Family, Financial Needs." New York Life Insurance, http://www.newyorklife.com/cda/0,3254,13769,00.html (site last accessed on November 20, 2009).

10. Farley and Haaga. *The American People*, p. 89.

11. Hamilton, K., and P. Wingert. "Can Generation Xers—Many of Them the Children of Divorce—Make Their Own Marriages Last?" Smart Marriages Archive, July 20, 1998, http://www.divorcereform.org/mel/agenxmarr.html (site last accessed on November 10, 2009).

12. http://en.wikipedia.org/wiki/Stagflation (site last accessed on November 10, 2009).

13. Altman, A. "The History of *Sesame Street.*" December 29, 2008, http://www.time.com/time/nation/article/0,8599,1868862,00.html (site last accessed on November 10, 2009).

14. Friedman, M. J. "*Sesame Street* Educates and Entertains Internationally." America.gov (U.S. Department of State Bureau of International Information Programs), April 8, 2006, http://www.america.gov/st/washfile-english/2006/April/20060405165756jmnamdeirf0.4207117.html (retrieved on October 10, 2009).

15. Myron, M. R., and P. L. Truax. "Anatomy of the 'Generation X' Consumer Age Group Demonstrates More-Conservative Buying Habits Than Their Parents." *Denver Business Journal*, April 24, 1998, http://www.bizjournals.com/denver/stories/1998/04/27/smallb4.html (site last accessed on November 10, 2009).

16. DeMarco, L. "Generation X Parents Outshine Baby Boomers." October 22, 2008, http://genxparents.blogspot.com/2008/10/agree-or-disagree.html (site last accessed on November 10, 2009).

17. Arndorder, J. "US Army to Drop 'Army of One' Advertising Campaign." *Advertising Age Magazine*, November 8, 2005.

18. Gardner, J. M. *Monthly Labor Review On Line*, June 1994, Vol. 117, No. 6, abstract, http://www.bls.gov/opub/mlr/1994/06/art1abs.htm (site last accessed November 20, 2009).

19. Shelton, C., and L. Shelton. *The NeXt Revolution: What Gen X Women Want at Work and How Their Boomer Bosses Can Help Them Get It*, as quoted by Anne Fisher in "What Do Gen Xers Want? Here's How Some of FORTUNE's 100 Best Companies to Work for Keep Young Up-and-Comers Happy." *Fortune* magazine, January 20, 2006, http://money.cnn.com/2006/01/17/news/companies/bestcos_genx/index.htm (site last accessed on November 10, 2009).

20. "Catalyst Study Dispels Myths About Generation X Professionals and Sheds

Light on What This New Generation of Leaders Seek at Work." http://www
.catalyst.org/press-release/43/catalyst-study-dispels-myths-about-generation
-x-professionals-and-sheds-light-on-what-this-new-generation-of-leaders-seek
-at-work (site last accessed on November 10, 2009).

21. Levoy, R. P. *222 Secrets of Hiring, Managing, and Retaining Great Employees in Healthcare Practices.* Sudbury, MA: Jones & Bartlett, 2006, p. 37.

22. NetApp Web site. http://www.netapp.com/us/company/careers/benefits.html (site last accessed on November 10, 2009).

23. http://www.plantemoran.com/pmcareers/inside/news/fortune.asp (site last accessed on November 10, 2009).

24. http://www.gore.com/en_xx/careers/graduates/working_at_gore.html (site last accessed on November 10, 2009).

25. Stevens, L. "Gen X Needs Training, Gen Y Supervision." *Business Review Western Michigan,* April 30, 2008, http://blog.mlive.com/wmbr/2008/04/gen_x_needs_training_gen_y_sup.html (site last accessed on November 10, 2009).

26. Zakomurnaya, Z. "Arthur D. Levinson, President and CEO, Genentech." April 10, 2007, http://www.good2work.com/article/2088 (site last accessed on November 10, 2009).

27. *Ibid.*

Chapter 5   Managing Generation X

1. Intel Policy Set. http://download.intel.com/pressroom/archive/backgrnd/Policy_Manual_2004_GCR.pdf, p. 23 (site no longer available).

2. Grossman, L. "Fatherhood 2.0." *Time,* October 4, 2007, http://www.time.com/time/magazine/article/0,9171,166 (site last accessed on November 14, 2009).

3. Sloan Work and Family Research Network, Boston College, Boston. http://wfnetwork.bc.edu/template.php?name=casestudy#AFLAC (site last accessed on November 10, 2009).

4. *Ibid.*

5. *Ibid.*

6. Castle N. G., J. Engberg, R. Anderson, and A. Men. "Job Satisfaction of Nurse Aides in Nursing Homes: Intent to Leave and Turnover." *The Gerontologist* 47 (2007): 193–204, http://gerontologist.gerontologyjournals.org/cgi/reprint/47/2/193.pdf (site last accessed on November 10, 2009).

7. Interview with Paul Berry, spokesperson for USAA, July 9, 2009. Permission granted to use.

8. https://www.quickenloanscareers.com/web/college-graduate.aspx (site last accessed on November 10, 2009).

9. Zemke, R., C. Raines, and B. Filipczak. *Generations at Work.* New York: AMACOM, March 2000, p. 115.

10. McKeown, J. L. *Retaining Top Employees.* New York: McGraw-Hill, 2002, p. 72.

11. Parkinson, C. N. *Parkinson's Law.* C. Northcote Parkinson is Raffles Professor of History at the University of Singapore. This article first appeared in *The Economist* in November 1955.

12. http://www.intel.com/jobs/usa/bencomp/benefits.htm#TimeOff (site last accessed on November 10, 2009).

13. http://money.cnn.com/magazines/fortune/bestcompanies/best_benefits/ (site last accessed on November 10, 2009).

14. http://www.accenture.com (site last accessed on November 10, 2009).

15. Rosenthal, R., and L. Jacobson. *Pygmalion in the Classroom.* New York: Irvington, 1992.

16. Twitchell, J. "Workplace Fun Is the Shoe That Fits at Zappos." *Las Vegas Sun*, January 26, 2009, http://www.lasvegassun.com/news/2009/jan/26/zappos com/ (site last accessed on November 10, 2009).

17. "Workers Prefer Generation X Bosses." August 9, 2007, http://www.smart company.com.au/information-technology/workers-prefer-gen-x-bosses -small-business-employees-take-less-time-off-for-babies-selling-on-ebay -the-easy-way-in-game-ads-work.html#boss (site last accessed on November 10, 2009).

18. Rigoli, E. "Down-Under Gen X Bosses the Best, Survey Shows." *ere.net*, August 9, 2007, http://www.ere.net/2007/08/09/down-under-gen-x-bosses -the-best-survey-shows/ (site last accessed on November 10, 2009).

Chapter 6   The Next Elephant in the Python

1. Banchero, S. "Harder to Get into Than Harvard." *Chicago Tribune,* February 28, 2008, http://archives.chicagotribune.com/2008/feb/26/news/chi-school -competition_26feb26 (site last accessed November 13, 2009). Excerpted with permission of the *Chicago Tribune*; copyright *Chicago Tribune*; all rights reserved.

2. Kees, M. "Is Your Child Overscheduled & Overstressed? U-M Expert Offers Tips on How to Tell—and What to Do." University of Michigan Health System, July 25, 2005, http://www.med.umich.edu/opm/newspage/2005/ hmchildstress.htm (site last accessed on November 13, 2009).

3. http://therapists.psychologytoday.com/rms/name/Nancy_Cowan_Weisman_ PhD_Marietta_Georgia_46573 (site last accessed on November 13, 2009).

4. www.harrisinteractive.com (site last accessed on November 13, 2009).

5. Junco, R., and J. Mastrodicasa. *Connecting to the Net.Generation: What Higher Education Professionals Need to Know About Today's Students.* Washington, DC: NASPA, 2007.

6. "Gen-Y Social Application Demand Continues to Grow as Facebook Plans Platform Redesign." *BNET,* June 2008, http://findarticles.com/p/articles/ mi_pwwi/is_200806/ai_n25498258/ (site no longer available).

7. "Gen-Y Recruiting, Listening Up, Virtual HR Learning, and Innovation Teams Take Top Honors at 2009 Arbor Awards for Excellence." *Reuters,* March 9, 2009, http://www.reuters.com/article/pressRelease/idUS105483 +09-Mar-2009+PRN20090309 (site last accessed on November 13, 2009).

8. Koc, E. L. "NACE Research: The Oldest Young Generation—A Report from the 2008 NACE Graduating Student Survey." NACE/WEB, May 2008, http:// www.naceweb.org/public/koc0508.htm (site no longer available).

9. Quotation via email from W. Stanton Smith, national director, Cross Generational Initiatives, Talent Innovation & Eminence, Deloitte LLP.

10. Koc. "NACE Research."

11. http://www.expertmagazine.com/ (site last accessed on November 13, 2009).

12. Robison, J. "What's Behind the Ritz-Carlton Mystique?" *Gallup Management Journal,* December 11, 2008, http://gmj.gallup.com/content/112906/ How-RitzCarlton-Manages-Mystique.aspx (site last accessed on November 13, 2009).

13. PricewaterhouseCoopers 2008. For more information visit PwC special microsite, where contents of all the Managing Tomorrow's People reports can be found including the Millennials report: www.pwc.com/managingpeople 2020 (site last accessed on November 13, 2009).

14. This information is from a Randstad/Harris interactive survey. The 2008 edition of Randstad USA's annual "World of Work" survey.

15. Confirmed by Kristie Richie, senior new business/communications director at Upshot.

16. "The Millennial Generation: Pro-Social and Empowered to Change the World." *The 2006 Cone Millennial Cause Study,* http://www.coneinc.com/ news/request.php?id=1090 (site last accessed on November 13, 2009).

17. http://www-03.ibm.com/employment (site last accessed on November 13, 2009).

18. http://www.loomstate.org/about/ (site last accessed on November 13, 2009).

19. 2008 Deloitte Volunteer IMPACT Survey. Permission to reprint granted.

20. https://www.salesforce.com (site last accessed on November 13, 2009).

21. ©Google Inc. Used with permission.

Chapter 7   Managing Generation Y

1. Direct quotation used with permission from Cam Marston.
2. http://money.cnn.com/galleries/2007/fortune/0705/gallery.great_for_new_grads .fortune/3.html (site last accessed on November 13, 2009).
3. http://money.cnn.com/galleries/2007/fortune/0705/gallery.great _for_new_ grads.fortune/12.html (site last accessed on November 13, 2009).
4. http://money.cnn.com/galleries/2007/fortune/0705/gallery.great_for_new_grads .fortune/14.html (site last accessed on November 13, 2009).
5. http://newsroom.cisco.com/dlls/2009/prod_062609.html (site last accessed on November 13, 2009).
6. Kupsh, J., and P. R. Graves. *Create High Impact Business Presentations.* Lincolnwood, IL: NTC LearningWorks, 1998. www.wplc.info/statistics/Net LibraryStatsSep2004.xls (site last accessed on November 13, 2009), p. 135.

Chapter 8   Old Dogs Have Lots to Offer

1. Drain, C. B. *Perianesthesia Nursing: A Critical Care Approach.* New York: Elsevier Health Sciences, 2003, p. 22.
2. Mithers, C. "Workplace Wars." *Ladies Home Journal,* May 2009, http://www .lhj.com/relationships/work/worklife-balance/generation-gaps-at-work/ (site last accessed on November 20, 2009).
3. "Volunteering with AARP." *AARP.org,* November 2008, http://www.aarp .org/makeadifference/volunteer/articles/volunteering_with_aarp.html (site last accessed on November 13, 2009).
4. Clarke, G. "The Silent Generation Revisited." *Time,* June 29, 1970, http:// www.time.com/time/magazine/article/0,9171,878847-1,00.html (site last accessed on November 13, 2009).
5. "Hiring Grey-Haired Employees." *Employer-Employee.com,* http://www .employer-employee.com/september2001tips.html (site last accessed on November 13, 2009).
6. HomeDepot.com. https://careers.homedepot.com/cg/content.do?p=aarp (site last accessed on November 13, 2009).
7. Freudenheim, M. "More Help Wanted: Older Workers Please Apply." *New York Times,* March 23, 2005, http://www.nytimes.com/2005/03/23/business/ 23older.html (site last accessed on November 13, 2009).
8. http://www.seniors4hire.org/featured/petco.asp (site last accessed on November 13, 2009).
9. Williams, S. L. "Jobs for Senior Citizens in Washington DC." March 13, 2008, http://www.associatedcontent.com/article/652531/jobs_for_senior_citi zens_in_washington.html?cat=12 (site last accessed on November 13, 2009).

10. JobBankUSA.com. http://www.jobbankusa.com/News/Hiring/valuable_re source_hiring_senior_citizens.html (site last accessed on November 13, 2009).

Chapter 9   Managing the Traditional Generation

1. McIntosh, B. *An Employer's Guide to Older Workers: How to Win Them Back and Convince Them to Stay.* www.doleta.gov/Seniors/other_docs/EmplGui de.pdf (site last accessed on November 13, 2009). School of Business Administration, University of Vermont, Burlington, VT 05405. mcintosh@bsad .uvm.edu.

2. Manpower Press Release: *Latest Manpower Research Shows Few U.S. Employers Retain, Recruit Older Workers Despite Feeling the Crunch from Talent Shortages.* http://www.manpower.com/investors/releasedetail.cfm?releaseid =238986 (site last accessed on November 13, 2009).

3. McIntosh. *An Employer's Guide.*

4. http://www.aarpinternational.org/conference_sub/Conference_sub_htm?doc _id-707438 (article no longer available).

5. http://www.southernmetalroofing.com/blog/?p=13 (site last accessed on November 13, 2009).

6. http://www.taen.org.uk/news/pr.php?action=fullnews&id=5494 (article no longer available).

7. Said, C. "Wanted: Retirees to Work: Employers Try to Prepare for Pending Exodus of Boomers." *San Francisco Chronicle,* April 29, 2005, http://www .sfgate.com/cgi-bin/article.cgi?file=/c/a/2005/04/29/BUGO7CH2691.DTL (site last accessed on November 13, 2009).

8. *Ibid.*

9. "Senior Citizens Lead Internet Growth, According to Nielsen/Net Ratings." November 20, 2003, www.nielsen-online.com/pr/pr_031120.pdf (site last accessed on November 20, 2009).

10. *Earthlink and AARP Washington Launch GenerationLink in Seattle.* http:// ir.earthlink.net/releasedetail.cfm?releaseid=249686 (site last accessed on November 13, 2009).

11. Childress, M. "Senior Citizens Learn About Computer Use: Experts Advise Them to Take Care When Giving Personal Information over Internet." *Charleston Daily Mail,* March 3, 2009, http://www.dailymail.com/News/ Kanawha/200903030082.

12. http://www.generationsonline.com (site last accessed on November 13, 2009).

13. Baucom, A., and R. J. Grosch. *Hospitality Design for the Graying Generation.* New York: John Wiley and Sons, 1996, p. 143.

14. Nelson, B. "One Management Style Does Not Fit All." *Meetingsnet*, January 1, 2007, http://meetingsnet.com/careers/generations/insurance_one_size _not_010107/ (article no longer available).
15. http://www.america.gov/st/develop-english/2009/June/20090630165619 cpataruk0.2550318.html (site last accessed on November 13, 2009).

Chapter 10   Cell Phones and Hanna Montana

1. http://en.proverbia.net/citasautor.asp?autor=16652 (site last accessed on November 13, 2009).
2. http://www.babyboomercaretaker.com/baby-boomer/generation-z/index .html.
3. Demarco, L. "Generation X Parents Outshine Baby Boomers." *Plain Dealer* (Cleveland), September 6, 2004.
4. *Ibid.*
5. Alexander, K. "The War on 'No': Is Child Centered Parenting Producing a Generation of Brats?" *Babble: The Magazine and Community for a New Generation of Parents,* http://www.babble.com/content/articles/. . ./No-Doesnt -Mean-No/ (site last accessed on November 20, 2009).
6. Reprinted with permission from Mike Brody, mikebro@erols.com.
7. http://www.nick.com/kids-choice-awards/beyonce-single-ladies.jhtml (site last accessed on November 13, 2009).
8. Madden, M., and A. Lenhart. "Teens and Distracted Driving." *Pew Internet .com,* http://www.pewinternet.org (site last accessed on November 20, 2009).
9. *Ibid.*
10. *Ibid.*
11. *How Teens Use Media: A Nielsen Report on the Myths and Realities of Teen Media Trends,* June 2009, http://blog.nielsen.com/nielsenwire/reports/nielsen _howteensusemedia_june09.pdf (site last accessed on November 13, 2009).
12. Hardesty, G. *The Orange County Register*, January 7, 2009.
13. Van den Bulck, J. "Adolescent Use of Mobile Phones for Calling and for Sending Text Messages After Lights Out: Results from a Prospective Cohort Study with a One-Year Follow-Up." *Sleep* 30 (2007): 1220–1223.
14. *Ibid.*
15. http://www.physorg.com/news132231126.html (site last accessed on November 13, 2009).
16. http://www.telegraph.co.uk/news/worldnews/2121298/Mobile-phone-addic tion-Clinic-treats-children.html#continue (site last accessed on November 13, 2009).
17. Hoffman, T. "Job Skills: Preparing Generation Z." *Computer World Careers,*

August 25, 2003, http://www.computerworld.com/action/article.do?com
mand=viewArticleBasic&articleId=84295 (site last accessed on November
13, 2009).

18. http://www.climatecrisis.net/ (site last accessed on November 13, 2009).

19. http://www.campparents.org/newsletter/0901/article3.html (site last accessed
on November 13, 2009).

20. http://www.lnt.org/programs/peak.php (site last accessed on November 13,
2009).

21. Chiras, D. D. *EcoKids: Raising Children Who Care for the Earth.* Gabriola
Island, BC, Canada: New Society Publishers, 2005, p. 17.

22. http://www.gloucestertimes.com/archivesearch/local_story_163093911 (site
last accessed on November 13, 2009).

23. http://www.greenchildrenshouse.com/mission.html (site last accessed on
November 13, 2009).

24. Iasevoli, B. "Green Preschools on the Rise." Columbia News Service, March
31, 2009, http://jscms.jrn.columbia.edu/cns/2009-03-31/iasevoli-greenschool
(article no longer available).

25. *Youth Helping America: The Role of Social Institutions in Teen Volunteering.*
http://www.nationalservice.gov/pdf/05_1130_LSA_YHA_SI_factsheet.pdf
(site last accessed on November 13, 2009).

26. http://www.teensturninggreen.org/about-us/teens-for-safe-cosmetics.html
(site last accessed on November 13, 2009).

27. http://greenteensusa.org/default.aspx (site last accessed on November 13,
2009).

28. Roth, D. "Trading Places." CNN Money, January 20, 2006, http://money
.cnn.com/2006/01/06/news/companies/bestcos_undercover/index.htm (site
last accessed on November 13, 2009).

Chapter 11   Managing the Linkster Generation

1. http://www.quotationspage.com/quote/2073.html (site last accessed on November 14, 2009).

2. Chen, X. P., and A. S. Tsui. "An Organizational Perspective of Multi-Level
Cultural Integration: Human Resource Management Practices in Cross-
Cultural Contexts." In F. J. Yammarino and F. Dansereau (Eds.), *Research
in Multilevel Issues*, vol. 5. New York: Elsevier, 2006, pp. 81–96.

3. Castina. "Gwen Stefani W Hotels Uniform Designer." Pop Crunch, September 15, 2008, http://www.popcrunch.com/gwen-stefani-w-hotels-uniform
-designer (site last accessed on November 13, 2009).

4. Sandison, N. "McDonald's Aims for Premium Image with Designer Uni-

forms." Brand Republic, April 23, 2008, http://www.brandrepublic.com/News/804087/ (article no longer available).

Chapter 12   Different Strokes for Different Folks

1. "How Jack Welch Runs GE: A Close-up Look at How America's #1 Manager Runs GE." June 8, 1998, http://www.businessweek.com/1998/23/b3581001 .htm (site last accessed on November 13, 2009).
2. Excerpt from *Saving Private Ryan*. © DreamWorks LLC and Paramount Pictures and Amblin Entertainment.

Appendix A

1. Johnson, L., and B. Phillips. *Absolute Honesty: Building a Corporate Culture That Values Straight Talk and Rewards Integrity.* New York: AMACOM Books, 2003.

Appendix B

1. Lancaster, L. C., and D. Stillman. *When Generations Collide: Who They Are. Why They Clash. How to Solve the Generational Puzzle at Work.* New York: Collins Business, 2003.
2. Schweitzer, T. "Report: Retiring Baby Boomers Expected to Hurt U.S. Companies." *Inc: Daily Resources for Entrepreneurs,* March 23, 2007, http://www.inc.com/news/articles/200703/boomers.html (site last accessed on November 13, 2009).
3. Greene, K. "Baby Boomers Delay Retirement." *Wall Street Journal,* September 22, 2008, http://online.wsj.com/article/SB122204345024061453.html (site last accessed on November 13, 2009).
4. Kittredge, B. M. "National Service Bill Will Expand Service Opportunities for Seniors." *U.S. Committee on Education and Labor,* March 8, 2009, http://edlabor.house.gov/blog/2009/03/give-act-will-expand-service-o-1.shtml (site last accessed on November 13, 2009).
5. Coupland, D. *Generation X: Tales for an Accelerated Culture.* New York: Macmillan, 1991.
6. Merriam-Webster's OnLine. http://www.merriam-webster.com/dictionary/meritocracy (site last accessed on November 13, 2009).
7. McKeown, J. L. *Retaining Top Employees.* New York: McGraw-Hill, 2002, p. 72.
8. Drain, C. B. *Perianesthesia Nursing: A Critical Care Approach.* New York: Elsevier Health Sciences, 2003, p. 22.

9. Mithers, C. "Workplace Wars." *Ladies' Home Journal,* May 2009.

10. "Volunteering with AARP." *AARP.org,* November 2008, http://www.aarp
.org/makeadifference/volunteer/articles/volunteering_with_aarp.html (site
last accessed on November 13, 2009).

11. Jayson, S. "It's Cooler Than Ever to Be a Tween, but Is Childhood Lost?"
USA Today, February 4, 2009, http://www.usatoday.com/news/health/2009-
02-03-tweens-behavior_N.htm (site last accessed on November 13, 2009).

12. http://www.babyboomercaretaker.com/baby-boomer/generation-z/index.html
(site last accessed on November 13, 2009).

Index